ERA OF EXPERIMENTATION

JEFFERSONIAN AMERICA

Jan Ellen Lewis, Peter S. Onuf, and

Andrew O'Shaughnessy, Editors

Era of
Experimentation

American Political Practices
in the Early Republic

DANIEL PEART

UNIVERSITY OF VIRGINIA PRESS *Charlottesville and London*

University of Virginia Press
© 2014 by the Rector and Visitors of the University of Virginia
Printed in the United States of America on acid-free paper

First published 2014

9 8 7 6 5 4 3 2 1

Library of Congress Cataloging-in-Publication Data
Peart, Daniel, 1985–
    Era of Experimentation : American political practices in the early republic /
Daniel Peart.
        p.   cm. — (Jeffersonian America)
    Includes bibliographical references and index.
    ISBN 978-0-8139-3560-7 (cloth : alk. paper) — ISBN 978-0-8139-3561-4 (e-book)
    1. United States—Politics and government—1815-1861. 2. Political parties—United
States—History—19th century. 3. Political participation—United States—History—
19th century. 4. Elections—United States—History—19th century. 5. Political culture—
United States—History—19th century. I. Title.
    E338.P37 2014
    320.97309'034—dc23

                                                                2013039748

CONTENTS

ACKNOWLEDGMENTS

You would not be reading this book today if the following people and institutions had not helped me to write it, and for that I owe them my thanks.

First off, it is proper that I recognize the invaluable financial support I received from the following sources: University College London; the Central Research Fund of the University of London; the Peter J. Parish Memorial Fund, administered by the Association of British American Nineteenth Century Historians; the British Association for American Studies; the Gilder Lehrman Institute of American History; the King V. Hostick Award, administered by the Illinois State Historical Society; the Barra Foundation International Fellowship, administered by the Library Company of Philadelphia and the Historical Society of Pennsylvania; and the Mellon Research Fellowship, administered by the Virginia Historical Society. I am grateful for their aid at the outset of my academic career.

For their unfailing willingness to assist a frequently bewildered British graduate student I'd like to thank the staff at the following U.S. archives: the Abraham Lincoln Presidential Library, the Boston Athenaeum, the Boston Public Library, the Chicago History Museum, the Edwardsville (IL) Public Library, the Historical Society of Pennsylvania, the Illinois History and Lincoln Collections at the University of Illinois, the Illinois State Archives, the Library Company of Philadelphia, the Library of Congress, the Library of Virginia, the Massachusetts Historical Society, the New York Historical Society, the New York Public Library, the Rare Book and Manuscript Library at the University of Pennsylvania, and the Virginia Historical Society. Special thanks must go to Tom Schwartz, of the Illinois State Historical Society, and Jim Green, of the Library Company of Philadelphia, for their efforts to make sure my stay at their respective institutions was both pleasant and productive. Most of all, though, I'd like to thank Cheryl, Debbie, and Glenna at the Abraham Lincoln Presidential Library and Judy (and her husband, Mike) at the Edwardsville Public Library for going out of their way to make me feel at home in the wonderful state of Illinois (which is, I discovered, almost as flat as the Fens of Lincolnshire, where I grew up). I cannot think of a finer example of American hospitality.

Unfortunately, there were many parts of the United States that I could not find time to visit. Fortunately, though, I was able to avail myself of the efficient remote-research facilities offered by the following archives: the Alabama Department of Archives and History, the Albert and Shirley Small Special Collections at the University of Virginia, the American Antiquarian Society, the Earl Gregg Swem Library at the College of William & Mary, the Georgia Historical Society, the Indiana State Library, the John Hay Library at Brown University, the Knox County (TN) Public Library, the Mississippi Department of Archives and History, the Missouri History Museum, and the University of Delaware Library. Thanks too to Heather at the Massachusetts Historical Society, who tracked down all of the information that I realized I needed after I had left Boston.

Several individuals helped me out when I came up against specific obstacles. Donald DeBats, Jeffrey Pasley, John Sacher, Jeffrey Selinger, and (on multiple occasions) Donald Ratcliffe graciously responded to queries on subjects that were only tangentially related to their own research. Mick Bignell facilitated my data collection by giving me the benefit of his IT know-how. And without the assistance of Phil Lampi, liberally requested and always cheerfully granted, I could never have conducted the analysis of voter turnout that provided the starting point for my thesis. By extension I am also grateful to all the staff who have contributed to making Phil's treasure trove of election returns freely available online via the A New Nation Votes project.

This book has been improved by feedback I received on papers presented at the American History seminar series at the Institute of Historical Research, the American Politics Group conference, the Association of British American Nineteenth Century Historians conference, the Commonwealth Fund conference at University College London, the "Ireland, America and the Worlds of Mathew Carey" conference at Trinity College Dublin, and the Society for Historians of the Early American Republic conference. It has also been improved by the thoughtful comments and criticism of Jonathan Chandler, Reeve Huston, Johann N. Neem, Andrew Robertson, and David Sim, all of whom generously agreed to read a full draft of the manuscript. And it wouldn't even be a book without the support of Stephen Conway and Adam

I. P. Smith, my supervisors at University College London. Though not a nineteenth-century specialist himself, Stephen was always willing to discuss my research at length, and his insightful questions frequently set me thinking about the subject in new and fruitful ways. As for Adam, it was he who first sparked my interest in the history of U.S. politics as an undergraduate student, and he has continued to shape my development as a historian ever since.

For all their help in preparing this book for publication, I'd like to thank Dick Holway and the rest of the editorial team at the University of Virginia Press, as well as Doug Bradburn for introducing me to them in the first place and Joanne Allen for her expert copy editing. Parts of chapter 3 have previously been published in "Looking Beyond Parties and Elections: The Making of United States Tariff Policy during the Early 1820s," *Journal of the Early Republic* 33 (Spring 2013): 87–108; I am grateful to the University of Pennsylvania Press and to the Society for Historians of the Early American Republic for their permission to reproduce those parts here. And thanks are due too to my own "editorial team" here in the United Kingdom. My sisters, Louise and Julia, served as dedicated proofreaders; any remaining errors I am certainly responsible for. And my girlfriend, Helen, has seen this project through from beginning to end and supported me every step of the way.

❖ All this leaves me with just one more acknowledgment to make. I'd like to dedicate this book to my mother, Amanda. She knows (or professes to know) practically nothing about American political practices in the early republic, but in every other way that she could she has contributed to making me the historian that I am today. Thank you.

ERA OF EXPERIMENTATION

The Election of President of the United States has at this season excited very little interest, either in the private circles, or in the newspapers," observed a correspondent to the *Richmond Enquirer* in November 1820. "There will be no contest," "Virginius" continued. "Mr. Monroe is as sure of his re-election, as his most sanguine hopes, or his warmest friends could possibly desire." In the eyes of the author, the president's success owed "as much to the present state of parties, as to the excellence of his administration." For Monroe's Republican predecessors, "party spirit was active and vigorous enough to present some opposition," and thus they "had to win their way to the Presidency through a sea of contest and competition." Ever since his elevation to the White House, however, the Federalist Party "have rather supported Mr. Monroe than opposed him; and they will as cheerfully give him their voices, on his re-election, as the sturdiest of the ancient republicans."[1]

Events would soon prove "Virginius" correct. James Monroe was returned to the presidential chair by near-universal acclamation. Even in the few states where Federalist slates triumphed at the polls, the victors willingly cast their ballots for the Republican candidate in the Electoral College. The Richmond writer's prophecy that Monroe "will not lose a vote in the Union" was spoiled only by a single recalcitrant elector in New Hampshire, who refused to support the incumbent on the grounds that he had "conducted, as president, very improperly."[2] This isolated instance of ill will aside, the 1820 election appeared to confirm the oft-repeated claim made three years previously by the Federalist editor Benjamin Russell that Monroe's presidency had ushered the United States into an "Era of Good Feelings."[3]

Subsequent studies have shown that "Era of Good Feelings" is a serious misnomer for the decade following the War of 1812, during which the federal government was racked by factional infighting and fraught with sectional tension.[4] Yet the phrase persists as convenient shorthand to describe a period that many historians now contend was defined by widespread apathy toward politics among the general populace. Indeed, this interpretation has become so entrenched that one recent survey of U.S. politics concludes that "the Era of Good Feelings . . . might more accurately be called the Era of No Feelings."[5]

"No Feelings" is certainly an apt characterization of popular sentiment with regard to Monroe's reelection. In the city of Richmond, capital of the president's native Virginia, the *Enquirer* reported that a mere seventeen tickets had been taken at the polls. "The election will be necessarily a very thin one throughout the State, and the Union, in consequence of a want of opposition," the editor predicted.[6] And so it transpired, with just one in ten of those Americans who were eligible to vote taking the trouble to do so. Four years later, there was little sign of improvement. In 1824 no less than five serious contenders competed for the White House, and newspapers trumpeted that the contest was "the all-absorbing topic of every circle."[7] Yet a full seven-tenths of the electorate failed to cast their ballots. "The election of a president is a great political curiosity," mused the venerable senator from Virginia John Taylor. "Partisans are zealous, and a great majority of the people indifferent."[8]

The particular apathy of Americans toward presidential elections during this period becomes even more conspicuous when placed in a broader context. Turnout surged in 1828, when "the People's President," Andrew Jackson, was hoisted into the White House, and again in the famous "Log Cabin and Hard Cider Campaign" of 1840. Thereafter, a participation rate of roughly 70–80 percent was sustained throughout the nineteenth century, before falling away significantly. And this trend was mirrored in midterm elections, where turnout between 1850 and 1898 averaged approximately 64 percent, several points below that in presidential contests but still much higher than would become customary during the twentieth century (fig. 1).[9]

Historians have used these turnout figures to divide America's political past in a way that foregrounds the relationship between popular participation in elections and the evolution of political parties. One of the first to suggest that "the decades from the 1830s to the early 1900s form a distinctive era in American political history" was Richard L. McCormick, who coined the phrase *Party Period* to describe a time "when parties dominated political participation" and "voting was more partisan and more widespread than ever before."[10] This conceptual framework has since been adopted by Joel

Fig. 1. Voter turnout in presidential elections

Sources: Burnham, "Presidential Elections, USA, 1788–2004."

Silbey, who argues that "the primacy of political parties was the dominant fact of this political era (and of no other)" and that as a result "Americans repeatedly turned out to vote in record numbers at all levels of electoral activity."[11] In a similar vein, William Gienapp asserts that whereas previously "few men were interested in politics, and fewer still actively participated in political affairs," the "full establishment" of a "party system" by 1840 meant that "for the first time politics assumed a central role in American life. . . . In structure and ideology, American politics had been democratized."[12]

More recently, the Party Period chronology has been challenged by scholars working on the conflict between Federalists and Republicans that preceded the Era of Good Feelings. Donald Ratcliffe has long contended that historians "underestimate how far the political experience of these years was structured by partisan divisions, how far these divisions penetrated into the electorate, and how significant the experiences of these years proved for subsequent party development."[13] He has since been joined by Andrew Robertson, Rosemarie Zagarri, and Jeffrey Pasley, who maintain that, in the words of the latter, "this early partisan political culture . . . was one of the most participatory and transformative that the United States has ever experienced, despite its utter lack of many elements that came to define party politics later."[14] In support of this claim Pasley produces evidence that while voter turnout in national elections remained relatively low, participation rates for state elections "approached 70 percent of adult white males" in many parts of the nation between 1800 and 1816.[15]

For all their differences, these conflicting interpretations share one important point in common: they identify political parties as responsible for increasing turnout in elections, whether they date this process to the first or the fourth decade of the nineteenth century. The assumption that competing parties opened public life to mass participation and made government more responsive to the people lies at the heart of much of what has been written on U.S. politics between the Revolution and the Civil War.[16] Amidst this "celebratory" narrative the Era of Good Feelings, during which the Republicans enjoyed unchallenged control over the national government, appears as merely a brief aberration. For one subscriber to the Party Period framework these years represent a final manifestation of the "deference to social elites and mass indifference" that characterized politics prior to the advent of the recognizably modern Democrat-Whig party system.[17] To a critic of that concept they appear as only a brief interlude of "political vacuousness" following the collapse of the Federalist opposition, during which popular participation, which had previously flourished, now "withered into apathy."[18] Without strenuous party competition to sustain their attention, it is generally agreed, most Americans simply would not have been interested in politics.

❖ Newly discovered evidence, however, reveals the "Era of No Feelings" to be nothing more than a myth. Over the past decade the New Nation Votes project has made available masses of election results from the early United States, many of which were previously assumed to be lost forever. When used in conjunction with census returns to calculate participation rates in congressional and gubernatorial elections from 1820 to 1825, the results are striking. Of the twenty-four states admitted to the Union by that time, twelve broke Pasley's 70 percent barrier *at least once* during this period, and eight maintained an *average* turnout that was equal to or in excess of the 64 percent witnessed in comparable contests during the Party Period (tables 1 and 2). Taken as a whole, these figures demolish the notion that the vast majority of citizens were simply not interested in politics during the early 1820s.[19]

Party competition on a national scale cannot have provided the stimulus for these remarkable participation rates. From the first administration of George Washington to the outbreak of hostilities with Britain in 1812,

TABLE 1. *States with at least one turnout of 70 percent or higher in congressional and gubernatorial elections, 1820–1825*

State	Single highest turnout (%)
Alabama	95
Rhode Island	89
Georgia	85
Illinois	83
Mississippi	82
Tennessee	80
Indiana	76
Missouri	76
Kentucky	74
New York	72
Maryland	72
Delaware	71

Sources: See appendix 1.

TABLE 2. *States with an average turnout of 64 percent or higher in congressional and gubernatorial elections, 1820–1825*

State	Average turnout (%)
Alabama	80
Tennessee	78
Missouri	74
Kentucky	72
Illinois	69
Indiana	66
Mississippi	65
Delaware	64

Sources: See appendix 1.

Note: Burnham's figure of 64 percent is for midterm elections only during the Party Period, while my figures include gubernatorial and congressional elections held in the presidential-election years 1820 and 1824. However, as we have already seen, turnout in these presidential elections was so low that it could hardly have exerted a coattails effect on turnout in the other types of election. Furthermore, only Massachusetts and New Jersey actually held presidential elections at the same time as other elections during this period, and neither appears in this table.

Federalists and Republicans had battled for control of the federal government. But the Hartford Convention scheme, in which Federalist leaders threatened disunion just as the war reached its climax, had forever damned their party's cause in the eyes of most contemporaries. No candidate would contest a presidential election under the banner of Federalism after 1816, and by the beginning of Monroe's second term Federalist numbers in Congress had dwindled to less than forty.[20] As "Virginius" aptly put it in his letter to the *Enquirer,* the Federalist Party "received its death blow during the war of 1812. . . . They have lingered ever since, in the councils of the nation, without strength and without hopes, as a political party."[21]

Descending the rungs of the federal system, the situation becomes more complex.[22] Most states had some experience of Federalist-Republican rivalry, but the extent to which conflict between these parties continued to shape the political landscape following the War of 1812 varied significantly. At one extreme stood Massachusetts and Delaware, where the Federalists proved capable of winning statewide elections long into the 1820s. At the other stood Virginia and the Carolinas, where even before the renewal of hostilities with Britain the Republicans had established a superiority so complete that party names lost all relevance. Falling between these two poles were states in the Mid-Atlantic region, where Federalist politicians clung to local strongholds and sought out alliances with dissident Republican factions for statewide contests, and in New England, where defeated partisans preferred to maintain their identity and retire *en masse* from electoral combat.

There were also, however, parts of the nation in which the old party enmities had rarely, if ever, exerted a meaningful influence on politics. In most instances this was true of states that had been admitted to the Union after the Republicans came to dominate the federal government and where there was therefore little incentive for local leaders to attach themselves to the ailing Federalist cause. In consequence, candidates for public office tended to run without reference to party, and formal devices of political management, such as caucuses and conventions, were practically unknown. In this regard, these states stood apart from their sisters, where both parties had experimented with various modes of organization, albeit in a relatively unsystematic manner.

When the new data on election turnout are incorporated into this picture, the inverse relationship between party activity and popular participation is immediately evident. Of the eight states with an average turnout equal to or in excess of 64 percent, the first seven were states in which the Federalist-Republican division had failed to take root. Delaware, where "the old parties still retained their original identity and undiminished vigor," comes in eighth, but Massachusetts, the only other state where this was also true, languishes in nineteenth place on the list.[23] As for New York, recently described by one scholar as "an advanced laboratory of political sophistication, where the foundations were being laid for the emergence of the mass political parties of the nineteenth century," it places only twelfth.[24] Pennsylvania, another state often identified as being at the forefront of new forms of partisan politics, comes in even lower, in fourteenth place (table 3).[25] Once again, party competition does not appear to have provided the stimulus for mass participation in politics; indeed, it seems to have had the opposite effect.

❖ Exposing the "Era of No Feelings" myth is just the beginning of this story. By severing the reflexive connection between parties and participation, it becomes possible to rethink the celebratory narrative in exciting new ways. Since before the Revolution, Americans have argued about the proper relationship between the people and their government and struggled to

TABLE 3. *Average turnout in congressional and gubernatorial elections in selected states, 1820–1825*

Rank	State	Average turnout (%)
1	Alabama	80
2	Tennessee	78
3	Missouri	74
4	Kentucky	72
5	Illinois	69
6	Indiana	66
7	Mississippi	65
8	Delaware	64
12	New York	59
14	Pennsylvania	55
19	Massachusetts	34

Sources: See appendix 1.

demarcate the legitimate methods by which citizens might engage in politics. Yet, too often these multiple and frequently contradictory meanings of democracy do not come across in the existing literature, which suggests a more linear, though by no means constant or uncontested, progression toward a "democratic" future defined by universal suffrage and a national two-party system. Democracy cannot be reduced to a simple count of who has the right to vote or how many choose to exercise that right at the ballot box. And while today's scholars have talked of the "incomplete" nature of public life in the United States before the "birth" of a "modern politics" defined by mass parties, contemporaries, deprived of the advantage of hindsight, cannot possibly have conceived of their experiences in this manner.[26] This book, then, seeks to understand these early Americans on their own terms and in so doing to recapture a political world of extraordinary creativity and diversity, a world that in some respects has been lost to us through the routinization of a politics bounded by parties and elections.[27]

Historians have tended to overlook the decade following the War of 1812 because it does not fit their orderly model of democratization, yet the huge variety in political thought and practice across the United States during this period is precisely what makes it so fascinating. With this in mind, I propose to explore four moments of high political excitement, all of which occurred during the early 1820s, in a bid to understand why contemporaries, when faced with a particular challenge or set of circumstances, chose to pursue one course of action over the range of alternatives at their disposal. Crucially, whatever the specific issue in dispute, all of these episodes have important implications for the meaning of popular sovereignty. The principle that the people should rule is enshrined in the opening line of the United States Constitution, but how this would work in practice was far from settled at the Philadelphia Convention in 1787 and remains the subject of much discussion even today.[28] At the same time, each episode highlights a different aspect of political life in early nineteenth-century America: the fierce contest that raged over the role of parties in politics; the possibilities that existed for mass political mobilization in the absence of parties; the contribution to governance made by modes of organization and participation beyond parties and elections; and the critical events that shaped the development of a national two-party system.

Chapter 1 focuses on competition between the Federalist and Republican parties and popular resistance to that framework in Boston. There, parties dominated the political process to a degree almost without parallel elsewhere in the Union. At the same time, turnout rates remained persistently low; throughout the early 1820s as few as one in five citizens cast their ballots in elections for congressional representatives, and even the highly charged, ultrapartisan contests for the state governorship frequently failed to attract a majority of those who were eligible to the polls. Clearly the standard party-equals-participation model, which provides the foundation for the celebratory narrative, does not apply in this case. Yet while historians have sometimes debated the extent to which parties promoted genuine political engagement among their supporters, little doubt has been cast on their efficacy in marshaling votes on election day.[29] This study, then, offers an opportunity to consider the circumstances in which parties might actually serve to channel, control, and even curb mass participation in politics.

Popular discontent with the established parties finally erupted in Boston in 1822 in the form of a protest movement calling itself the "Middling Interest." These insurgents demanded the reform of party machinery to give rank-and-file members a greater say in the selection of candidates for office and called for those in power to be held accountable to their constituents. This was undeniably a form of antipartisanship, but it was not one borne of the usual sources identified by historians, namely, a commitment to the increasingly outdated values of the Founding Fathers or an idealistic devotion to evangelical Protestantism.[30] The men who gave voice to the Middling Interest derived their convictions not from theoretical treatises or utopian sermons but from practical experience of party rule. And their solution was not to entirely reject party as a model for political action but rather to organize themselves as a third party, running their own tickets at the polls and borrowing extensively from the campaign tools of their opponents. The story of the Middling Interest illustrates that partisanship and antipartisanship cannot be reduced to a simply dichotomy and at the same time demonstrates the determination of ordinary Americans to fashion a political system that fulfilled their expectations of popular sovereignty.

As resentment toward parties boiled over in Boston, one thousand miles to the west residents of Illinois took pride in keeping their politics free from partisan interference. As chapter 2 reveals, however, this meant that when advocates of a scheme to legalize slavery in the state succeeded in forcing a popular referendum on the issue, their opponents were faced with the challenge of mobilizing a mass electorate in the absence of existing mechanisms for this purpose. They responded swiftly, establishing a network of antislavery societies to sway public opinion and taking steps to secure the nomination of suitable candidates for the legislature in a bid to sweep the proslavery faction from office. These efforts were rewarded with a decisive victory at the polls in August 1824, as more than 80 percent of the electorate turned out to vote in an historic result which ensured that the future home of Abraham Lincoln would remain free from human bondage.

The celebratory narrative centers on the emergence of mass political parties, but events in Illinois remind us that this was just one element of an explosion of civic activity during the half-century that followed the Declaration of Independence. As relations with Britain deteriorated, Patriot groups such as the Sons of Liberty demonstrated that the people could play an active role in public life beyond that of "the mob."[31] When peace was restored, the inhabitants of the new United States continued to put the lessons they had learned to good use, joining with their fellow citizens to overcome fresh challenges and exploit new opportunities. Their endeavors were spurred by visions of human progress associated with the Enlightenment and a burst of evangelical fervor in the shape of the Second Great Awakening.[32] The federal government also played its part by sponsoring improvements to the national infrastructure and subsidizing the burgeoning newspaper press.[33] By the time Alexis de Tocqueville embarked on his celebrated tour of the United States in 1831, voluntary organizations had become the bedrock of civic life. "Americans of all ages, all conditions, and all dispositions constantly form associations," the Frenchman famously wrote, and their creations were made to serve all manner of purposes, "commercial and manufacturing[,] . . . religious, moral, serious, futile, general, or restricted, enormous or diminutive."[34]

The importance of self-created societies to reform movements like abolitionism and temperance has long been recognized, but historians have tended to treat these moral crusades as exceptions to the party-drive norm of American political life. Only recently has substantial work been undertaken to explore the considerable overlap between the two. Some studies have shown how voluntary associations were put to work for explicitly partisan ends, for example, providing the infrastructure to sustain conflict between

Federalist and Republican coalitions in Philadelphia that lacked alternative means of reaching out to ordinary citizens.[35] Others have demonstrated the dialectical relationship that existed between parties and nonpartisan movements in terms of personnel, tactics, and organizational techniques.[36] The success of the antislavery campaign in Illinois provides yet more evidence of the creativity of political activists working outside the confines of two-party politics and testifies to the capacity of early Americans to make real the promise of popular sovereignty even in the absence of political parties.[37]

If parties were unpopular in Massachusetts and irrelevant in Illinois, what role did they play in governing the nation? This question provides the starting point for chapter 3, which examines the battle over federal tariff policy between supporters of protective duties for domestic industry and those who favored free trade. The tariff dispute focuses attention on the connection between parties, elections, and policymaking that lies at the heart of the celebratory narrative. According to Richard L. McCormick, "The same party organizations that mobilized citizens on election day also structured their receipt of government goods. . . . The policy equivalent of patronage, distribution strengthened the parties and helped build bridges between their voters, leaders, and representatives in office."[38] Subscribers to this interpretation, however, have often struggled to establish a strong correlation between the three elements in this equation. As Gerald Grob states, "Few historians who hold a representational model of the American political system have been able to demonstrate empirically that policy expectations and demands of citizens in the decades before the Civil War were first identified by legislators, who then processed them into policies that conformed to popular expectations."[39]

The "representational" model, as Grob calls it, rests on two problematic assumptions. The first is that parties neatly translate popular opinion into government programs. In fact, contemporaries found them to be notoriously poor forums for the formulation of public policy. The primary goal of any major party is to gain power by winning elections. This necessitates appealing to as diverse an audience as possible, which tends to disincline parties to take a decisive stance on any issue that might alienate potential supporters. American parties are particularly prone to this tendency because of the federated structure of their political system, which forces national leaders to offer state and local organizations considerable autonomy in exchange for their backing.[40] And during the early nineteenth-century, when parties only came together to contest elections and otherwise lacked a permanent institutional presence, campaigning took even greater precedence over policymaking.[41] The attention of historians is inevitably drawn to the relatively few issues on which parties divided sharply, but in the national and state legislatures most bills became law with little or no interference from party leaders.[42]

The second problematic assumption that underlies the "representational" model is that a close relationship exists between election results and the legislative agenda. Studies of nineteenth-century politics naturally emphasize voting as the most obvious form of popular participation, at least to modern eyes. Yet elections occur only infrequently and can involve a bewildering array of issues, which makes them an impractical means of influencing the everyday business of policymaking. This, of course, was precisely the point for the architects of the Constitution, who intended that the people would exercise their sovereignty at the polls and then leave their chosen leaders to govern on their behalf. In the eyes of the Founding Fathers, "officials were set off from their constituents as rulers who should do what was best for the public good, not what was most popular. The ballot box would assure that rulers did not abuse their trust with impunity; elections would not serve as referenda."[43] Consequently, many accounts that purport to describe the democratization of the United States during this period actually offer a curiously sterile version of popular participation in politics in which "the people" appear around election time only to vanish into obscurity again the moment the polls close.

Over the past fifteen years, it is true, a methodological shift has taken place as historians have broadened their definition of political activity to include such novel subjects as clothing, civic rituals, and even the making of a "Mammoth Cheese."[44] However, this research has tended to focus on how its subjects acquired and projected a political identity rather than on what one critique of this approach has called the "classic considerations of political life . . . who gets what, why, and how?"[45] The conflict over the tariff, in contrast, provides a case study of contemporaries who were determined to play an active role in the policymaking process. Protectionists and free traders alike sought to mobilize support through nonpartisan voluntary associations operating on a national scale and made extensive use of petitioning and lobbying to promote their respective causes. Unlike fashion, festivals, and *fromage,* these devices offered Americans direct access to the highest levels of government in a manner that circumvented party control of the polling place. This episode, then, presents an opportunity to look beyond parties and elections and appreciate the many and diverse ways in which early Americans sought to participate in governing the nation.

Following these three different manifestations of popular dissatisfaction with parties, chapter 4 explores the origins of a new national two-party system in the presidential election of 1824. Accounts of party development tend to pass swiftly over this contest, dwelling only on the result, namely, that with several candidates in the field and none able to secure a majority in the Electoral College, John Quincy Adams was elevated to the presidency by the House of Representatives despite Andrew Jackson's having led in the popular vote. This set the stage for an acrimonious rematch between the two men in 1828, from which Jackson emerged triumphant, having conspired with his loyal lieutenant, Martin Van Buren, to lay the foundations for the creation of the Democratic Party. During Jackson's eight years in the White House, his many enemies would themselves coalesce around the rival standard of the Whig Party, and the short-lived Era of Good Feelings would fast become a distant memory.

Yet this story is not as straightforward as it is often presented—far from it. Few historians care to mention that the 1824 election found Jackson and Van Buren on opposing sides of the political arena, with party the chief issue that divided them. On that occasion the tone of Jackson's campaign was decidedly antipartisan, as he pledged to overthrow the rule of career politicians and return power to the people. Van Buren, meanwhile, was straining to prop up the candidacy of the unpopular secretary of the treasury, William H. Crawford, with the machinery of party. In consequence, the celebratory narrative has a schizophrenic quality to it. Jackson is lauded for resisting the rise of party in 1824 and then for facilitating it in 1828. Crawford, conversely, is condemned for his efforts to build the very party that historians praise his rival for constructing four years later. First party is the problem; then it is the solution. Only by teasing out these ironies in the historical record can we begin to understand how political parties came to dominate, though never to monopolize, U.S. politics in the decades that followed.

The celebratory narrative that dominates the existing literature, with its narrow focus on parties and elections, fails to capture the full variety of

American political practices during the early 1820s. Far from being an "Era of No Feelings," this was a period of vitality and innovation, with fluid forms and uncertain outcomes. It was, in sum, an Era of Experimentation, in which a political system organized around two competing national parties was only one of many possible futures for a generation of Americans grappling with the democratic potential inherent in that famous phrase: "We the People."

1 | " 'WE THE PEOPLE' HAVE NO POLITICAL EXISTENCE"
The Rise and Fall of the Middling Interest in Boston, Massachusetts

The following satirical article, a parody on the fugitive slave advertisements that filled the southern press, appeared in a Boston newspaper four days after the congressional election of 1820:

> DESERTED from the federal cause, on 23d inst. SIX HUNDRED legal voters, principally merchants and mechanics. They have no other excuse for their conduct, than that the overseers, who have lately taken the management upon their shoulders, have threatened them with *gagging*, if they refused obedience. They may be known by their attachment to the good old federal politics of '96, which they are fond of exhibiting on all occasions, and a certain obstinacy and perverseness, which they, agreeable to the obsolete nomenclature, denominate *independence*. Whoever will take up said runaways and return them to the overseers shall receive the thanks of the GENERAL (*alias* Central) COMMITTEE, and the promise of an invitation to the next Primary Caucus, in case any vacancy should happen in the present Ward Delegations.[1]

Historians, with few exceptions, have treated this period as one in which parties were weak or nonexistent. So why, in critiquing the relationship between local Federalist leaders and their constituents, did the *New-England Galaxy* choose as the most appropriate analogy that of overseers and slaves?

To the editor of the *Galaxy* and his readers, the notion that parties played an insignificant role in politics would have seemed absurd. For two decades at least, political life in Boston had been defined by a struggle between rival Federalist and Republican organizations. Modern scholars are apt to consider institutionalized two-party competition as proof of a flourishing democratic politics. Many Bostonians, however, did not share this faith. They believed that the existing political arrangements were designed to concentrate power in the hands of a few and to rob the many of their right both to choose those who would govern over them and to regulate their conduct once in office. For this reason, a large section of the town's residents spent the early 1820s in open revolt against the established party system. The banner under which these protestors rallied was the Middling Interest.

The Middling Interest did not seek to do away with parties entirely. Instead, they proposed to transform them from impediments to popular rule into instruments for implementing the will of the people. Modeling their organization on that of their opponents, the insurgents enjoyed an initial spell of electoral success. Ultimately, though, the movement's failure to overcome the obstacles of operating in a political environment so accustomed to two-party competition ensured that its career would be short-lived. Nonetheless, the rise and fall of the Middling Interest illustrates the extent to which the practical implications of popular sovereignty remained subject to dispute during this period and provides an opportunity to explore some of the many meanings attached to both partisanship and antipartisanship.

❖ As President Monroe coasted toward almost unanimous election to a second term, party conflict raged unabated in Massachusetts.[2] The Federalists clung to control of both the executive and legislative branches of government, but statewide contests for the governor's mansion were always closely fought affairs, and the Republicans consistently racked up healthy minorities in both the Massachusetts General Court and the state's delegation to Congress. With each Federalist failure elsewhere in the Union, the situation became more fraught. To Republican partisans, every lost election represented another missed opportunity for Massachusetts to rejoin the national mainstream. For Federalists, just one slip could spell the end of their party's very existence.

Nowhere did that existence seem less in peril, however, than in the town of Boston. The Republican ticket had not tasted success there since the heady days of Thomas Jefferson's first tenure in the White House. Presiding over this bastion of Federalism was an exclusive group of party grandees fronted by Harrison Gray Otis, Thomas Handasyd Perkins, and William Sullivan. Although these three names had been rendered notorious throughout the nation by their association with the ill-fated Hartford Convention, at home they represented the pinnacle of social prestige and political power.[3] Looking back sixty years later, Josiah Quincy Jr., whose father was also a sometime member of the Federalist inner circle and would play a principal role in the drama about to unfold, recalled that "in the third decade of the century Boston was a synonym for certain individuals and families, who ruled it with undisputed sway."[4]

The role of party in sustaining this oligarchy has often been downplayed by historians. One typical account talks of "an elite accustomed to leading by nods and gestures" who "did not need an organized political party."[5] The reality was somewhat different, however, as this description of Federalist nominating practices from the *Boston Commercial Gazette* suggests:

> The Federal party is thus organized—The Federal electors assemble in their respective wards, and choose a member of the general committee, and from seven to ten persons to constitute the ward committees. The general committee assemble some days before an election, and send a circular to the several ward committees, with twenty or thirty blank notifications and in all cases, the same number to each of the wards, to be filled up by the ward committees, and sent *at their discretion* to citizens in their wards, to meet with the general committee and the ward committees, in caucus, to nominate candidates.—At this caucus the mode of proceeding is, to nominate as many candidates as the assembly sees fit and then to mark against the names. The individual (or individuals, if more than one office is to be chosen) who has the highest number of marks is considered the candidate.[6]

Here, then, was a party with an established organizational framework and formalized procedures for choosing candidates for public office. The pyramidal structure of multiple local committees reporting to a single central body, all of which were ostensibly elected by the membership, closely resembles that of today's parties. The same is true of the nominating method itself, which involved party leaders meeting with delegates chosen from each ward of the town to select candidates on the principle of majority rule. Boston's prolonged electoral calendar required that this process be repeated several times a year, with municipal offices to be filled every March, the governor and state senators chosen in April, state representatives in May, and then the biennial contest for a seat in the United States Congress held in the fall.[7] Yet this punishing schedule did not prevent the party from exerting its control over all levels of electoral activity. According to the *Galaxy,* "In Massachusetts, and more especially in Boston, all the candidates for office, from the chief magistrate of the state down to the *keeper of the town bell,* are selected by the 'Central Committee.'"[8]

The Republican Party in Boston was organized in a similar manner. The Republican Institution served as a counterpart to the Federalists' General Committee and likewise sat atop a pyramidal structure reaching down into the wards. To the public eye, the Republicans' nominating process appeared somewhat less regular than that of their adversaries, with electoral tickets put forward by assemblages variously described as "a convention of the Republican Electors" or "a very full meeting of Republican Citizens" or simply appearing as if from thin air for endorsement in the Republican press.[9] As far as critics of party rule were concerned, however, the differences were negligible. "The 'Republican Institution' of Boston" and "the federal 'primary caucus,'" declared the *Galaxy,* "are the same in purpose, the same in effect, equal in power and glory, and are of no use but to perpetuate an ill-gotten ascendancy, by distributing patronage and rewards to their respective tools and pandars."[10]

Equal in importance to nominating machinery was the political newspaper, which provided a continuing institutional presence outside electoral campaigns for these early parties. In Boston the Federalists enjoyed the favor of the *Columbian Centinel,* the *Commercial Gazette,* and the *Boston Daily Advertiser,* while their Republican opponents could count on the *Boston Patriot* and the *American Statesman.* Friendly editors might hope to receive a direct reward for their service, perhaps an appointment to public office or a lucrative printing contract, or they might simply expect a boost in subscription and advertising revenue from fellow partisans. In return, newspapers advertised party activities for those who wished to attend and reported the proceedings for the benefit of those who could not. They informed the faithful of nominations and other party decisions and provided a forum for the discussion of public issues. And as each polling day approached, partisan editors endeavored to whip the electorate into a state of fervor, exhorting each and every voter to turn out and back the party ticket. These men were "full-time, year-round politicians, running businesses devoted to politics" and serving as "principal spokesman, supplier of ideology, and enforcer of discipline" for their parties.[11]

In the absence of recruiting arms of their own, both the Federalists and the Republicans also looked to fraternal societies and volunteer militia companies to attract new members and sustain their interest between elections. A classic example is the Washington Benevolent Societies, more than two hundred of which were established throughout the nation during the first two decades of the nineteenth century.[12] The stated purpose of these ostensibly nonpartisan societies was to "alleviate the sufferings of unfortunate individuals" through charitable assistance, but their true object was to broaden the base of the Federalist Party.[13] The Boston branch was founded in 1812, and within a year it boasted a membership of fifteen hundred. "The *'Washington Benevolent Societies,'* so called, were established to answer the purpose of a political party, and . . . are in direct opposition both to *Washington* and *Benevolence,*" complained one Republican newspaper. "The *fund,* said to be raised for *benevolent* purposes, is . . . expended in paying for *banners, votes, ribbands,* and other vapid trumpery to make up a show."[14]

As this source suggests, putting on a show was another way for Federalist and Republican leaders to connect with their constituents. "Both nascent parties invented new rites that expressed their different views: the Federalists' tributes to Washington, the Democratic-Republicans' fetes in honor of the French Revolution, [and] both parties' competing July Fourth celebrations," explains the historian David Waldstreicher.[15] This was certainly the case in Boston, where the Republicans, observing "with much regret, that the Fourth of July anniversary orations in this town were pronounced exclusively by orators of an opposite party" and "finding, as they did, that this influence was spreading its baneful effects over the minds of the rising generation," took to holding their own separate commemorations in the early nineteenth century.[16] Public occasions such as these provided politicians with a platform for addressing prospective voters and also allowed the parties to display their strength in numbers, in full knowledge that the proceedings would be published far and wide in the next day's newspapers.

When polling day arrived, both Boston parties worked hard to ensure the greatest possible support for their candidates. The Federalist ward committees were directed to "ascertain and make a list of all the Federal Voters in their respective Wards" and to "see that the names of all these voters are put upon the Lists of Voters, required by law . . . and the names of ALIENS, (if any) stricken off."[17] Requiring eligible voters to register in advance and

{19

prove their place of residency was one of the many ways in which parties sought to regulate the electoral process during the nineteenth century, and Massachusetts was a pioneer in this respect.[18] Volunteer activists were also encouraged "to patrole the Wards on the Day of election, remind our busy, and forgetful brethren, that they are voters, and that it is their duty, in honor, and conscience, to exercise their elective rights."[19] Tickets were prepared in advance and agents appointed to distribute them as citizens approached the ballot box. Taken in totality, these arrangements are a far cry from the now-familiar portrait of "an elite accustomed to leading by nods and gestures."

This is not to say, however, that "nods and gestures" played an insignificant part in the Federalists' political success. Harrison Gray Otis in particular was acutely aware that the party's ascendancy relied on an adroit union of political management and public display. Federalist power, he observed in 1822:

> depends upon the influence and example of the most respectable persons in the various walks and professions who have long been habituated to act together—The force of these persons is increased by the sympathy and enthusiasm of numbers, and by a feeling of shame or self reproach which attends to the consciousness of a *known* dereliction of duty—The class which is *acted upon* by this example and influence realize a pride and pleasure in shewing their colors upon a general review, which they cannot feel when trained in a gun house—The old leaders have learned the art of giving a salutary impulse to the whole body when collected together—This impulse ought to be a unit, to procure unity of action—It is easier to manage the town of B[oston] by a *Lancastrian* system of political discipline than to institute numerous schools.[20]

The "Lancastrian system" to which Otis referred was an educational model promoted by the contemporary reformer Joseph Lancaster. Lancaster argued that large numbers of children of mixed abilities could be taught successfully in one room by a single schoolmaster assisted by the more advanced students in the class. According to Otis, this was precisely how Boston politics should operate. In his analogy, Faneuil Hall, the town's sole designated polling place, was the classroom, and the Federalist leaders were the schoolmaster and his assistants, who by their "example" and their "influence" provided a "salutary impulse" to their students, the pliable electorate.

Otis's letter indicates that a political organization that was extremely so-phisticated by the standards of the day could still effectively integrate ele-ments of an older style of politics characterized by "nods and gestures." The Federalists, and their Republican opponents too, relied on a committee sys-tem to nominate candidates for office, newspapers and voluntary associa-tions to drum up support for those candidates, and a network of agents to translate that support into success at the polls. But the whole system was underpinned by a faith that the rank and file would follow the lead given to them by those at the head of the party hierarchy. For Otis and his associates, the people's role in politics was to be "acted upon," a notion that put them fundamentally at odds with the emerging Middling Interest.

❖ The first sign of opposition to the Federalist oligarchy emerged from the choice of municipal officers in March 1820.[21] The town's Board of Selectmen was subject to annual election, but it was customary for incumbents to be returned several times in succession. On this occasion, the seven members who ran for reelection under the Federalist standard had served for an aver-age of nine terms each, with two boasting thirty-nine years of experience between them.[22] To their surprise, however, this distinguished record proved insufficient to stay the hand of disgruntled voters who objected to the board's efforts to ban the practice of sales at auction, an action taken at the behest of prominent merchants who resented the auctioneers for undercutting their prices.[23] The disaffected from both political parties joined together in sup-port of a "Union Ticket," which swept to victory at the polls.[24] Apologists for the old board were quick to complain that "strict integrity and undeviating devotion to public good, have never failed to create an host of enemies."[25] Only the *Galaxy*, whose editor, Joseph T. Buckingham, would prove to be the most vocal supporter of the nascent protest movement, cast the result as an incipient challenge to "the [Federalist] *Central Committee* who stand behind the scenes during the exhibition of our *puppet-show elections.*"[26]

Dissident Federalists returned to the party fold for the state elections in April and May, but discontent resurfaced in the congressional contest held in the fall. After the two major parties each nominated a lawyer as their can-didate, a third group of men dared to make their own recommendation. At a meeting chaired by the Federalist distiller David Ellis they endorsed the Republican merchant Samuel A. Wells, arguing that "as this District is almost entirely composed of *Merchants, Mechanics,* and others dependent on *Commerce,* it ought to be represented by a *commercial* man."[27] This barb was no doubt directed at the previous Federalist incumbent, who had recently voted for a federal tariff bill that promised enormous profits for a few manufacturers at the expense, many Bostonians believed, of the transatlantic trade upon which their livelihood depended.[28] Wells outpaced his Republican rival, Henry Orne, in the town of Boston and obtained sufficient votes in the three-way race to deny the Federalist candidate, Benjamin Gorham, an outright majority.[29] Although Gorham won the required runoff comfortably, the *Galaxy* remained defiant, comparing recent events in Boston to Latin America's ongoing struggle to free itself from European dominion with the observation that "this is an age of revolution, and great fires are sometimes kindled by a very small spark."[30]

Amidst continued rumblings of resentment the Federalists carried the elections of 1821 without upset, but in the spring of 1822 popular resistance to party rule assumed unprecedented proportions. The catalyst was a long-standing and seemingly innocuous law that restricted the construction of wooden buildings greater than ten feet in height within municipal boundaries. Many Bostonians favored a repeal of the regulation in the belief that it would provide jobs in construction and cheaper housing, and in June 1821 a town meeting voted to petition the Massachusetts General Court to that effect. Wealthy residents resisted the measure, however, publicly arguing that it would expose the town to increased risk of fire and privately fearing that it would reduce the rental income they earned from their own brick properties. When the matter came before the legislature, the town's own delegation displayed a notable reluctance to press the case for repeal. "How astonished were the petitioners, to hear, when the bill was brought in, that it was entirely contrary to the expectations and wishes of a great majority of the town," remarked a correspondent in the *Galaxy,* adding that "this astonishment was not diminished when it was found that the greater part of the representatives from Boston chose to be absent on this occasion."[31]

In January 1822 a second attempt was made to revise the wooden-buildings code. Once again a town meeting voted overwhelmingly to petition the General Court, this time adding the specific proviso that the town's "Senators & Representatives [be] *directed* to use their influence in procuring the passage of [the] bill."[32] Once again Boston's political chiefs maneuvered to block the change, this time by organizing a counterpetition. And once again, contrary to their instructions, members of the Boston delegation in the legislature either absented themselves or voted in opposition, thereby consigning the proposal to a second defeat.

But the issue would not die. By March 1822 support for repeal was such that more than five thousand signatures had been collected for a third petition, a figure in excess of half of the town's electorate.[33] Belatedly, the Federalist leadership began to realize the precariousness of their situation. Writing from Washington, where he was serving in the United State Senate, Otis warned William Sullivan that "if you mean to prevent the triumph of the revolutionary movement . . . you ought to let the advocates for wooden buildings . . . understand that your opposition will be withdrawn." "The wooden project cannot be resisted for any length of time—and as in the case of other popular hallucinations, the mischief must be yielded to, or others will follow in train," he predicted, adding, "I fear the Devil will break loose."[34]

❖ This reluctant concession proved too little too late. The dispute had now outgrown the original problem of restrictions on wooden buildings. In *An Exposition of the Principles and Views of the Middling Interest,* a pamphlet that served as a self-proclaimed manifesto for the developing insurgency, the anonymous author explained that the town's political elite had shown their true character when "in defiance of the authority of precedent usage, and the plainest of all constitutional injunctions, the request to the Senators and the instructions to the Representatives of Boston, . . . were received by them as though they were irresponsible to their constituents."[35] That the malefactors in this particular instance were Federalists did little to spare their partisan opponents from mounting popular anger. "The Federalists have their aristocracy, and the Republicans have theirs," a rebel handbill reminded its readers, "but they are both equally united on some occasions against the Middling Interest. . . . Their object is power to be used for themselves, as they have done, and not always for the benefit of the people."[36] In consequence, the emerging protest movement transcended petty rivalries. "It was composed of federalists and republicans and some who had not for years taken any part in politics," a newspaper correspondent observed, all of whom "had become justly alarmed at an invasion of one of their dearest rights—'the right to INSTRUCT their Representatives,' as expressed in the CONSTITUTION."[37]

To appreciate the scale of the revolt, it is necessary to understand what this commentator meant by *"the right to* INSTRUCT *their Representatives."* The phrase refers to the practice of constituents' instructing their elected representative on how to act in regard to a particular political issue.[38] Originating in Britain, this custom had never been fully accepted there because it clashed with the concept of virtual representation, which held that members of Parliament should consider the good of the whole nation rather than merely communicate the sentiment of a small part. The American colonies, in contrast, subscribed much more closely to the notion of actual representation, which considered a legislator to be little more than the agent of his constituents, and in this context the practice flourished. By the time of the Revolution, instruction had become so commonplace that several states wrote it into their new constitutions. One of these was Massachusetts, Article XIX of whose state constitution of 1780 affirmed that "the people have a right, in an orderly and peaceable manner, to assemble to consult upon the common good; give instructions to their representatives, and to request of the legislative body, by the way of addresses, petitions, or remonstrances, redress of the wrongs done them, and of the grievances they suffer."[39]

This passage provided the Middling Interest with a constitutional foundation for their claim that legislators were bound to respect the wishes of their constituents. "It is in vain [our opponents] object, that this doctrine may make a mere automaton of a Representative, deprive him of all power of deliberation, and even of the boasted right of speaking and acting for himself," declared the *Defence of the Exposition of the Middling Interest,* a pamphlet published shortly after the *Exposition* and dealing almost exclusively with the dispute over instruction. "While a representative has as much good sense and sound political integrity as his constituents, he need apprehend no interference, if he fulfils their wishes," avowed the author, "and when he ceases to do this, the sooner he becomes an automaton, the better."[40] Likewise, the argument that the General Court must be "the *general* guardians of the public welfare" and therefore could not "transfer *their discretion*" to one small part of the commonwealth was easily swept aside.[41] "If that clause [Article XIX] was ever applicable," the *Defence* maintained, "it was in the instances complained of, when the INSTRUCTIONS related to municipal regulations in which no one but Boston could be materially interested."[42]

Defenders of the Boston delegation struck back by disputing the practicality of instruction. "Nothing is more easy," alleged "A Citizen," "than for a combination of interested persons to carry by surprise in a town meeting, which seldom contains more than one quarter of the legal voters, any measure in favor of which such a combination should have been excited." If a general referendum were taken on the question of repeal, the writer confidently predicted, "a large majority would be found against it." Why, then, should a section of the town be permitted to dictate the conduct of representatives elected by the whole?[43]

This argument was angrily rejected by Buckingham, who contended that the five thousand signatures gathered by the wooden-buildings petitioners "incontestably proved, that a large majority of the voters (of those at least who care any thing about the business) are in favor of the present unreasonable, unjust, and oppressive restrictions being removed."[44] Yet this claim could hardly be substantiated, since there was no guarantee that all of the signatories were actually qualified to vote. Unlike the strict laws governing access to the ballot box, there were few formal guidelines in place during this period to determine whether a petition or set of instructions was legitimate. Consequently, while only a brave or foolhardy politician would deny that the voice of the people should be obeyed in principle, many found it possible to evade this responsibility in practice by questioning whether it was truly "the people," in their sovereign capacity, who had spoken or whether their mantle had merely been falsely assumed by an interested minority.

Even more pressing for the Middling Interest was the problem of what to do with legislators who refused to follow instructions. The Massachusetts Constitution affirmed the people's right to "give instructions to their representatives," but the corresponding obligation of representatives to carry out those instructions was at best implicit. Furthermore, as the *Defence* acknowledged, "there are no constitutional means of enforcing the obedience to such instructions; because a representative has a constitutional right to keep his seat to the end of his term." In the opinion of that author, a formal mechanism for compulsion was unnecessary, because every representative on assuming office took an oath to uphold the constitution, and "consequently in as much as we have established the constitutional right to give instructions, and a correspondent obligation to obey them, obedience to such instructions is one of the duties which every representative solemnly swears to fulfil." If a legislator should feel unable to follow a set of instructions, the *Defence* concluded, "let him address his constituents, frankly avow his scruples, and withdraw from an agency, which he can no longer execute in conformity with their views."[45]

This voluntary check was clearly inadequate, however, for members of the Boston delegation in the legislature had refused to comply with instructions and, far from resigning, were now offering themselves as candidates for another term. The only remaining option was for voters to signal their displeasure at the polls. Consequently, the insurgents sought to make this the sole issue in the coming selection of state senators. On 11 March a "large and respectable meeting of citizens from all the wards in Boston" took place, with the Federalist glazier Michael Roulstone in the chair and the coachmaker William W. Blake acting as secretary. Those present adopted a resolution that "men in civil society are in danger of being led by party names to act contrary to their true interests" and put forward their own slate of senatorial candidates in opposition to the regular Federalist list.[46] The reelection of the chief offenders, "which as patriots they ought to decline," a rebel flyer announced to voters, "would set a dangerous example to the Commonwealth and to your country. You sanction their error. You acknowledge the principle that 'instructions to representatives and that on a municipal concern, are not binding.' You relinquish in this the dearest right in your Constitution!"[47]

In contrast, loyal partisans were adamant that the wooden-buildings dispute should not be allowed to intrude upon the senatorial election. "We do not think it right, on the one hand, to present a petition soliciting our friendship, and on the strength of that very petition, in the other, to impose on us a list of men, for no other purpose than to carry down the measure," protested the editor of the *Commercial Gazette*.[48] "The question ought not to be simply, 'Whether we shall have permission to erect commodious wooden buildings?,'" lectured another correspondent in the same paper, "but whether we will choose men to rule over us, who are emphatically, 'honest, capable, and faithful to the constitution;' men who will not pledge themselves to vote for particular schemes, but who will look to the interests of the community at large."[49]

These remarks reflect a conservative vision of the political process in which the people were expected to elect the best men to public office and then defer to their judgment in matters of policy. This attitude was epitomized by "One of the Remonstrants against any wooden houses," who doubted whether instructions and petitions could ever be compatible with good government. What "would be the state of our Legislature, if petitions should be circulated on any great question, . . . and 300,000 petitioners were applicants for the law? Could the Legislature act freely, and advisedly in such a case?" the author inquired. "There is no use in town meetings—none in deliberative legislative proceedings, if such a course should be deemed proper, and should be generally resorted to," he continued. "Of all this the petitioners seem not to be aware, and they have had the imprudence to believe that by the mere force of numbers they can carry a question adverse to the great interests of the town and of the republic at large."[50] In essence, this writer was prioritizing the welfare of the community, as defined by the town's political leaders, above the dictates of public opinion, or "mere force of numbers." The republican principle of popular sovereignty, in his eyes, did not necessarily equate with the democratic practice of majority rule.

The Middling Interest completely rejected this model of politics. "Our Republic is simply a government of the people," declared the *Exposition;* ". . . the majority are, and of right ought to be, sovereign; and . . . there is not, nor can be danger in trusting to the majority, when every voter in the Commonwealth is left free to form, express and act upon his own opinions of men and measures."[51] The right of instruction served as a practical articulation of the sovereignty of the people by providing for their active and ongoing participation in government between elections. Taking aim at Boston's established party leadership, the *Defence* maintained that "the adherents to THE FEW, deny this right; because they believe the people must be managed, and that THE FEW are better able to direct public affairs: while more liberal men assert this right; because they believe in the competency of the people to judge for themselves." The wooden-buildings dispute, therefore, involved nothing less than "a question on the fundamental principles of our government; whether the power of the State resides in the people; or is vested at every election beyond their controul in the representatives elected."[52] In pointed contrast to their opponents, the Middling Interest embraced an expansive interpretation of the democratic potential inherent in the idea of popular sovereignty.

The "Middling Interest Ticket" received more than 43 percent of the ballots cast in the senatorial election on 1 April 1822. Typically accustomed to commanding a two-thirds share of the vote, the Federalist slate limped home on this occasion with barely half; a scattering of support for Republican candidates actually robbed two of the six Federalist nominees of the absolute majority they needed to take office. Reflecting on the result, a correspondent to the *Patriot* gleefully remarked that "though [the Federalists] may boast of a partial victory, it is such a victory as Pyrrhus gained over the Romans, when he said, 'another such victory and I am ruined.'"[53] Sure enough, just days after this letter was published the Middling Interest would go on to inflict another, even more damaging blow against party rule in Boston.

❖ The year 1822 was a momentous year in Boston's history, for the furor over wooden buildings played out against the backdrop of the town's incorporation as a city.[54] Calls for incorporation dated back to the mid-seventeenth century but had always been forestalled by popular fears that such a move would further consolidate power in the hands of a select circle of politicians. Late in 1821 the town's managers tried once again. The increased size of the municipality, they argued, made the present mode of administration, which relied on town meetings in which all adult males could have their say on any public issue, impractical. The only solution was "to change the government of the town in all matters of Legislation from a *simple democracy* to a *Representative Republic*" by replacing the town meeting with an elected board of aldermen and mayor.[55]

In light of the evident restlessness among Boston's citizenry, this might seem like an inauspicious occasion for party grandees to have pushed for a complete overhaul of the town's political structure. But the architects of incorporation were convinced that such a reform would prevent the recurrence of unwelcome incidents like the sales-at-auction debacle. By and large, these sentiments were shared by Federalist and Republican leaders alike. "I do not perceive any feeling of political parties to be operative in forming opinions on the proposed change," Sullivan informed Otis, echoing the opinion of Gerry Fairbanks, a Republican activist appointed to the committee charged with drawing up a plan for city government, that "the thing has not in any of its details taken a party turn."[56] One major obstacle remained, however. Before they could solicit the General Court to pass a bill of incorporation, the proposal's backers required the approval of Boston's citizens expressed in a town meeting.

Debate over the measure continued for three days.[57] Time and again men of middling circumstances came forward to proclaim that they would not support the plan unless it was rewritten to include a provision for voting in wards. Past elections had always taken place at Faneuil Hall, the Federalist classroom of Otis's metaphor. Those in favor of this change pointed out, quite sensibly, that if the increased size of the town made it no longer practical to govern through town meetings, then it was equally unreasonable to expect an electorate of several thousand to cast their ballots at a single polling place. Even more importantly, they argued, ward voting would take power back from political parties and return it to the people. "This measure will prevent intrigue, will cut up caucuses," avowed one speaker. "The election will then be at our doors—we can step in with our leather aprons on—can choose a man of our own sentiments—one whom we know."[58]

When news of the ward-voting scheme reached Washington, Otis was struck "full of fears" and immediately put pen to paper in praise of the "Lancastrian system" of political management.[59] The Federalist leaders back home in Boston, however, did not share his concerns. "So long as the present majority in the town continue," Sullivan reassured his anxious friend, candidates for office "will be agreed on, in caucus;—proper measures will be taken to have this agreement understood at the ward meetings; and we ought not, I think, to apprehend that voters will not understand who they should vote for, or be less disposed to vote, than if the meetings were in Faneuil Hall."[60] Ward voting was written into the draft charter, the town meeting signaled its concurrence, and the proposal was passed by the state legislature with the proviso that it be ratified by a popular referendum. On 4 March 1822 Boston voted 2,797 to 1,881 in favor of becoming a city.[61]

Any sense of satisfaction felt by the Federalist leadership would prove short-lived, however. Emboldened by their victory on ward voting and their impressive showing in the recent senatorial contest, discontented elements resolved to challenge the established parties' stranglehold over the choice of municipal officers under the new charter, which would occur on 8 April. To ensure bipartisan support for incorporation, and to avoid an unseemly struggle for places in the inaugural administration, Federalist organizers had struck a deal with their Republican counterparts to include three Republicans on their ticket for aldermen. In return, the Republicans pledged to allow their ostensible opponents to choose the five remaining aldermen and also the city's inaugural mayor.[62] The latter position, both sides understood, would be filled by Otis. As one observer subsequently recalled, "A plan had been formed by a number of politicians, that he [Otis] should be the first mayor, as a stepping stone to the Governor's Chair, & would then have the arrangement of the City offices & salaries & could then reward partisans who had pressed the City Charter through the Legislature for this purpose."[63]

This elitist caballing was precisely the sort of conduct that the Middling Interest perceived as robbing the people of their rightful role in the political process. The pyramidal nominating structure employed by both existing parties, the *Galaxy* proclaimed, was a sham. "These nominations all originate in an insurance office, or at some rich man's parlor fire, where the wine and the compliments circulate liberally," Buckingham explained. "For decency's sake, a convention is then called of the ward committees, with some dozen of their neighbors whom they can trust with the secrets of the general committee, and whom they know will fall in with the views of the junto." But this introduced only the semblance of inclusiveness, for "these ward committees are usually nominated by some impudent brazen-lung'd toad eater, who is sent to the ward meeting for that purpose. The moderator of a caucus has *convenient ears;* he never hears the name of an independent man; but he can hear *whispers* from the well known, tried and faithful servants of the aristocracy, or he can, upon an emergency, take *nods* and *winks* for a nomination." In consequence, the editor concluded, "not one of the Middling Interest has, in fact, any more voice or influence in the nomination than the man in the moon."[64]

The columns of the *Galaxy* had long provided an open forum for fulminations against "the present system, by which the junto, who are only lovers of themselves, manage to monopolize those offices, which, for the honor of the town and the good of its citizens should be given only to men of talents, and patriotism."[65] "This system has been pursued in Boston twenty years, more or less," Buckingham complained in 1820, "and for the whole of that period there never has been a single free and uncontrolled election."[66] The mayoral election in 1822 offered an opportunity to shatter this monopoly. Knowing full well that the Federalist leadership favored Otis, the proprietor of the *Galaxy* publicly declared his preference for the party maverick Josiah Quincy.[67] Meanwhile, behind the scenes, a "Committee of citizens headed by a Carpenter" approached the erstwhile candidate, and he consented to stand.[68] "Quincy has thrown himself into the hands of the 'Midling or Medling

Interest,'" an astonished Thomas Handasyd Perkins reported to Otis.[69] The contest was on.

Federalist commentators professed bemusement at the selection of Quincy as the standard-bearer for the insurgency. "Admitting that there is such a thing as the middling interest, distinct from the interest of the federalists of Boston, is there any thing in the character, habits, associations or politics of Mr. Quincy, that can connect him with it more than Mr. Otis?" inquired the *Daily Advertiser*.[70] But as Quincy's daughter Eliza perceptively observed, the crucial difference between the two candidates was that her father "was a Federalist from principle but too independent to join in party measures."[71] His consistent refusal to bow to the dictates of the General Committee had led to numerous run-ins with the party hierarchy, including being unceremoniously dumped from the Federalist senatorial ticket in 1820 after several years of service, and by early 1822 he had been relegated to the unfancied post of municipal court judge. Nonetheless, he remained well known to the Boston electorate, and his Federalist credentials would appeal to dissident partisans who could never bring themselves to support a Republican. When he was approached by the Middling Interest delegation, Quincy cannot have been unaware of the open secret that Otis was being groomed for the mayoralty, but once again he demonstrated his "inveterate habit of thinking for himself" by defying the party grandees in a bid to resurrect his own political prospects.[72]

At their candidate's behest, members of the Middling Interest led by the merchant William Sturgis, whom Perkins described as Quincy's "great 'slang wanger,'" made one final attempt to have their voice heard within the Federalist Party by challenging Otis's formal nomination at the primary caucus.[73] The fact that they considered this a realistic prospect demonstrates just how far disillusionment had spread among the party rank and file. When the ballots were counted, Otis was declared the victor by the slender margin of 175 to 170, but Quincy's supporters cried foul. The *Galaxy* reported that Otis's friends, "after the marking for candidates was declared to be closed, persuaded others to come and mark for their favorite candidate, thus turning the scale against the candidate who had a majority of the marks."[74] "It is this kind of management which has produced a division in the ranks of federalism, and sown the seeds of a new party, which, like the fabled teeth of the giant, will soon spring up and become an army that will overpower its predecessor," Buckingham commented.[75] The rebels refused to abide by the caucus decision and pledged to back Quincy as their candidate for mayor under the Middling Interest banner, thus signaling their intent to abandon the Federalist Party since it could not be reformed from within.

The full force of the Federalist machine was unleashed on Otis's behalf. "Mr. Otis' partisans were very angry, that the people should presume to interfere with their plans & between the two parties the City was thrown into a most violent commotion," Eliza Quincy recorded.[76] The Federalist candidate himself was still absent in Washington, and in any case contemporary protocol would have prevented him from personally campaigning. Instead, as an anonymous wit remarked, "those who aspired to be Mayor, left [it] wholly to their agents to manage the public, and anxiously awaited the rising of the popular breeze."[77] According to Eliza, "Mr Otis' sons & sons in law distributed votes & every effort was made for his election." This led to an amusing encounter on the day before the ballot, when the Quincy family ran into Harrison Gray Otis Jr. on their return from church. "Where are you going so fast, Otis," Josiah demanded, to which the younger Otis responded, "Working against you Sir, as hard as I can." "Very well," came Quincy's laconic reply, "only take care you don't work *too hard*."[78]

The Federalist press also threw its whole weight behind Otis. After the contest concluded, the *Galaxy* complained that "the leading federal editors have entirely excluded from their columns every communication in favor of Mr. Quincy, nor have they even deigned to mention that he was a candidate, till the day of election; and then, only to oppose him." Freedom of the press was considered to be a cornerstone of republican government, and the conduct of the Federalist newspapers provided critics with yet more evidence that the party's leadership cared little for the sovereignty of the people when their own interests were at stake. "It would have been fair, in our humble opinion, for the editors of the town, to have permitted the friends of both these gentlemen to advocate publickly their respective claims, and to offer to the consideration of the citizens at large, the reasons which induced a preference to either," Buckingham declared. "We hope we shall never feel impelled to adopt that narrow-minded, exclusive sort of policy, which would seal up the press of this free and enlightened country, against the expression of the will and sentiments of a majority of citizens, and open it only at the will and pleasure of a cabal."[79]

In making the case for Otis, Federalist writers cast the choice primarily in terms of loyalty to party. While the senator's "distinguished talents and character" were alone sufficient to qualify him for the office, announced the *Boston Daily Advertiser,* "there is another ground on which we feel more conclusively bound to urge his election.—He is the regularly nominated candidate, at a meeting in which all the federalists of the town were duly represented and as such is entitled to the support of the federal party."[80] These arguments were echoed by the *Commercial Gazette.* "As citizens and as federalists, we feel impelled, by a more positive and imperious duty than we owe to any *individual* on earth, however estimable in his public or private character, to resist the nomination of [Quincy] for this office," proclaimed the editor. "Federalists . . . who feel an interest in the concerns of the party, and who wish to preserve its integrity, have but one course to pursue;—to give the *regularly nominated Candidate* their cordial support."[81] Statements such as these demonstrate the extent to which political parties and in particular the idea of party discipline were already embedded into the fabric of Boston politics by this point.

The Federalist efforts were to no avail, however, for Quincy outpolled Otis by 1,736 to 1,384 in the final count. Narrowly denied an outright victory by a few hundred votes cast for other candidates in traditionally Republican wards, the frontrunner disappointed his followers by deciding that he would rather withdraw than go in by a small majority on the second ballot, leaving the way open for a compromise candidate, John Phillips, a notional Federalist who commanded the respect of all parties. Nonetheless, the scale of Otis's defeat could not be disguised; in the wake of their upset in the senatorial elections, the Federalist share of the vote had slipped still further, to less than 40 percent. "The Junta people in Boston, as they are called, have met with a total overthrow," exulted the New York senator and party politico Martin Van Buren, who certainly knew a thing or two about juntas. On the other side of the partisan divide, a despondent Christopher Gore, a Federalist patriarch of Waltham, Massachusetts, gloomily predicted that "what little of old Federalism remained will soon be extinct."[82]

The events surrounding the Boston mayoral election of 1822 reflect the broader concerns that many Americans had about party management of the electoral process.[83] "The Republican Institution and the Central Committee . . . have taken from the good citizens of the town all the labor of investigation into the characters and claims of candidates for officers," lamented Buckingham, "and he who would not give his vote as one or other of these self-created bodies of aristocrats and demagogues should dictate, might as well stay at home."[84] The pyramidal structure of party organization offered the illusion of popular control, but on closer inspection it often proved to be nothing more than "a formula for self-replicating petty oligarchs."[85] And far from promoting free debate about men and measures, the partisan press frequently seemed more concerned with stifling dissent among the rank and file; unquestioning devotion to party was the order of the day.[86] But in endeavoring to squeeze the people out of any meaningful participation in the choice of public officers, the Boston parties overreached themselves and provoked the populist revolt that came within a whisker of placing its own candidate in the mayoralty.

❖ For loyal Federalists the emergence of the Middling Interest proved utterly mystifying. Moved to put pen to paper by the confusion surrounding the mayoral election, Leverett Saltonstall, of nearby Salem, inquired of an associate, "What are you coming to in Boston? Quincy v. Otis! This is too bad. There must be something in this business of which we at a distance are wholly ignorant." "I supposed," Saltonstall added, "that nothing could be wanting but the consent of Otis to choose him Mayor by an immense majority."[87] This conviction was shared by Perkins, who wrote to Otis, in Washington, on the eve of the contest to reassure him that "but for the most improper conduct of Quincy, the Election of the Mayor would have been unanimous."[88] These assessments attribute too much agency to Quincy, however, and serve only to verify their authors' ignorance of popular feeling in Boston. Accustomed to taking the lead in politics, party grandees naturally assumed that Quincy's mayoral candidacy was the cause, rather than merely a consequence, of the Middling Interest revolt.

In truth, the protest movement began to take shape long before Quincy accepted the nomination for mayor, and its members harbored more profound aims than simply realizing his political ambitions. In many ways the Middling Interest was typified by Joseph T. Buckingham.[89] Born into poverty in 1779, Buckingham took up a printing apprenticeship at the age of sixteen. After two decades, and several false starts, he began publication of his own newspaper, the *Galaxy*, in 1817.[90] The venture proved highly successful, and

Buckingham soon counted subscribers across the Union, but his sympathies always remained with the laboring classes, and he was proud to serve as secretary, vice-president, and finally president of the Massachusetts Charitable Mechanic Association.[91] In politics, Buckingham was a Federalist by principle but never a member of the party's inner circle. On national issues he criticized counterparts such as Benjamin Russell, editor of the rival *Centinel,* who promoted conciliation with the Republican administration in Washington. In local affairs the roles were reversed. Russell, a member of the Federalist General Committee, defended the status quo, whereas Buckingham condemned party control of the political process and backed the Middling Interest. Committed to retaining his independence, however, Buckingham would never seek public office, unlike Russell, who was rewarded with a seat in the Massachusetts Senate for his loyalty to party.

Writing for the *Galaxy,* Buckingham described the Middling Interest as encompassing "those classes of society, of whatever profession, which have not amassed wealth enough to live without industry and labor, and which are not so poor as to be dependent on charity."[92] Modern research has confirmed that when Boston's wards are ranked from wealthiest to poorest, those closest to the center of this scale provided the insurgency with its main electoral strength.[93] Little biographical information survives for individuals like Ellis, Roulstone, Blake, and Sturgis, who took an active role in organizing the movement, but data mined from city directories and tax records suggest that they were also drawn from a different socioeconomic stratum than their counterparts in the established parties. In terms of occupation, 59 percent of the identifiable leaders of the Middling Interest may be categorized as small producers, shopkeepers, or laborers, which is more than twice the proportion of these three classes in the upper echelons of the Federalist machine although almost identical to their presence in the Republican Party. As for wealth, the median tax assessment levied on Middling Interest activists was slightly more than ten dollars, whereas the equivalent for Republicans was almost twice that amount, and for the Federalists it was nearly double again (table 4).

Socioeconomic divisions do not tell the whole story, however. "It has been sneeringly said, that the Middling Interest is an array of the POOR against the RICH," acknowledged the author of the *Exposition,* but "on the contrary, the Middling Interest are as ready to admit the just influence of rich men as the

TABLE 4. *Profile of political organizers in Boston, Massachusetts, 1820–1824*

	Federalist Party	Republican Party	Middling Interest
Median tax assessment ($)	36.76	19.79	10.29
Mean tax assessment ($)	64.92	45.51	20.97
Number of organizers assessed over $100 (% of total)	9 (25)	3 (10)	0 (0)
Occupation (% of total)			
Gentleman	9	4	0
Professional	30	18	23
Financial or commercial service provider	30	14	18
Editor	3	4	0
Small producer or storekeeper	21	46	45
Mechanic (laborer)	6	14	14

Sources: Boston Directory; Buckingham, *Annals;* "Members of the Massachusetts Charitable Mechanic Association 1819," in Jenkins, *Address;* Rohrbach, *Boston Taxpayers in 1821;* various newspaper articles.

FEW, who affect to enroll all of them in their ranks." "On this subject, we hold that rich men acquire no political influence justly by their wealth alone," the writer explained, but this did not preclude any individual, rich or poor, from exercising an influence proportionate to "the soundness of his judgment, the fairness of his mind, and his ability to be useful."[94] This claim is borne out by the men the movement nominated for office; in neither wealth nor occupation was there much difference between candidates backed by the rebels and those endorsed by the two established parties (table 5). When Middling Interest polemicists took aim at a host of unpopular measures, including imprisonment for debt, inequitable tax assessments, inflated judicial fees, and of course the restrictions on wooden buildings, they were not seeking to drive their well-to-do neighbors from office but simply to make them accountable to their constituents.[95]

Similarly, the Middling Interest did not reject the concept of party absolutely; they merely renounced the uses to which it had been put by Boston's political elite.[96] Some die-hard Federalists muttered darkly of a Republican plot, declaring that the movement "only unites the Old Democratic party

TABLE 5. *Profile of candidates for public office in Boston, Massachusetts, 1820–1824*

	Federalist Party	Republican Party	Middling Interest
Median tax assessment ($)	53.74	50.58	50.58
Mean tax assessment ($)	96.04	115.86	68.58
Number of candidates assessed over $100 (% of total)	57 (29)	41 (21)	18 (17)
Profession (as % of total)			
Gentleman	6	5	7
Professional	24	20	18
Financial or commercial service provider	46	45	47
Editor	4	2	0
Small producer or storekeeper	15	25	20
Mechanic (laborer)	4	4	8

Source: See table 4.

under a new name."[97] Most commentators, however, whether friend or foe to the insurgency, accepted that it was dominated by former Federalists who had lost faith in their party leaders. The *Commercial Gazette* interrupted an appeal to those "who range themselves under the name of the 'middling interest'" to observe that "we mean those of them who are federalists, and they in fact constitute the mass of that body."[98] Likewise, the *Galaxy* informed its readers that "the great majority of the [Middling Interest] party consists of those federalists, who having seldom or never been . . . consulted in the selection of candidates previous to important elections, have thought fit to withdraw from a party which had never used them but as humble instruments to effect purposes in which the mechanics and middling classes of the people had no concern." "If some of the democratic party choose to vote for the Middling Interest candidates," Buckingham added innocently, "we know not any method by which they can be prevented."[99]

Those who spoke for the movement willingly conceded that "the utility of political parties in all free governments, is as little to be disputed, as their pernicious and deplorable effects when carried to extreme."[100] As one Middling Interest meeting recorded, *Federalist* and *Republican* were "names which might have originally arisen from a difference of opinion with equally patriotic motives."[101] But that time had passed. "What distinction is there *now* between a *federalist* and a *democrat,* but the name?" queried the *Galaxy.* "There seems to be no difference of opinion with regard to the policy which our national administration ought to, and does, pursue," the editor continued, "and it is difficult to ascertain to which of the great political parties a man belongs, unless you sound him upon the policy of Adams and Hamilton, of Jefferson and Madison."[102] The only remaining obstacle to political progress, the protestors concluded, was "a few aspiring demagogues, [who] are anxious to keep alive the flame of old party animosities, for the advantage of themselves and their relatives or dependents."[103]

The object of the Middling Interest, then, as expressed in the *Exposition,* was "the suppression of party spirit, and the violence and overbearing domination of those, who seek power for the gratification of possessing it, and use the influence it gives, to controul freedom of opinion and independence of suffrage." "They who wish success to the cause of the Middling or General Interest," the author explained, "are disposed to try the experiment of supporting good measures by whomsoever adopted, without regard to any old party names, which from obvious causes has ceased to be significant."[104] Likewise, the *Bostonian & Mechanics' Journal,* another newspaper sympathetic to the rebels, informed its readers that in the election of representatives "it matters not to what party the candidate attaches himself, so [long as] he be a suitable person to discharge the duties of the office for which he is nominated."[105] This philosophy was of course antithetical to the oft-repeated mantra of the partisan press that maintaining party regularity must take precedence over personal preferences for candidates and policies.

But for all their rhetorical appeals to "freedom of opinion and independence of suffrage," the rebels were well aware that they could not be successful unless they matched their opponents in organization. "No one, it is presumed, can object to the *principle* of such an organization of the town, or city," Buckingham had commented on the account of Federalist nominating procedures published in the *Commercial Gazette* following the mayoral election of 1822. "It is the exclusive and one-sided policy which has been *practised* under this organization, that is a subject of complaint."[106] Shortly thereafter, notices were posted in the press inviting "those who are favorable to the Middling Interest" to attend meetings "for the purpose of carrying into effect a system of Organization."[107] The result was the adoption of a formal constitution for the movement. Having "made themselves conspicuous by two or three troublesome ebullitions of a bad spirit," one astonished observer reported, "this band of murmurers have actually become an organized party calling themselves 'the Middling Interest.'"[108]

The Constitution of the Middling Interest Association established an organizational structure that bore an uncanny resemblance to that of their Federalist opponents.[109] The document provided for three types of committees:

1. A Ward Committee, consisting of twenty-four persons in each ward.
2. A Select Committee, of thirteen—consisting of one person from each ward, and one person elected by the Committee at large.
3. A General Committee, to consist of the Ward and Select Committees, who are to assemble at the request of the Select Committee.

The function of the General Committee, a mirror of the Federalist primary caucus, was "to take into consideration all elections, and to give a fair expression of sentiment in proposing, for candidates, men of approved fidelity to the common cause—the nomination of such being made, they shall be marked for, at all times; and the highest number of marks shall be supported." The Ward Committees were required "to appoint Vote Distributors, Rallying Committees, and all other Committees preparatory to an election [and] to attend that all persons, duly qualified, favorable to the Middling Interest, have names inserted on the Ward Lists." The Select Committee served to coordinate the electioneering efforts of the Ward Committees and was evidently intended to provide central direction to the movement, much like the Federalists' General Committee.

Determined to prove that party could serve as a vehicle for popular rule, the Middling Interest sought to distinguish themselves from their more established counterparts in two ways. First, they institutionalized the principle of rotation in office. Their constitution mandated not only that all committeemen were to be chosen annually by the members in their respective wards but also that "one third at least of all the several Committees (including such persons as may have resigned) shall be ineligible for office for the next political year."[110] This decision was evidently calculated to appeal to those who denounced the Federalist leadership for "cling[ing] to the honours and offices in the gift of the party with an affection stronger than death."[111]

Second, Middling Interest spokesmen placed great emphasis on the movement's responsiveness to popular sentiment in the nomination of candidates. Typical of this publicity campaign was a handbill circulated prior to the choice of state senators in March 1822 announcing that "a considerable number of gentlemen from every ward in Boston, have been for several weeks engaged to ascertain the voice of the community; and had it been possible they would have extended the enquiry to every individual citizen." "Your opinion was wished for if it was not obtained," the author assured his readers.[112] The insurgents were also careful to break the trend of party insiders' monopolizing nominations for public office. Less than one-fifth of the men who are identifiable as serving on Middling Interest committees also found a place on an electoral ticket endorsed by the movement during its lifetime, compared with almost one-third of Republican Party activists and approaching half of the Federalist leadership during the same period.[113] The underlying message was clear: the Middling Interest, unlike the existing major parties, would represent the interests of the many rather than the few.

Federalist commentators, of course, denied the need for any revolution in Boston politics. "We have seen nothing material in [the Constitution of the Association] which is not to be found in the bill of rights of the state, and has not been made the ruling principle of federalists for years," claimed the editor of the *Commercial Gazette*.[114] In a speech before a Federalist caucus shortly following his defeat in the mayoral election, Otis launched a stinging attack on those he held responsible for his embarrassment. "These warm opposers of an *imaginary* privileged order, by their proposals plain would make a real privileged order," he protested. "For what is substantially a privileged order? It is one which elects, or from which only are to be elected, all the officers of Government." "It is proposed by their written constitution to secure this power to the middling interest," Otis observed, conveniently neglecting to mention that the Federalist and Republican parties both openly sought this same power for themselves. "Suppose I should propose to strike out the word 'middling' in this pamphlet and insert the word 'monied,'" he concluded, brandishing a copy of the movement's constitution, "I am persuaded that I should be overwhelmed by the burst of indignation that would resound from every part of this hall."[115]

Buckingham reacted to Otis's speech with disbelief. "Wealth has a natural influence of itself," he retorted through the *Galaxy*, "and can always command the services of mediocrity, without any combination of its possessors; but who ever heard that the middling classes of society could control the rich, or even maintain their own rights, without an association for self-defence."[116] Here the editor was returning to an argument that had found expression in the columns of his paper before. Months prior to the formation of the Middling Interest Association "Brutus" had written to complain that in Boston "a few men, signalized only by their superior wealth and ostentation, trample upon opinion, upon principle and upon the great body of the people." "Every effort to relieve the public of this monstrous Incubus will be unavailing while the people are asleep," the writer had predicted. But "let the majesty of popular resentment be once aroused to a sense of the indignity we suffer, and the danger which awaits," he promised, "and we shall then see Aristocracy and Aristocrats hurled from office and from influence; and virtue and talents, at the will of the people assume their just control."[117]

"Brutus," Buckingham, and all those who flocked to the Middling Interest standard shared one thing in common: a conviction that only by associating together could disenchanted citizens break the hold of party leaders over the political process. This version of antipartisanship was not a protest against "party" in the abstract but a demand that parties be made to serve the public as a whole rather than the whim of a few self-interested individuals. To triumph over a privileged minority, the rebels recognized, the masses must be mobilized or face the prospect of political oblivion. Without organization, as "Brutus" perceptively observed, "'We the people' have no political existence."[118]

❖ By the summer of 1822 the future of the Middling Interest appeared promising. The insurgents had tasted success at the polls, most recently securing eight seats in the May elections for the Massachusetts House of Representatives; they had established a formal institutional structure; and they had fashioned a public identity that set them apart from their main competitors. Yet just as the fortunes of the movement reached their peak, flaws in the design were also fast becoming apparent.

One critical problem was the protestors' lack of a loyal press organ, an imperative requirement for any serious political organization. At the outset, the only newspaperman sympathetic to the rebels was Buckingham, and he charted such an independent course with the *Galaxy* that his support could never be relied upon; in March 1822, for example, he offered only lukewarm endorsement to the Middling Interest senatorial ticket, while suggesting several substitutions.[119] The lack of coverage given to Quincy's mayoral campaign by the Boston press a month later further exposed this weakness in the editorial department. Shortly afterward, the defect appeared to be remedied with the establishment of the *Bostonian,* which announced that "it will be one of the purposes of this paper to support, by candid and temperate discussion, the principles of the Middling Interest; or, in other words, to assert the Constitutional rights of the MANY, in opposition to the covert and insidious *influence of the few.*"[120] Within a year, however, the editor was accused of having "deserted the object of our paper, which was the interest of the Mechanics," and sold out to the Republicans. "We have never been the tool of a party," he protested fervently, but evidently many of his patrons remained unconvinced.[121]

The trials faced by the *Bostonian* highlight an even more fundamental problem confronting the Middling Interest: how to hold together a movement composed of men who had previously been members of two competing political parties. When the rebels met to coordinate their strategy in the 1820 congressional election, a spectator reported that the rival factions "kept their positions in distinct bodies . . . [and] not unresembling game cocks, alternately crowed, and flapped their wings."[122] Republican correspondents complained that the Federalist-dominated Middling Interest were "not fully ascertaining the feelings and views of the great body of their associates," most notably in their choice of Quincy, a man "whose whole political life has rendered him obnoxious to the republican party," for mayor in 1822.[123] Others seemed to participate only to cause trouble, such as the orator who interrupted one Middling Interest meeting to announce that "he wanted no *federalists* to vote on his side, neither should he vote on theirs; that he never had voted for a *federalist,* nor ever would."[124]

In the fall of 1822 the movement suffered a setback when its candidate for Congress was soundly beaten by the rising star of Federalism, Daniel Webster. The 1823 municipal elections offered a prime chance for redemption, however; the Federalists were in disarray, having just lost control of both the Massachusetts governorship and the state legislature for the first time in a decade. In their desperation, some party leaders were even prepared to forgive Quincy his previous treachery. According to Eliza Quincy, "Mr. Sullivan

& other Federalists came & requested Mr. Quincy to consent to stand for mayor as the last hope of that party."[125] In response, the Middling Interest met in conference with the Republican Party and nominated George Blake as their joint candidate. Come election day, the rebel ticket benefited from an accession of Republican voters, but this was outweighed by the loss of dissident Federalists seduced back into the party fold by Quincy's defection. The latter triumphed by a substantial margin, made all the more impressive by the *Galaxy*'s claim that "the *particular* friends of Mr. Otis, we understand, either absented themselves from the polls, or gave their votes for the democratic candidate!"[126]

Otis had forecast the failure of the Middling Interest in his speech of May 1822. "Three parties can no more continue in a country, than three men can continue to fight in single combat," the defeated mayoral candidate had declared. "It will happen of necessity, that two must beat the other, before they can fight themselves, and perhaps in that very act, they become such friends, as to bury the hatchet."[127] Historians have often assumed that the leaders of the first American parties, guided by a republican ideology that taught that political life required the subordination of private interests to the common pursuit of a unitary public good, never truly accepted the legitimacy of partisan competition.[128] Yet here Otis classified the insurgency as unnatural specifically because it did not fit into a political order structured around a contest between two established parties. In response, even Buckingham was forced to admit that the prospects for the movement were uncertain. "Under its present organization, [the Middling Interest Association] cannot long continue," he observed. "The materials are too discordant to amalgamate. Some have joined it from principle and others from policy. We are satisfied that men of opposite political sentiments can not long act in concert, and that a dissolution or an expurgation must shortly take place."[129]

Developments outside Boston would hasten that dissolution. As John Lowell, another Federalist leader, observed to Otis, certain "milk & water [i.e., diluted] Federalists" might take pleasure in "joining with ye Democrats [to] mortify us, & carry a man offensive to us" on occasion, but "*they* know, that on the *power* of the *party* their very existence as publick men depends." "What would Q[uincy] & P[hillips] & all the P's & Q's become, if Democracy gets as well seated in the saddle as [it] is in N York?" he pondered. "They will never again be heard of. They will eat no more Corporation dinners, nor be regaled any longer with the odoriferous praises upon which they have subsisted heretofore." The Republican victory in the 1823 state elections was hugely damaging to the insurgency, therefore, as Federalist dissidents rallied to their party's standard in a bid to restore their previous ascendancy. When forced to decide between loyalty to party and permanent political obscurity, as Lowell had predicted, Quincy chose the former, and consequently "the 'oi Polloi' must follow us, because they have *no one else* to follow."[130] Within a year the Middling Interest, as an independent political force, was spent. There could be, it seems, no enduring place for a third party in Boston's political world.

❖ Despite the movement's limited life span, modern scholars have hailed the Middling Interest for "making the city a more democratic polity."[131] This conclusion fits neatly into the trajectory of progress that characterizes the celebratory narrative of early U.S. politics, but there is limited evidence to support it. Josiah Quincy certainly proved far less responsive to public opinion than the men who relaunched his political career might have wished; after one old supporter approached him following his election in 1823 to "beg him not to lose his popularity which gave him such a power to be useful," the new mayor "only laughed & told him popularity was the last thing he should think of, he should do whatever he considered his duty, & the people might turn him out as soon as they pleased."[132] When Quincy finally did step down in 1828, his successor was none other than his old nemesis, Harrison Gray Otis, a sign that the Middling Interest had done little to shake the patrician set's hold over local politics. The Bostonian elite, writes the historian Ronald Story, "achieve[d] an ascendance which stood ... dramatically athwart the egalitarian, individualistic, democratizing tendencies which were once thought, with some justification, to have characterized the age."[133] The triumph of party in this instance, even with the reformist pressures generated by popular insurgency, can hardly be read as the triumph of democracy.

In truth, the Middling Interest took shape at a time when popular participation in Massachusetts politics was waning. During the first fifteen years of the nineteenth century, as the well-organized Federalist and Republican parties engaged in fierce competition, turnout in statewide elections began frequently to exceed 50 percent of the eligible electorate for the first time, peaking at 67 percent in 1812.[134] In the years from 1820 to 1824, in contrast, the highest recorded turnout was 57 percent, and on two occasions the figure slipped to as low as 40 percent. Yet the Federalist and Republican parties of this later period were no less organized and no less competitive than their predecessors. If the first set of data provides compelling evidence for the role parties played in opening public life to mass participation, the second set proves that the presence of an entrenched two-party system is not on its own sufficient to sustain popular engagement in politics.

The problem faced by both major parties following the War of 1812 was that they had outgrown the important points of conflict that previously energized them. This was a theme to which Joseph T. Buckingham returned time and again in the columns of the *New-England Galaxy.* "Men who have always belonged to the federal party, who joined it in early life, find it difficult to break off early associations," he acknowledged. "They undoubtedly sometimes vote for its candidates more from affection to their friends and a wish to save the party from the mortification of a defeat than from any other motive."[135] But "young men who are now coming forward in life, do not feel all the excitements, that govern the conduct of their fathers."[136] This increasingly large share of the electorate could have little stake in a system in which "before it can be decided to support any candidate, it is necessary to look hard, and see whether he advocated or opposed the famous embargo and gun-boat system.—whether he belonged to the Jacobin Club of 1796, or the Hartford Convention of 1814."[137] With less and less to differentiate between Federalist and Republican positions on public issues, at both the federal and state levels, party leaders became ever more reliant upon an appeal to old loyalties to mobilize their supporters just as these loyalties were themselves losing their meaning.

The result was a clear decline in participation rates in Massachusetts. "The majority of the people in the state seldom trouble their heads about public matters unless private, and personal interest is to be in some shape or another affected," Buckingham lamented in 1820, shortly before the Middling Interest burst onto the scene. "They mind their own domestic concerns," he continued,

> and leave the affairs of state to be settled by juntos, caucuses, central committees, and a few demagogues, who, having by management, seated themselves in office, are determined to keep their places and establish

themselves as perpetual dictators. Whatever is said by General ——, or Major ——, or the Hon. Mr. ——, or . . . Esq. is received as right and expedient; and if there should happen to be a slight difference of opinion, as to the measure proposed, it is wrong to suggest it, because opposition duly weakens and divides the party, and hurts the feelings of these honorable and patriotic gentlemen.[138]

In this reading, party appears as a tool for managing, not promoting, popular engagement in politics. Nominating practices were manipulated to concentrate the choice of candidates in the hands of a small circle of men, while the doctrine of party discipline served as a means for stifling dissent. In essence, Buckingham's analysis anticipates that of some modern commentators; many citizens, in his experience, were all too ready to relegate their political fate to the care of a few career politicians who ruled through the medium of party.[139]

The Middling Interest promised to change all that, as the practice of politics itself became a source of conflict. The movement drew strength not from an abstract opposition to the very concept of party but from a deeply felt disillusionment with the established parties in Boston, prompted by their failure to address real issues of popular concern. The United States Constitution proclaimed that the people were sovereign in principle, but it was left to supporters of the insurgency to adopt an expansive interpretation of what this should mean in practice. Most importantly, they championed the right of instruction as a guarantee that citizens could play a continuing role in government between elections. "We claim from our constitutional agents some deference to the known will of the majority," thundered the movement's manifesto.[140] But this view did not find favor with the town's established political leadership; in their eyes, to paraphrase the historian Edmund Morgan, instructions were "a little too literally the voice of the people."[141] Ultimately the Middling Interest challenge may have faded without making Boston significantly more democratic. The very existence of the movement, however, demonstrates that contemporaries viewed the meaning of popular sovereignty as something to be contested and were more than willing to experiment with new forms of organization when old ones were found wanting.

2 "LET US UNITE LIKE ONE MAN"
Organizing the Opposition to Slavery in Illinois

On 2 August 1824 the citizens of Illinois were called upon to decide whether to summon a constitutional convention in order to open their state to slavery. At "the elections through the State, the utmost exertions prevailed, but no riots," recorded one observer. "The aged and crippled were carried to the polls, and men voted on this occasion that had not seen the ballot box before in twenty years."[1] Modern scholars have identified the establishment of political parties as a necessary precondition for mass engagement in politics. If this were true, then few parts of the United States during the early 1820s would have experienced lower rates of participation than Illinois, for parties were anathema in the Prairie State. Yet the "convention question" brought more than four-fifths of the eligible electorate out to vote, a turnout far in excess of any witnessed around the same time in Massachusetts, where, as we saw in the previous chapter, two-party competition defined the political arena. Popular participation, it would seem, was flourishing in the absence of parties.

The very fact that the question whether to legalize slavery was to be determined by a referendum underscores the fundamental American faith in the sovereignty of the people. Pro- and antislavery activists alike accepted this framework and applied their energies to securing a popular mandate. Despite lacking practice in the arts of partisan combat, the protagonists in this struggle were schooled in an associational tradition stretching back to the American Revolution. Drawing on this shared experience, both sides experimented with different methods of rallying support, but ultimately it was the opponents of a convention who proved most effective at disseminating their message and mobilizing voters on election day. Their success demonstrates that contemporaries were not dependent upon parties to put the principle of majority rule into practice.

❖ Prior to the convention campaign, politics in Illinois had assumed little importance beyond a biennial scramble for office. Since the state's entrance into the Union in 1818 the political landscape had been dominated by the mutual enmity of its two U.S. senators, Ninian Edwards and Jesse B. Thomas, the major point of dispute being neither principle nor policy but the distribution of federal patronage. The Federalist-Republican division had never penetrated deeply into the Prairie State, where all politicians of note claimed allegiance to the Jeffersonian persuasion. Those factional alignments that did develop out of the Edwards-Thomas rivalry were loosely defined and lacked dedicated popular followings. Parties of the kind that existed in Massachusetts were wholly unknown.[2]

This absence of parties ensured that entry into politics remained largely unregulated. "We are all politicians, we are all candidates—and the policy of the nation is the peculiar study of every wight, whether of the plebeian or patrician order," proclaimed "Rattlebrain" in the *Kaskaskia Republican*.[3] There were no nominating caucuses or conventions; instead, as one resident explained succinctly to a distant relative, "every person offers who chooses for any office."[4] Nor could ambitious men simply rely on the power of party loyalties to carry their election. Every applicant for public favor "is obliged to ride over the whole state or district, as the case may be, attending every log rolling, petty muster, or barbecue; where he is expected to make what is called a stump speech wheather he possesses a talent for that sublime species of eloquence or not," wrote Nathanial Buckmaster, reporting to his brother on his own bid for a minor post in local government. "He must relate his political experience, and recapitulate his political creed, which he takes care shall always coincide with that of his hearers," Buckmaster continued, and "this, together with the right of instruction, will bare out the candidate."[5] This practice of openly courting the electorate, including an explicit nod to the latter's right to direct the conduct of their elected representatives through instruction, was designed to affirm the practical sovereignty of the people in a manner that would have been repugnant to the Federalist grandees of Boston.

For political commentators in Illinois, the experience of Massachusetts provided a salutary lesson on the danger of parties. "Whoever has seen, as we have, how regularly drilled and organized, is the system of elective nomination in the eastern states, . . . would see how specious, how plausable, and yet how pernicious, is this course," observed "Zero" in the *Illinois Intelligencer.* "Instead of the direct individual influence of the candidate, on the community at large, arising from the open declarations of his pen; his public demonstrations of the interests of his country at *the Hustings* . . . instead of all this, he is enshrined as the Juggernaut of his party." In a passage that could have come straight from the pen of Joseph Buckingham, the writer went on to deplore the "little private caucuses" that "cut and dried" the choice of candidate long before the actual nominating meeting took place. "Experience has shewn," he concluded, that "caucuses, nominations or delegations . . . are political machines in the hands of the designing, the wealthy, and the vicious, by which they essay to influence, guide, and govern popular opinion." And "Zero" was not alone in this conviction. "Nomination by delegates, is a party measure," concluded "A Republican" in the *Edwardsville Spectator,* and its introduction into the state would substitute "the will of the *few,* for the will of the *many.*"[6]

Having moved to Illinois in 1821, the New England emigrant Horatio Newhall was struck by the enthusiasm that politics generated among his new neighbors. Writing the following year to family members who had stayed behind, Newhall declared that "when party politics were at the highest pitch in Massachusetts, there was, probably, never an election more warmly contested than our next election will be for *all* our state and national officers.—Wherever you go you hear of nothing else."[7] In the 1822 race for the governorship to which Newhall referred, four candidates took to the field, one of whom was Edward Coles, a well-to-do Virginian who had moved to Illinois in order to emancipate his own slaves. Coles loudly proclaimed his independence from both the Edwards and Thomas factions, yet he still emerged victorious from a lengthy campaign conducted through extensive speaking tours and in the columns of the state's few newspapers. In the final count, two-thirds of the electorate turned out to cast their ballots, a figure significantly in excess of the four in ten who had bothered to participate in the equivalent contest in Massachusetts earlier that year.

Coles's significance lies in his determination to confront the issue that lurked beneath the surface of Illinois politics: slavery. During its territorial stage Illinois had attracted a small but influential slaveholding population. These men, who included both Edwards and Thomas, were disproportionately represented in the convention that met in 1818 to draft the new state's constitution. Constrained by the Northwest Ordinance, this document formally prohibited the introduction of slavery into Illinois, but it allowed for the continued employment of those enslaved persons already present in the state, along with additional bound labor hired in from outside to work in the lucrative salt mines. The practical effect was to establish the institution in all but name, and the number of slaves had actually increased by the taking of the next federal census in 1820.[8] No wonder, then, that Newhall, taking stock of his new home in 1821, concluded that "many of our most influential public officers are dear lovers of Slavery and would gladly introduce into this State the same system which prevails at the South."[9]

Little had changed one year later, when the recently installed Governor Coles unexpectedly called for the total abolition of all forms of forced servitude in Illinois. Seeking to turn the situation to their advantage, a coterie of conspirators in the predominately proslavery legislature responded by proposing that another constitutional convention be summoned to settle the question, hoping that the convention would favor the full legalization of the institution. The motives of these men are not clear. Some may have planned to profit personally from land sales to the expected flood of slaveholding migrants; others might sincerely have believed the measure was necessary to resurrect the state's failing economic fortunes. Rumors also circulated that the lessees of the Salines were secretly backing the scheme because their temporary permit to import bound labor was shortly due to expire.[10] Whatever the truth of these allegations, it seems likely that the proslavery faction were acting on their own initiative rather than responding to popular pressure. The General Assembly records for that session contain no mention of any petitions on the subject, and the issue of slavery had not featured prominently in the recent state elections.[11]

The introduction of a resolution to call a constitutional convention provoked a struggle in the legislature that anticipated the intensity of the conflict that would soon consume the state. The antislavery minority, recognizing that the design of the movers was to establish rather than to eliminate the "peculiar institution," immediately vowed to defeat the plan. Advocates of a convention responded by dispatching agents to the constituencies of their adversaries to solicit signatures for letters instructing the latter to reverse their stance.[12] This early effort to enlist the power of public opinion proved successful in swaying several doubters, and on 11 February 1823 the proslavery men finally felt sufficiently confident to press their cause in earnest. To their dismay, however, they fell one vote short of the two-thirds majority required. The reason for this reversal was quickly discovered. Nicholas Hansen, the representative from Pike County, who had supported the convention resolution on previous readings in exchange for certain concessions for his constituents, had now defected after negotiating a better deal.

Enraged, several prominent conventionists assembled that evening at the head of a mob. They proceeded to burn Hansen in effigy and then marched to the residences of their chief opponents, where, as a contemporary later recalled, "they manifested their contempt and displeasure by a confused medley of groans, wailings, and lamentations."[13] This demonstration, one observer concluded, was intended "to confirm the timid" on their own side by "making the impression that it was *safer* to go the whole than shrink."[14] The next day, a member of the convention faction moved that the House reconsider its ruling on the contested election that had originally secured Hansen his seat. Since this only required a simple majority to overturn, the anticonventionist minority were powerless to prevent the replacement of Hansen by a reliable proslavery man who had been summoned for just such an eventuality.[15] As Abraham Lincoln passed his fourteenth birthday in an Indiana log cabin, the legislature of his future home state proceeded to approve the convention resolution by twenty-four votes to twelve. Both camps would now take their case to the people, who would give their verdict on the proposal to hold a constitutional convention at the next state elections in August 1824.[16]

❖ The popular campaign may be conveniently divided into two distinct though connected and overlapping phases. The first of these was defined by the efforts of each side to disseminate its message in order to directly influence the outcome of the referendum. Here, the antislavery forces faced some significant obstacles. Although less than 1 percent of the state's inhabitants actually owned slaves, approximately two-thirds had been born in the South and retained "many of the prejudices they imbibed in infancy."[17] In this respect at least, concluded George Flower, one of the founders of a community of English emigrants, Illinois was in large parts "as much a slave-state as any of the states south of the Ohio River." And frontier conditions only made the task of securing a popular majority against a convention even more formidable. "Settlements were far apart; but few took newspapers, and fewer read them; personal communication was infrequent," Flower recorded. "The country people were all engaged in their daily labor, not dreaming of any impending change in our system of laws and government."[18]

These problems were discussed at a conference of the antislavery members of the legislature upon the adjournment of the session. "It was all important that there should be a consultation on the spot, before the separation which would very soon occur, in order to make some arrangement of a plan of operations for the campaign which was now open," recalled Thomas Lippincott, secretary to the Senate and a fervent opponent of a convention. Lippincott was no career politician; indeed he would never hold an elective office above the county level. But he did possess an abiding abhorrence of slavery. "Never, probably, since our revolutionary fathers met to consider their rights and wrongs and dangers," he added, "has a meeting of free citizens convened to consider a political question, been more completely under a sense of responsibility."[19]

Just as it had been for the Middling Interest in Boston, the state of the press was a major concern. According to Lippincott, "It was deemed important—indispensable—that we should have at least one paper which should not only be accessible to us, but wholly and heartily on our side; pledged, not by promises, but by principle." Such a paper was identified in the shape of the *Edwardsville Spectator*, edited by the staunchly antislavery Hooper Warren, and those present at the anticonventionist meeting immediately pledged the not inconsiderable sum of two thousand dollars, raised among themselves, to "increase the circulation" and thus "diffuse the information more."[20] In all other respects, however, the situation appeared bleak. When one of the owners of the *Illinois Intelligencer* criticized the eviction of Hansen from the legislature, the proslavery majority responded by stripping him of the state printing contract and forcing the sale of his half of the paper to a man more sympathetic to their cause.[21] No such chicanery was required to persuade the state's three other newspapers, all of whom came out in favor of a convention.[22]

To redress this imbalance, Lippincott remembered, it was decided at the anticonventionist meeting that "we must have some sort of organization: some plan by which we could communicate with each other and with the people."[23] Other opponents of slavery were independently reaching similar conclusions. "If a correspondence could be set on foot among the friends of freedom scattered over the State, they might strengthen and inform each other, and the influence of good feeling might be increased," wrote Morris Birkbeck, another English expatriate, to Coles.[24] The governor concurred, observing that "the people are daily making up their minds and committing themselves by taking sides. Whilst this is going on we ought not to lay on our arms, and let the enemy undermine the feelings and judgment of the people, and thus sap the foundations of our strength."[25] Shortly thereafter, however, Coles left Illinois for a lengthy sojourn in his native Virginia, so the task of putting this plan into practice was left in the hands of active men like Lippincott, who had dispersed to their various localities with renewed vigor.[26]

The fruits of their labor were first evidenced on 22 March 1823, when a number of citizens of St. Clair County convened to form "the St. Clair Society to prevent the further extension of Slavery in the state of Illinois." The group's constitution explained that "the principal means to be used to accomplish the objects of the society, shall be, by disseminating light and knowledge on the subject of slavery, by cool and dispassionate reasoning, by circulating pamphlets, handbills, and other publications."[27] This faith in the political efficacy of educative efforts reflected a contemporary consensus that placed an informed citizenry at the heart of any republican regime. In its own inaugural address a similar association instituted shortly afterward in Monroe County announced, "We believe that such societies may do good by disseminating political information; for in a representative government founded upon the virtues of the people, they need only to be informed of its abuses to correct them."[28]

In this spirit, sister societies were swiftly established throughout the state until they numbered fifteen in all. "Each society had its confidential [*sic*] correspondents in each precinct," the Baptist minister John Mason Peck later recalled, "and every succeeding month, accurate knowledge was obtained at the office in Belleville [in St. Clair County], of the state and progress of the question." Peck, who was raised in Connecticut and sent west by the Baptist Missionary Convention in 1817, played a pivotal role in the formation of the antislavery network. Owing to his occupation, the preacher had, in his own words, "occasion to travel into nearly every county in the State during the pendency of the question" and could "without being known as a partisan easily find out who could be depended upon for correspondents."[29] Of this he took full advantage. According to Lippincott, Peck "traversed the State, over and over, and everywhere scattered publications, talked and preached, and argued with his forcible logic, spreading light and influence every where, exposing the schemes of political adventurers and the horror of slavery."[30]

Peck's role in the struggle underscores the important contribution religious groups made to the explosion of civic activity that occurred in the early United States. At the dawn of the nineteenth century, ministers from many different denominations joined in a crusade to rejuvenate religious feeling and reform social morals, in a process that scholars refer to as the Second Great Awakening. The chief agency for this movement was the voluntary association, and the decades that followed the War of 1812 witnessed the foundation of such behemoths as the American Bible Society and the American Tract Society, which provided a model for popular mobilization on a national scale. These institutions dispatched agents far and wide to encourage the formation of local auxiliaries; while traveling across Illinois speaking out against slavery, for example, Peck also spent his time establishing county Bible societies. Through activities such as these, evangelists encouraged their congregations to see public opinion as responsive not merely to a restricted circle of political leaders but also to effective organizing at a grassroots level. It is they, as much as the men who directed the nation's first major parties, who deserve credit for translating the principle of popular sovereignty into practice.[31]

❖ The extraordinary wealth of sources left by residents of Madison County, Illinois, allows us to take a more in-depth look at the activities of the anticonventionists there. Situated midway up the state's western border with Missouri, Madison was, according to one contemporary account, "a fertile and healthy country, well watered and timbered, and gently undulating, presenting at once to the agriculturalist the most desirable place for settlement."[32] The area predominately attracted migrants from the South and had one of the highest concentrations of slaveholders in the state. But it was also home to a fair sprinkling of New Englanders and New Yorkers, along with the colony of English families led by Flower and Birkbeck.[33] Edwardsville, the county seat, was one of the few sizeable towns in Illinois and consequently would become a focal point for both camps during the convention contest.

The antislavery forces struck first, with the organization on 28 June 1823 of "The Madison Association to oppose the introduction of Slavery in Illinois."[34] The constitution of the new society was typical of the constitutions of its counterparts throughout the state and indeed of voluntary associations of all types during this period. The organization was headed by a Board of Managers made up of several officers with specialized functions: a president, two vice presidents, a corresponding secretary, and a recording secretary. The holders of these posts were to be elected biannually. Meetings of the full society were scheduled quarterly, and those of the Board of Managers, monthly. The funds of the society, raised by voluntary contributions from subscribers, were "to be disbursed as a majority of the members of the society, or Board of Managers shall direct." Finally, the members were empowered to make such by-laws for the regulation of the society as they saw fit. The beauty of this model, so widely replicated for so many different purposes by nineteenth-century Americans, was its simplicity. But for its name, the Madison Association could just as easily have been formed to fight fires, to administer charity, or to exploit some opportunity for profit as to oppose the introduction of slavery.

The society was established at a public meeting of the citizens of Madison County. Evidently, though, many of the details had been orchestrated in advance, for the committees appointed to draft a constitution and a lengthy public address both completed their required tasks with remarkable haste. Most likely, the proceedings in Madison followed the pattern set by those in St. Clair. There, Peck revealed, a "preliminary meeting" was arranged between "a number of gentleman in the county known to be opposed to slavery." At this private conclave "the outlines of a plan of operations was proposed, and a committee was appointed to draft a constitution." Only once this work was finished was it decided to "call a general meeting," at which the society was duly organized.[35] Thus, while care was taken by the protagonists to present the creation of the societies as a spontaneous expression of popular enthusiasm against slavery, it appears reasonable to conclude that they were in fact the creation of a core of committed activists in each locality seeking an agency through which to cultivate public opinion.

Eighteen individuals were named as performing some role in the Madison Association during its fourteen-month life span.[36] The identities of these men, for men they all were, provide some idea of the type of person who led the fight against the convention scheme in Illinois. The most important were the five officers who together constituted the Board of Managers. Though subject to regular election, these posts were held by the same men throughout, with the exception of one individual who died in the interim. Of the six board members total, three had previously served in some capacity in the state legislature, one of whom was also the president of the state agricultural society and another, Lippincott, the founder of the first Sunday school in Illinois. The remaining three were, respectively, a postmaster, a tavern owner, and "a mechanic of good intelligence and unblemished character ... [who was] well and generally liked."[37] These were men of sound reputation who would have commanded the respect of their neighbors, a supposition corroborated by the presence of four of them on the committee chosen to welcome Revolutionary General LaFayette to Illinois on his commemorative tour of the nation in 1825.[38]

The chief architects of the Madison Association were also accustomed to filling positions of public leadership. The duties of local government during this period involved most adult white males in one way or another, and it was the principal members of the Madison Association who frequently filled prominent roles such as those of county commissioner and grand-jury foreman. Collectively, they also boasted considerable experience in managing other community organizations. Three held offices in the county chapter of the state agricultural society, and five served on the board of the Madison Auxiliary Bible Society. Only one of these men could accurately be described as a career politician, but all were eager to take an active part in the struggle against slavery.[39]

In the absence of surviving records, it is impossible to know how sizeable the membership of the Madison Association actually was. The fact that there was no subscription fee suggests that the organizers hoped to recruit as much support as possible. In nearby Morgan County the local antislavery society counted 140 signatures on its constitution, roughly one-third of the number of ballots that would be cast against a convention in the culminating election.[40] Such an early show of strength was important, for, as Lippincott observed, "there are not a few who love to be on the strongest side."[41] Beyond this, though, as the published proceedings of meetings in Madison make clear, the involvement of most members was confined to receiving reports and reelecting the existing officers, leaving the Board of Managers free to run the organization as they saw fit.[42]

The declared purpose of the Madison Association was to "use all honorable means to present the [convention] question in what we conceive to be its true light and character."[43] The primary medium for these efforts was the *Spectator*. According to Lippincott, "There was a knot of half a dozen persons at Edwardsville, and vicinity, who agreed among themselves to keep the *Spectator* supplied with matter, and to act in conjunction with the editor."[44] Newspaper proprietors, most of whom lacked a paid staff of their own, were heavily dependent upon volunteer correspondents to fill their columns. As was customary at the time, many of the protagonists in this debate wrote under a pseudonym, and consequently it was easy for the chief contributors to keep up a steady stream of arguments against slavery without revealing their identities. Coles, for example, later admitted that he had letters published under several different aliases, while Birkbeck was known to have used at least three assumed names in addition to his own.[45]

Where the reach of the press proved inadequate, the Board of Managers was also empowered "to adopt such measures relative to the publication of tracts on the subject of the introduction of slavery into Illinois, as may be necessary to disseminate useful information."[46] Coles used his contacts with antislavery activists elsewhere in the Union to arrange for the delivery of six thousand pamphlets from out of state, a substantial figure given that the entire Illinois electorate only numbered about fifteen thousand.[47] The Madison Association and its sister societies presumably assumed a primary role in their distribution, an inference supported by Coles's also informing Birkbeck that "our society at Edwardsville intends having another and large edition of [your tract] reprinted for the purpose of having it extensively circulated."[48] In addition, the group orchestrated the publication of five hundred copies of a third pamphlet, composed of antislavery pieces by local authors.[49] The effectiveness of these efforts is confirmed by the complaints of their opponents. "A Friend to Religion" lamented in the *Intelligencer*, "I can, of late, scarcely step into a churchyard, on the Sabbath day, before the usual hour for public worship, without beholding a newspaper or hand bill spread before the eyes of the congregation."[50] "The convention question . . . is a dish which is daily nay hourly served up," recorded Horatio Newhall four months before the crucial referendum. "It furnishes all our food for conversation, for read-ing and for newspaper scribblings."[51]

Aside from disseminating antislavery publications, the societies had other useful functions. As corresponding secretary for the Madison Association, Lippincott was expected "to correspond with friends in other parts, and re-ceive such contributions as might be sent for the purpose of meeting the expense of publishing and circulating information."[52] Communication be-tween the various groups was important because it allowed them to allo-cate their scarce resources where they were most needed. Midway through the campaign, for example, the Edgar County Society reported that "in this County the Spectator is generally read, from which source we get much use-ful information. But in all probability a few copies of pamphlets against Slav-ery wants still."[53] Lippincott also sought assistance from further afield. Put in touch with the Philadelphia philanthropist Roberts Vaux by Coles, Lip-pincott wrote Vaux to ask for "such information on the comparative prices of land in Pennsylvania and Maryland, & other slaveholding and nonslavehold-ing states, as may be within your reach."[54] These data provided the basis for an address to the public that Lippincott published under the auspices of the Madison Association in the *Spectator*.[55]

The Madison Association and its sister societies constituted the center-piece of the antislavery strategy. In its inaugural address, the St. Clair Soci-ety announced that "apprehending the danger to which we are exposed (not from the majority of the people but from political intrigue) we have been induced to systemize our measures, form a society and thus concentrate our efforts to prevent the further introduction of slavery."[56] Association, as this quote suggests, was the natural response of early nineteenth-century Ameri-cans when faced with a problem in the public sphere. Alexis de Tocqueville attributed this proclivity to the U.S. political system. In aristocracies, he wrote, the privileged classes "do not need to combine in order to act," but in a democracy "all the citizens are independent and feeble; they can do hardly anything by themselves."[57] In consequence, the convention question played out in a culture in which, in the words of one modern study, "widely shared knowledge of standardized associational routines allowed members to be-come instant civic organizers."[58] This knowledge was certainly put to good use by the opponents of slavery. According to Peck, "The Anti-Convention party had the whole State under their control, and the question virtually decided, before their opponents got up a public organization."[59]

❖ The St. Clair Society's claim that the convention scheme was born "not from the majority of the people but from political intrigue" provides a timely reminder that this was a political world defined by pursuit of the public good. As Johann Neem has recently observed, historians tend to give the impression that "America's voluntary tradition emerged naturally out of the democratic ideals of the American Revolution," but in truth contemporaries remained "uneasy about becoming a nation of joiners" for a long time thereafter.[60] The famous distinction drawn by James Madison in *The Federalist Papers* between "the people" and a "faction," the latter referring to a collection of individuals "actuated by some common impulse of passion, or of interest, adverse to . . . the permanent and aggregate interests of the community," left little room for the exercise of political power by self-created societies.[61] For this reason, those involved in the antislavery associations knew they would have to rationalize their conduct carefully or risk denunciation as charlatans seeking political advancement for their own advantage.

As a point of comparison, Middling Interest supporters in Boston spent remarkably little time defending their decision to associate. The movement's constitution simply declared that "the People have a Right at all times to assemble and consult upon the common Good."[62] This right was indeed enumerated in the Massachusetts Constitution, but Neem argues that the founding generation understood the practices of assembly and association very differently. "The freedom of assembly was a communal right," he explains; "it allowed an oppressed community to express its collective will. Unlike the modern freedom of association, the freedom of assembly did not protect the rights of minorities or dissidents to associate to oppose the majority's will."[63] By the early 1820s, however, after nearly three decades of partisan conflict, this distinction had collapsed. Citizens of Massachusetts had become accustomed to all manner of associations, including parties, playing a prominent role in public life, and so the Middling Interest were not pressed to justify their own existence.

Illinois, in contrast, lacked the same experience of party competition, and contemporaries continued to regard with suspicion any organization that might put the interests of its members before the welfare of the whole community. The Madison Association sought to calm these fears in its first public address. "In associating together, for the purpose of expressing our combined opinions on subjects involving the highest interests of the state, we only exercise a right guaranteed to us by the form and spirit of our government," the subscribers affirmed. According to this script, the society made no claim to special privilege; it was merely an assembly of persons collectively exercising a right to which each was individually entitled: freedom of speech. The document continued, "You will not therefore charge us of offering our opinions as the *dictum* of an aristocratic association, but merely as the reasons which govern us in opposing the calling of a convention at the present juncture." The purpose of the society was to promote rational deliberation of the convention question and thus arrive at a true understanding of the public good. "Permit us to hope," the address concluded, "that you will give our arguments a fair and candid examination, as emanating from men who have a community of interests with you."[64]

The crucial argument put forward by the Madison Association, however cautiously expressed, was that civic societies could play a positive role in politics. This view challenged the more conservative vision, favored, as we saw, by Federalist leaders in Boston, that the people should limit their participation to the election of representatives. The latter position was categorically rejected by the Monroe Society in its own address. "When [the people] cease to be the sentinels of their own rights, they have virtually surrendered them to the mercy of their rulers; whose ambitious views will seldom accord with their happiness," declared the members. Elected representatives could not always be relied upon to pursue the public good, and "it is, therefore, not only the right of a free people, but their duty, as honest citizens, to express freely their abhorrence and detestation of those faithless public servants, who, forgetful of the responsibility of their stations, unblushingly trifle with the high confidence reposed in them by their fellow citizens." Without constant vigilance, the republic would certainly fail, for "the people . . . are the only regenerators of corrupt government."[65]

This rhetorical strategy seems to have proved successful, for the anti-conventionist associations attracted relatively little public censure. Where opposition did appear, it incorporated all the traditional tropes of antipartyism. Typical was a satirical piece supposedly written by the secretary of the

St. Clair Society, which proclaimed that the populist rhetoric of the society was merely a front for an attempt to promote the selfish ambitions of a few politicians. The author accused the managers of conducting all their significant transactions in secret and without the other members present. The true object of the society, he announced, was to prevent "a continuation of the disagreeable situation in which we have heretofore been placed, as office hunters, envying and striving one against the other."[66] Yet allegations such as these could have little force when the societies to which they referred possessed no electoral function, a point to which we shall return shortly.

The conventionists themselves were slow to organize, but the success of their adversaries spurred them into action. Just weeks after the formation of the Madison Association, proslavery agents were said to be acting as "recruiting sergeants" in that county.[67] Then in December 1823, writing from the state capital, Coles alerted Vaux that "nearly all the leading friends of a convention have been assembled here and have held caucuses for the purpose of deliberating upon the best means of promoting the success of their favorite measures."[68] The product of these discussions, the governor subsequently reported to Birkbeck, was the implementation of a committee system of "five persons in county, with a request that these five appoint three in each election precinct, for the purpose of diffusing their doctrines, embodying their forces, and acting with the greatest concert and effort."[69] At the head of this chain, it was rumored, stood a shadowy Central Committee of ten, although neither the origins of this body nor the extent of its powers was discussed in the conventionist press.[70]

The centralized structure and secretive character of the proslavery organization provoked condemnation from contemporary commentators. "A Voter," writing in the *Intelligencer,* accused the Central Committee of establishing a "system of espionage" in the manner of "a well trained army, by guards and pickets, corps of advance and reserve." The language of this complaint raised the specter of arbitrary martial authority exercised over an unwilling citizenry, an image sure to resonate with a generation of readers brought up on the rhetoric of the American Revolution. The parallels to Middling Interest critiques of the Federalist Party in Boston, which boasted its own Central Committee, are also readily apparent. "Can public good be the primary object of that party, whose measures are born in silence and concealed in darkness?" the author inquired.[71] By choosing to concentrate their organization-building at the county level, to conduct their business in public, and to open their doors to all who wished to participate, the anticonventionists were able to spare themselves such censure.

In closing his description to Birkbeck of the conventionist plans, Coles remarked that "when bad men conspire, good men should be watchful."[72] This simple phrase perfectly captures the ambiguous position of political organization in the early United States. On the one hand, collaboration between self-interested individuals seeking to subvert the purposes of government for their own private ends was something to be put down wherever possible. On the other, self-created societies offered a medium through which ordinary citizens could maintain a public presence between elections and guard against the corruption of those in power. The act of association provoked such strong debate because it was, in essence, a form of political alchemy, transforming men who were insignificant as individuals into that all-powerful body "the people."[73]

❖ As the months passed, the activity of the anticonventionists began to tell. "The free party have been as industrious as possible," Newhall noted in May 1823, "and a pretty considerable change has taken place in public sentiment."[74] By September of that year Coles too was confident that "if the question were now decided, . . . a majority of the people would be opposed to it."[75] Yet victory in the referendum alone would not suffice, for as Warren warned readers of the *Spectator*, "There is nothing to prevent the next legislature from renewing the contest, by the adoption of another resolution for again taking the sense of the people on the subject." "Although the opposition of the people to that measure is constantly increasing, and its failure more certain," the editor proclaimed, "the friends of freedom ought to take care not to elect those who may re-enact the scenes of last winter."[76] This shift in emphasis heralded the second phase of the campaign, which was defined by the entrance of organizational efforts directly into the electoral sphere.

The antislavery associations had quite self-consciously shunned the issue of securing control of the legislature in order to shield themselves from accusations that they had been created to serve the political fortunes of ambitious office seekers. This attitude was encapsulated in the inaugural address of the Monroe Society, which announced that "we should lament to see these societies converted into little dark scenes of political intrigue, for the purpose of promoting men, and not measures."[77] Of all the groups established in 1823, only one, in Morgan County, made reference to the forthcoming elections. Article 9 of the Morganian Society's constitution stated that members would consider "neither local or political distinction of parties in the selection of candidates for office, save one, which requireth that he shall be decidedly opposed to slavery."[78] Yet even this pledge was entirely voluntary, for no institutional mechanism was put in place to ensure subscribers' compliance. Instead, the anticonventionists concentrated their initial efforts solely on securing a popular majority against the convention scheme in the referendum.

The problem identified by Warren could not be ignored indefinitely, however. Once again the first step toward organization appears to have taken place in St. Clair County. There, on 27 December 1823, a public meeting resolved that "the present crisis of our state requires that the friends of freedom concentrate their vote at the next election" and called on local residents to assemble "for the purpose of devising some method of selecting candidates."[79] As with the antislavery societies, this proposal was soon taken up in other counties across the state. Writing in support of the scheme, a resident of Bond County explained that the usual practice of self-nomination could not be countenanced, for multiple anticonventionist candidates might put themselves forward and split the vote, thereby allowing a proslavery man to triumph. Some new "antidote to disunion" was needed.[80]

The solution the anticonventionists settled on was to implement their own version of the pyramidal nominating system employed by the major political parties in Massachusetts and elsewhere. The *Spectator* provides a particularly detailed account of this process in Madison County. At an initial public meeting called for 21 February 1824, committees were appointed to each of the county's five electoral districts with the task of collecting the citizens to choose delegates to a countywide nominating convention. These district meetings were held one month later, five delegates were appointed by each, and the twenty-five-strong nominating committee convened on 27 March to select three candidates for the Illinois legislature. Their chosen slate was then presented to a general meeting of the citizens of the county, held on the same day in Edwardsville, for ratification.[81] By constructing their nomination from the grass roots up, rather than simply putting forward a ticket on their own initiative, local anticonventionist activists evidently sought to involve as many Madison voters as possible and thus demonstrate their responsiveness to public opinion.

The Madison Association remained institutionally independent from the nominating system employed in the county. Neither made any mention of the other in its proceedings, despite an extensive overlap in personnel; all five surviving officers of the antislavery society were involved in some capacity in the various nominating conventions, and Curtiss Blakeman, George Churchill, and William Otwell, the three men selected for the anticonventionist ticket for the legislature, were all members of the Madison Association. Yet the formal separation of powers was maintained; the society existed to sway public opinion on the convention question, the nominating system to concentrate the antislavery vote on a single slate of candidates chosen by the people. This distinction lent credence to the anticonventionists' defense that their only ambition was promotion of the common good and not pursuit of public office.

The electoral arrangements adopted by the Madison County anticonventionists were immediately tested by the self-nomination of another candidate, Benaiah Robinson, who also claimed to oppose the convention.[82] Robinson was almost certainly a proslavery agent in disguise, for the conventionists never added a third name to their own ticket of Emanuel West and John Todd, put forward by the Central Committee, it would seem, without any popular consultation.[83] At the 1822 elections in Madison, with four seats in the legislature up for grabs, the citizens had scattered their votes among thirteen individuals. In 1824, in contrast, not a single ballot was cast for anyone other than the six men named above. A similar pattern is evident elsewhere in the state; in St. Clair, for example, the three anticonventionist candidates were separated by only fifteen votes, and their opponents by only seventeen, with just ten scattered ballots among nearly three thousand cast.[84] Organized nomination, whether by delegate conventions or simple public meetings, was an innovation introduced to Illinois by the opponents of slavery and proved to be remarkably effective.[85]

❖ Unlike their earlier efforts to disseminate their message, the anticonventionists' entry into the electoral sphere provoked a storm of criticism. The immediate response of their opponents was that the contest over slavery bore no relation to the elevation of men to public office. The editor of the *Republican Advocate,* for example, claimed that since the members of the next legislature were constitutionally bound to carry out the decision of the popular referendum, their personal sentiments on the issue were irrelevant.[86] Fanciful as it may seem, this notion had some precedent. For the Founding Fathers, a candidate's opinion on particular matters of policy was immaterial; the only subject worthy of a voter's consideration was whether the candidate possessed the character to govern wisely. This was the argument employed by Federalist leaders in Boston when they sought to preserve their electoral fortunes in the face of popular outrage over the wooden-buildings issue. In Illinois it was encapsulated by the pointed declaration of a conventionist meeting in Kaskaskia that "an honest difference of opinion will never remove our fellow men from a seat in our affections, nor as a general rule, deny to them the benefit of our suffrages."[87]

These arguments were summarily dismissed by antislavery commentators. "Independently of every other reason, we should vote against convention men for the next legislature, because if a majority of such men are elected we will have the scenes of last winter acted over again and a new convention again recommended," wrote one correspondent in the *Spectator,* echoing Warren's earlier caution. But, he continued, the state elections also offered an opportunity to "express our disapprobation of the measure still more strongly" by punishing those originally responsible.[88] The idea that elections could serve as referenda on specific issues was not something that the architects of the United States Constitution, who intended for those in power to act independent of popular opinion, would have approved of, but it reflected the increasing determination of many Americans to draw out the democratic implications of republicanism.

The crucial question, however, was what role organized nominations should play within this schema. There was no constitutional foundation for any form of nomination in Illinois or elsewhere in the Union, because contemporary protocol forbade the active pursuit of office as evidence of unseemly ambition, but in practice candidates clearly needed some method of publicizing their availability. Self-nomination had been accepted by most, because the individual merely placed his name before the community, often under the pretense of reluctantly acceding to the urging of his friends, and voters retained their right to choose between those that offered or even draft

in someone else. Nominations by public meeting, in contrast, were suscep-
tible to control by an aristocratic clique who might engineer the selection
of their favorite and then force all those present to pledge their support to
him, depriving the people of their sovereignty. This was the argument that
had previously been wielded so decisively against organized nominations
by commentators such as "Zero" and "A Republican," and it was the same
reasoning now deployed by the conventionists against their opponents. "It
remains to be seen whether the honest yeomanry of this county will tamely
submit to this species of dictation," trumpeted the *Illinois Republican*, mouth-
piece of the proslavery contingent in Madison.[89]

The anticonventionists rushed to refute this charge. "There has not been
the slightest shadow of advantage taken of the people in any of the proceedings," avowed "Nathan" in the *Spectator*. "Nothing was transacted under
cover," the writer explained. "Every meeting preparatory to the business has
been held in the day time, with open doors, and the proceedings published
in *form*." The local citizens "were publicly notified, and pressingly solicited
by advertisements of several weeks standing, to attend unanimously; and I
rejoice to be enabled to state that they did attend, and their voices were heard
from every part of the county."[90] The mode of nomination was also defended
by Warren, who claimed that by allowing for the popular election of delegates to the nominating committee and then referring the ticket back to a
public meeting for ratification, "the citizens ... have a direct and effectual
voice in the nomination, and may prevent the exercise of an undue influence in the selection of candidates."[91] "By the logic of this editor, therefore,"
he concluded, "it remains to be seen whether the majority will submit to be
dictated to—by *themselves*."[92]

The most controversial aspect of the anticonventionists' conduct was not
the nominating method itself but the associated condition that "NO MAN
who sets up in opposition to the nomination should be countenanced or
supported by the party."[93] "Jack No Party" took issue with this dictum on
the grounds that the proslavery faction, in a gesture of "brotherly love," had
signaled their willingness to recommend for office men who were known
to oppose the calling of a convention. "Why must your party get up county
meetings, and take so much pains to concentrate your votes, and shew so
much illiberality as not to receive acts of kindness and good will from your

opponents?" he demanded of Warren.[94] Anticonventionist correspondents countered that it was precisely to prevent such dubious schemes that organized nominations were necessary. "If a great many candidates opposed to slavery, should be voted for," wrote "Junius," "our opponents, who obey implicitly the decrees of their secret county juntoes, and who by that means concentrate their votes upon a single ticket, would elect their own candidates, notwithstanding the decided majority which we possess."[95]

Even among the anticonventionists the topic of organized nominations proved controversial. Some considered the practice to be merely a temporary expedient necessitated by the extraordinary contest at hand. "When the times are not so momentous as the present; when subjects of minor importance only are before the public; when no general voice of disapprobation against public men or public measures is required, we may more safely trust to the divided suffrage of the people," a resident of Bond County assured the readers of the *Spectator*.[96] Others, however, disagreed. "Why should you wait for the most forward to volunteer their services, and to tell you that they are the best qualified to do your business?" inquired a group of anticonventionists in St. Clair. "Is it not better to be your own judges, and do it yourselves?"[97] It was Warren, though, who went furthest toward articulating an acceptance of organized nominations as routine. "We have not the slightest objection to the conventionists holding meetings, and agreeing upon the candidate whom they will support," he declared, "we have no wish to interfere with their nominations; nor have they any right to meddle with ours."[98]

At the root of these disputes, indeed at the root of all disputes over political practice during this period, was the issue whether the proposed innovation served to express or to subvert the sovereignty of the people. Critics of organized nomination condemned it as an attempt to introduce parties into Illinois and thereby to rob the people of their rightful place in the political process. This view was epitomized by "Vive le Convention," who complained that the anticonventionists' bid to control nominations demonstrated that "the best interests of the country are to be sacrificed upon the altar of *party* for the sake of keeping a few men high in office." "Men and not principles are the idols," he lamented, and "this monster *party* has such unbounded influence, that one man opposes a convention because his friend does—not even can a constable be appointed, or a sheriff elected, but *party takes her rule.*" "Let there be no party but 'we the people,'" the writer counseled, "and let every consideration but the *good of the whole* be sacrificed upon the great convention question."[99]

The anticonventionists, in contrast, relied on the same argument that they had used to justify their right to associate: that organized nominations were necessary to provide the people with a political voice. "Let us never give them [the conventionists] occasion to boast, that although we are vastly superior in *numbers,* yet their superiority in *management* has enabled them to gain a victory," proclaimed "Junius."[100] Just like "Brutus" and his fellow Middling Interest men in Boston, this essayist believed that the people could only exercise their sovereignty effectively through organization. This call became the rallying cry of the campaign against slavery. "In times like the present, when every species of address and management is resorted to, to induce you to tear up the foundations of civil government," explained the St. Clair anticonventionists, "it becomes the duty of all citizens friendly to good order, and the best interests of society, to unite in their exertions . . . and endeavor to apply the proper corrective for the abuses." "Our country calls upon us for action," the authors of the address avowed, "let us stand forth in all our strength; let us unite like one man, and our exertions will be the more effectual."[101]

❖ The debates over the antislavery societies and organized nominations form part of a larger struggle between the two sides to identify their cause with that of the people. As Lippincott later recalled, "The one idea, constantly held up, and to be met and refuted everywhere, was, that the anticonventionists were *trying to defeat the will of the people!*"[102] "Who are those opposed to a Convention? It is those who believe they ou[gh]t to rule, and not the people," insisted "Convention" in the *Intelligencer.* As proof of this allegation, the author pointed to the conduct of those legislators, including Churchill of Madison, who had voted against the convention resolution despite receiving instructions to the contrary from their constituents. "Is it not the avowed and open principle of the federalists, that the right to instruct is not with the people?" he inquired, attempting to tar the anticonventionist cause with the name of a party that had never been popular in Illinois.[103] This theme was also taken up by "Truth," who claimed that "if doctrines like these should prevail, the standard of FEDERALISM would be erected in our land, and the people would be disarmed of their sovereignty."[104] Thus, opposition to the convention, denial of the right of instruction, and support for Federalism were linked by conventionist writers in an unholy conspiracy against the liberties of the people.

Yet in truth the anticonventionists were no more inclined to deny the principle of popular sovereignty than their opponents. "Instead of stating explicitly the *object* of the measure, they [the conventionists] merely insist on the *right* of the people to vote for it," complained Warren more than a year after the passage of the convention resolution, adding that "we defy the advocates of the measure to produce a single article wherein its opponents, directly or indirectly, deny this right."[105] A few months later, the newly appointed anticonventionist editor of the *Intelligencer,* David Blackwell, reminded his readers "*that the people are sovereign,* is a plain truth which no man of sense will deny; but it does not follow, that the people will have a convention, merely because they may have one." "Who are the people?" he continued, "the conventionists? No. Both parties together are the people; and we recognize in our happy government, the voice of the majority, as the will of the people, to which all must submit."[106]

Meanwhile, other commentators attempted the delicate task of defending Churchill against the charge that he had acted improperly by opposing the convention resolution without denying the right of constituents to instruct their representatives. "I confess it would be rather a hazard to attack this principle, which is so popular, even to clip its wings, or to confine it to its proper bounds; more especially, as any such attempt has already been threatened with the reproachful epithet of Federalist or Aristocrat," observed "A Friend to ORDER." Nonetheless, he suggested, "in order for instructions to be *binding,* they ought to be taken by the vote of all the electors by whom the representative was chosen."[107] This certainly did not apply to Churchill's case, in which conventionist agents were alleged to have "set down the names of a considerable number of boys, strangers, citizens of other counties and states, and citizens who did not vote in Madison county in the last election," and even engaged in "*forging a number of signatures.*"[108] Just as it had in the wooden-buildings episode in Massachusetts, the right of instruction became a subject for heated debate during the convention contest, as commentators clashed over how to translate principle into practice.

The commitment of the antislavery forces to majority rule is best demonstrated by their refusal to rely on the Northwest Ordinance. Passed by

Congress in 1787, this act prohibited all forms of involuntary servitude in the Northwest Territory, out of which the state of Illinois was later carved. Whether the Ordinance continued to apply once Illinois was admitted to statehood was uncertain, but when Eastern newspapers caught wind of the plot to introduce slavery several loudly proclaimed that the federal government would never allow it. In contrast, anticonventionist publicists within the state, by and large, made little reference to the Ordinance. Indeed, Coles actually pleaded with a friend in Philadelphia to "prevail on the newspaper writers to let this question alone" for fear that it might "arouse the feelings of State pride, and State rights, and that natural love of unrestrained liberty and independence which is common to our countrymen, and especially to our frontier settlers, who of all men in the world have the strongest jealousy of authority and aversion to restraint."[109] By accepting the terms of the referendum, the anticonventionists reaffirmed their faith in the sovereignty of the people and urged them to exercise their right to decide positively against the legalization of slavery.[110]

On 2 August 1824, after eighteen long months of campaigning, the day of reckoning finally arrived. "The election was a hot time," Lippincott recorded. "The weather was warm enough, being early in August, and the people were heated with excitement."[111] Newspapers exhorted every voter to "be at his post."[112] The proslavery forces distributed printed tickets, previously unknown in Illinois, under the title "People's Ballot."[113] But when all the votes were counted, the result was a clear, if closely contested, victory for their opponents. The statewide totals stood at 6,650 to 4,997, or 57 percent against a constitutional convention. In Madison County 914 ballots were cast, of which 563, or 62 percent, were opposed to a revision of the constitution, and all three antislavery candidates won seats in the legislature. A conservative estimate puts turnout across the state at 80 percent; it may well have been even higher.[114]

The climactic elections signaled the complete cessation of operations of the friends of freedom. "The question being decided in August," Peck later remembered, "the anti-convention party disbanded, [and] the county societies died."[115] At a dinner held to celebrate the success of an antislavery candidate for the legislature in Morgan County, one participant offered a toast: "The Freedom of Election—Unshackled from the drill and coercion of Jacobin Clubs, however plausible the names of Washington, Benevolent, St.

Tammany, Cincinnati or Morganian Societies may appear."[116] The repeated
cheers that greeted this salute stand as testament to the continued strength of
antiparty sentiment in the state. Voluntary associations and organized nominations had proven useful to concentrate the people's voice in a crisis, but
unlike their counterparts in Massachusetts, few citizens of Illinois were willing to accept such devices as a permanent fixture in politics.

❖ The Illinois convention contest was a triumph of democracy. "When the
votes were counted, and it was ascertained that the people had decided not to
call a Convention for the purpose of opening our State to Slavery, there was
a great calm," Thomas Lippincott recorded. "The defeated party submitted
quietly; the triumphant rejoiced without noise or show."[117] Yet the absence
of political parties means that the episode sits uneasily amidst the celebratory narrative of early U.S. politics, in which party and democracy go hand
in hand. Consequently, many modern accounts of the contest have, perhaps
unwittingly, treated it as a relic of an older, more deferential, top-down style
of politics by seeking their explanation for the anticonventionists' success in
the charismatic leadership of Governor Edward Coles.[118] In this they merely
follow a precedent established by Coles himself, who in a memoir penned
late in life modestly recorded, "I was chiefly instrumental in preventing a call
of a convention, and making Illinois a slave holding state."[119] Yet ultimately it
was the Illinois electorate, not the governor, who made the critical decision.
The real heroes of this story were men like Thomas Lippincott, Hooper Warren, and John Mason Peck, who embraced the challenge of constructing an
antislavery political organization from the grass roots up and ensured that
the voice of the people would be heard.

In his subsequent account of the campaign, Lippincott somewhat surpris-
ingly claimed that the friends of freedom had been "a band drawn together
by affinity, and not bound by organized association."[120] Whatever the motives that compelled the anticonventionists to unite, however, the act of association was critical to their ultimate success. For an individual to attempt
to influence the course of politics was dangerous, raising the specter of self-
interest. But an association of individuals could plausibly profess to represent
the one body that might legitimately dictate to government: the people. Likewise, public nominations could be presented as a more accurate reflection of
the popular will than the practice of allowing any man to declare himself a

candidate and work for his own election. Just as they did in Boston, defenders of these forms of organization in Illinois argued that they were necessary to secure the rule of the majority against intriguing minorities. "Were societies to be formed, and corresponding committees appointed" across the state, declared the St. Clair Society in its opening address, "it is fondly hoped that the designs of the slave party would fall before the majesty of the people."[121]

Taken together, the voluntary societies and nominating machinery employed by the opponents of a convention fulfilled many of the functions that modern scholars attribute to parties: they coordinated campaign activities, communicated the antislavery message to the electorate, and brought voters to the ballot box. Yet they did this without effecting the centralization of power that turned the Middling Interest against the established parties in Boston. As Lippincott said of the initial meeting of the antislavery minority in the legislature, "No [central] society was formed that I know of, no leaders chosen; no particular plan of operations; only that all should do their best, especially in their own localities."[122] By placing their faith in grassroots activism, the anticonventionists encouraged an expansive interpretation of the meaning of popular sovereignty, for as Johann Neem observes, "In learning how to volunteer, ordinary people learned to think and to act as citizens. They ensured that citizenship in a democracy would not be confined to voting and to office holding."[123]

One man who never underestimated the value of the anticonventionists' organizational efforts was John Mason Peck. Thirty years later he offered some telling advice to a member of the newly formed Republican Party. "If I was in your *position* and the vigor of life as I was in 1823–4," the preacher wrote, "I would have an organization in every county and a 'club' in every precinct. Organize, organize, organize. Making stump speeches does well enough to arouse the people, but quiet and private arrangements will produce the votes."[124] Peck was certainly correct on the latter point. *Organize* was the watchword of the convention campaign, and the electorate responded by turning out in record numbers. The achievement of the friends of freedom in mobilizing a popular majority against the calling of a convention demonstrates that mass participation in politics was not dependent upon the presence of a competitive two-party system.

3 | "ASSOCIATE YOURSELVES THROUGHOUT THE NATION"
The Struggle to Shape Federal Tariff Policy in Pennsylvania and Virginia

Reflecting during the summer of 1820 on the recent defeat of the Baldwin tariff bill in Congress, the Philadelphia printer Mathew Carey, a vocal advocate of protection for American manufactures, was in no doubt as to the culprit. In a lengthy "Prefatory Address" to his latest pamphlet in favor of increased import duties, Carey railed against the "miserable spirit of party" that had once again proved fatal to the protectionist cause. "This distinction between federalism and democracy, has, in great measure, subsided," he claimed, with much justification. "Good men of both parties, think nearly alike on the affairs of government," and the only persons who "wish to perpetuate the distinction" are "some of the printers of newspapers, and men who enjoy the sweets of public office, or who aspire after them." Yet to Carey's distress, party names continued to hold their charm at the ballot box in spite of their irrelevance to policy or principles. "When your establishments are sold by the sheriff at a fourth part of their cost—your families in a state of suffering—your workmen reduced to abject penury and wretchedness," he implored his intended audience, "what will it avail you that your state legislators and members of congress are democrats?" "The vital interests of a great nation," the Philadelphia penman concluded, "are too valuable to be offered a sacrifice to any man or any party."[1]

Carey was far from alone in holding these views. The Panic of 1819, a global financial crisis, provoked fierce public debate over federal tariff policy, as a host of nonpartisan organizations, including agricultural societies, chambers of commerce, and protectionist associations, competed to influence deliberations in Congress. Rather than restricting their efforts to the polling place, these groups encouraged citizens to maintain a constant pressure on legislators through activities such as petitioning and lobbying. This chapter charts their activities in Pennsylvania, the epicenter of protectionism, and Virginia, where support for free trade was strongest. It serves to illustrate both the reluctance of many Americans to leave the business of policymaking to their chosen representatives and their readiness to look beyond parties and elections in their bid to shape the course of government.

❖ Prior to the Panic of 1819, federal tariff policy generated little controversy. Since the First Congress a tax on imports had been generally accepted as a means of raising government revenue. Even the enactment of additional duties following the War of 1812 that were explicitly designed to safeguard from foreign competition the infant industries that had sprung up during that conflict encountered negligible opposition in the national legislature. A few representatives from the slave states protested that their region would see little benefit from the measure, but many supported it in order "to give some protection to those establishments which had greatly helped save us in time of war, and without which no nation on earth can ever be truly independent or safe."[2]

This relative consensus would not survive the financial crisis. With consumer demand crippled at home and abroad, the commodity price index plummeted and bankruptcies multiplied.[3] "So far as property was concerned," reported Carey, "the devastation caused by an invading army could not exceed the destruction that was exhibited in various parts of the United States," with manufacturing-oriented Pennsylvania hit harder than most.[4] "This distress pervades every part of the Union, every class of society. . . . It is like the atmosphere which surrounds us—all must inhale it, and none can escape it," echoed Speaker of the House Henry Clay, the champion of protectionism in Congress.[5] Only a further increase to the tariff, these men and their allies argued, could save the American economy. Such a policy would "restrain the excessive influx of foreign products, by which we have been made so dependent upon transatlantic markets; have incurred an enormous balance of trade against us; have been drained of our specie, deranged in our finances, exhausted, and brought to the near prospect of general impoverishment."[6]

Not all contemporaries accepted this assessment, however. The Panic also proved calamitous for Virginia, which, like much of the South, was dependent upon the production of staple crops for sale overseas. "The times! the times! no dividends!" wailed one resident of the Old Dominion, Francis

Corbin, in 1820. "We are all broke—, I believe—, in the Country, as well as in the Towns. . . . I fear we here in the Slave holding States are going on from bad to worse!"[7] Many planters were skeptical of claims that delivering protection to a handful of manufactories north of the Mason-Dixon line would salve their own distress. The proposed policy, they argued, would "produce a tax highly impolitic in its nature, partial in its operation, and oppressive in its effects: a tax, in fact, to be levied principally on the great body of agriculturalists . . . who are the chief consumers of all foreign imports."[8] And these critics were joined by merchants like Corbin, who feared a decline in their already faltering business under the impact of increased duties. Together, this constituency argued that the solution to the Panic should instead be sought in free trade, which would permit agriculture, commerce, and manufacturing each to flourish in its own sphere.

By this point there was virtually no difference between the two major political parties on the question of tariff policy. Originally, protection for manufactures had formed part of the Federalist vision of an activist state, while Republicans had rejected government intervention in the economy. Over time, however, these distinctions became blurred. As Federalism retreated into its New England stronghold it inherited that region's commercial bias toward free trade, while Republican politicians became more sympathetic toward protectionism in a bid to attract new constituencies. Following the Hartford Convention debacle, party cohesion on both sides evaporated. In the final roll call on the Baldwin tariff bill in 1820, Republican members of Congress, who held a clear majority of seats in both the House and the Senate, divided almost evenly, while their Federalist counterparts favored it by a margin of two to one. Significantly, the chief architect of that bill, Representative Henry Baldwin of Pittsburgh, Pennsylvania, had been elected by a bipartisan coalition with the explicit aim of protecting local manufactories.[9]

Sectional identity offers a more reliable but far from perfect guide to the voting record of individual legislators on the tariff. Debate on the Baldwin bill followed closely on Missouri's hotly contested application for admission to the Union as a slave state, and many scholars have naturally assumed that support for increased duties and opposition to slavery extension were henceforth linked in southern minds as measures of northern oppression.[10] This interpretation is partially borne out by the fact that three-quarters of the free-state contingent in Congress supported tariff reform, and roughly the same proportion of delegates from the slave states opposed it. Yet the defection rate on both sides was substantial; the Mid-Atlantic and Old Northwest regions may have been united in favor, but New England remained divided, and while the cotton-producing states of the Deep South flocked to the free-trade standard, some of their Border State counterparts proved more reluctant to follow (table 6). Former president James Madison even predicted that the tariff struggle might "mitigate the alienation threatened by the Missouri controversy," because it "divides the nation in so checkered a manner, that its issue cannot be very serious."[11]

The failure of the tariff issue to fit neatly into prevailing categories of analysis did not escape the notice of contemporaries. "The subject of domestick manufactures—the reasons for their encouragement, and for 'letting them alone'— . . . are themes of great and growing importance, on which, however, our notions appear to be less distinct, than on any other leading question of national concern," observed the editor of the *Illinois Gazette* in 1824. "Pennsylvania, a state entirely democratick, is unanimous for a new tariff, while Virginia, equally democratick, is equally unanimous against it. Massachusetts, recently a federal state, in like manner is opposed, and Connecticut, also federal, is in favor of it." The answer to the puzzle was not to be found in section or party, the writer suggested, but in "interest, the governor of men's opinions, [which] has brought about these new relations." "Those states, whose principal occupation and source of wealth is commerce, and such agricultural states as chiefly turn their attention to the production of staples for a foreign market, form the party opposed to the tariff," he surmised, "while the states purely manufacturing, and such agricultural ones as are less dependent upon foreign countries for the disposal of their productions, are in favor of it."[12]

This use of the term *interest* reflects a political culture in transition. During the Revolutionary era *interest* was generally understood to refer to "the personal following that a leading man or a prominent family could influence."[13] Half a century later, however, the word had taken on a more abstract meaning, encompassing a supralocal combination of individuals bound by a shared motive for political action. It was in this context, for example, that Representative George Holcombe declared the tariff question to be "combated on [the floor of the House] by three interests essentially distinct; the agricultural interest of the South, the manufacturing interest of the East, and

TABLE 6. *Breakdown of key votes on the Baldwin tariff bill in the Sixteenth Congress, by party and section*

Party or section	Supported passage	Opposed passage	Did not vote
Party			
Federalist	21	10	3
Republican	91	90	15
Section			
Free states			
New England	24	21	6
Other free states	72	3	1
Slave states			
Delaware, Kentucky, and Maryland	12	11	4
Other slave states	4	65	7

Sources: 35 Annals of Cong. 672 (1820) and 36 Annals of Cong. 2155–56 (1820); partisan affiliations from BDUSC.

Note: This table presents combined totals from the House vote to pass the tariff bill on 29 April 1820 and the Senate vote to postpone consideration of the bill on 4 May 1820. In the latter case, members voting to postpone were taken as being opposed to the passage of the bill, and members voting against postponement as supporting the bill.

the general interest of commerce and navigation."[14] Given the relative balance of pro- and antitariff forces in Congress and the willingness of legislators to break the bonds of party and section on the issue, clear potential existed for such "interests" to exert an important, perhaps even decisive influence on policymaking. To do so, however, they would need to organize.

❖ Organized pressure for protection was not new in 1819. Efforts to establish manufacturing in America predated the Revolution, and that conflict provided a critical stimulus by expanding the domestic market just as it insulated the infant industries from foreign competition. When peace returned in 1783, this new constituency sought legislative intervention to preserve their advantageous position and secured the passage of high tariffs in several states under the Articles of Confederation. With the ratification of the United States Constitution, however, the power to set import duties was reserved to the federal government. From this point the campaign for a general protective policy largely died away, to be replaced by localized projects competing with one another for public support in the form of legal privileges and land grants.[15]

This situation was transformed by the Panic and by the tireless endeavor of Mathew Carey. Born in Ireland, Carey emigrated to the United States in 1784 and entered public life as a Federalist newspaper editor during the 1790s. After defecting in protest against that party's Anglophile sympathies he spent some time in the Republican ranks but departed when his support for the rechartering of the Bank of the United States in 1810 put him at odds with many of his fellow partisans. Disenchanted by his experiences, Carey set to work writing *The Olive Branch,* a disquisition on the dangers of partisanship that censured Federalist and Republican alike. "I believe it is a sound political maxim," he stated, "that *a thoroughgoing party-man never was a perfectly honest politician;* for there hardly ever yet was a party free from errors and crimes, more or less gross, in exact proportion to the folly or the wickedness of its leaders."[16] This sentiment evidently struck a popular chord, for *The Olive Branch* sold more copies than any previous political treatise.[17]

Following the financial crisis, Carey became convinced that only tariff reform could save the American economy from ruin. To this end, he was instrumental in the founding of two protectionist organizations, or "interest groups," as we might call them today, in his home state of Pennsylvania. The first of these was the Philadelphia Society for the Promotion of National Industry, established in the spring of 1819. The Philadelphia Society was atypical of the protariff associations that would soon proliferate throughout the nation. It was privately organized without publicity, and membership was restricted to just ten individuals, each of whom was required to subscribe the extraordinary sum of one hundred dollars. There is no indication that an official constitution or a regular schedule of meetings was ever agreed upon, and by all accounts the group seems to have functioned more as an informal club for like-minded individuals. Carey later recalled that the original plan was to "examine the various works written on [political economy]; to select the principal maxims they contained; and to publish them as a sort of manual or analysis for the use of legislators and citizens generally."[18] This project was soon judged unfeasible, however, and instead the society began churning out essay after essay in favor of protection, almost all of them written by Carey.[19]

Much more common in terms of both its organization and its activities was the Pennsylvania Society for the Encouragement of American Manufactures, which took shape in the autumn. This association evidently sought to attract the largest possible membership; its creation was widely publicized, the subscription fee was set at just fifty cents, and more than one hundred agents were appointed to actively solicit additional signatures to the constitution. The structure of the society followed the same template employed by the anticonventionists in Illinois. Officers were elected to fulfill the functions of president, vice president, treasurer, and secretary, while the main burden of business fell on a thirty-man Board of Manufactures, which was granted sweeping powers to "appoint from their number, committees for the purpose of correspondence, for the collection of information, and for such other objects as shall be calculated to promote the intentions of the association."[20] Carey served as the head of this committee, which included seven of the nine other members of the Philadelphia Society. Regular meetings were scheduled quarterly, but the board met much more frequently.[21]

The structural differences between these two protectionist societies and the fact that they retained distinct identities despite their overlapping personnel reflects the dual strategy adopted by Carey and his fellow activists. The unconcealed purpose of the Philadelphia Society was to convert public opinion and, if possible, individual legislators to the cause of increased duties. For this reason, the size of its membership was far less important than the resources each member could contribute to its publishing efforts. Whatever the original intent of the other participants, the onus of preparing the pamphlets clearly fell on one individual; Carey would later recollect that "few of the members were able to write for the press" and "all the ideas I received from the whole of the members would not fill a page."[22] Nonetheless, the financial assistance that his collaborators provided was critical, because publishing was an expensive business, especially when the product was distributed without concern for profit. The society's receipt book reveals that in the first year of its existence it paid out $842.25, almost all of which was for paper, binding, and other printing costs, and recouped only $42.50 from sales.[23]

The Pennsylvania Society, in contrast, sought to present itself as an unmediated expression of existing popular sentiment for protection. The organization was established at a "Public Meeting without Distinction of Party," open to all persons "who are disposed to support and encourage American manufactures."[24] Of the thirty-one members of the board for whom an occupation can be identified, less than half were engaged in some form of manufacturing, with a range of other professions also represented, including commerce, law, medicine, politics, and publishing.[25] This composition was surely intended to signal that increased duties would benefit the community as a whole. The founders also took care to further demonstrate their nonpartisan credentials by choosing two Federalists and three Republicans for their five principal offices.[26] Once again the message was clear: this association would not be merely an adjunct to some existing party, as were the Washington Benevolent Societies, discussed previously, but an independent force with its own political objective.[27]

Unfortunately, no records exist from which to calculate the size of the Pennsylvania Society's membership, though a similar organization in Delaware claimed more than one thousand subscribers.[28] We do know that all who affixed their names to the constitution pledged "to give a preference to American manufactures" in their private consumption and, in addition to their annual dues, could be expected to contribute the weight of their names to any action taken on their behalf by the board, such as the adoption of a petition to Congress.[29] Those present at the original public meeting also resolved "that at all future elections, for members of the state legislature or congress of the United States, we will vote for no man who is known to be unfriendly to the support and protection of domestic manufactures."[30] Politicians with an eye for popular favor could hardly miss the suggestion that there were potentially many ways for an association like the Pennsylvania Society to convert its numerical strength into an advantage for the cause.

The protectionist movement swiftly spread outside Pennsylvania. As with the antislavery associations in Illinois, the typical procedure was for a few like-minded individuals to lay their plans in private and then give notice of their intent to form a society in order to drum up public support. Often the initiators were prompted in their endeavor by friends elsewhere, for the business dealings of the manufacturing community ensured that a nationwide correspondence network through which ideas could be disseminated was already in place. Carey played a pivotal role in this expansion, offering advice and encouragement to allies in all parts of the Union through an extraordinary volume of personal correspondence.[31] Another critical stimulus was provided by sympathetic newspapers, which eagerly reported the foundation of protariff associations and ensured a wider circulation for their constitutions and addresses.[32] Through these means, even those citizens who lacked experience in organizing could easily follow the example set by others elsewhere. By the opening of the Sixteenth Congress in December 1819, statewide societies had been established in nine states, along with many smaller ones that differed in little besides name and location.[33]

❖ Contemporaries who opposed any alteration to the tariff observed these proceedings with mounting alarm. "The universal cry of the Manufacturers from all parts of the country, is for *protecting duties*," cautioned "A Friend to Commerce" in the *Boston Daily Advertiser*, "and they are exerting all their energies by their numerous petitions, resolves and addresses, to obtain further aid and encouragement from Congress and to enlist the public voice in their favor—societies are forming, conventions organizing, and no means left unemployed for effecting their object."[34] If anything, free traders tended to overestimate the coordination of their adversaries. Representative Ezekiel Whitman of Massachusetts warned his colleagues in Congress of "an association in Philadelphia, calling itself a Society for the Promotion of National Industry, [which] has its branches in every part of the Union, with which it corresponds, and which it directs, and instigates, and sets in motion, by the means of pamphlets and newspaper essays."[35]

According to Thomas Ritchie, the influential editor of the *Richmond Enquirer*, the solution was simple: "the only plan by which Agriculture can effectually resist the encroachments of the Manufacturers, is to oppose combination with combination."[36] This argument echoed that of the Virginia planter and political theorist John Taylor of Caroline, who in his 1813 treatise *Arator* had recommended "establishing Agricultural societies in each Congressional district, for the purpose of considering and explaining respectfully to Congress, what does [agriculture] good, and what does it harm, in imitation of other interests."[37] At the time of publication Taylor was out of favor in the Old Dominion, having split with the dominant Jeffersonian wing of the Republican Party, and many, including Ritchie, dismissed him as a crank. But with the protectionist campaign swelling to a crescendo, Taylor's views suddenly came into vogue, and Virginians turned expectantly to the state's agricultural societies for salvation.[38]

Agricultural societies, or associations of gentleman farmers meeting regularly to exchange advice and reward good practice, were commonplace in eighteenth-century Britain, and a few such groups were established in America prior to the Revolution. After the United States gained independence, societies continued to flourish sporadically in various parts of the country, but in Virginia none seems to have survived the War of 1812. Over the decade that followed, however, at least sixteen local associations would be founded in the state, in addition to the Virginia Society, a revival of a previously defunct statewide organization effected in 1817, and the United Agricultural Societies, a federated body comprising delegations from several county societies, established in 1820. The latter appears to have been something of a rival to the Virginia Society, for there was little overlap in membership between the two, but both would act in tandem, if not in concert, against the tariff bill of 1820.[39]

This spurt of association-building was not solely the product of agitation over the tariff. Virginia agriculture was in crisis during this period, as planters abandoned the state's exhausted soils for the fertile cotton belt of the new Southwest in droves. Yet the political function of the new societies was also made explicit in many cases. "The object of the Society shall be to promote the interest and improvement of agriculture, husbandry, and rural economy," affirmed the constitution of the Roanoke Agricultural Society, "by supporting its rights in opposition to the interested clamors of the manufacturers, who unjustly claim the exclusive protection of the government, to the manifest injury of the great body of the American people."[40] Likewise, the United Agricultural Societies announced their formation "not more for the improvement of the practice, than for the protection of the *rights and interests* of Agriculture . . . for it is more essential to preserve our present income, limited as it is, to our own uses, than to increase it tenfold, for the benefit of others." "Agricultural societies connected by representation," the authors of this address concluded, "will furnish the means to resist invasions, which heretofore, have seldom failed of success."[41]

Like their protectionist counterparts, the agricultural societies followed a standard model. Each possessed the usual complement of officers, a regular schedule of general meetings, and a smaller committee to handle routine business. The main difference between them and their opponents was a higher subscription fee, which typically ranged between two and five dollars. Since Virginia was one of the few states to retain a property-holding qualification for suffrage, it would not be a surprise if the founders of the state's agricultural societies envisaged a similar connection between economic independence and civic worth.[42] The natural consequence, of course, was that membership tended to be more restricted; the Virginia Society listed 244 subscribers in 1818, while the constituent bodies of the United Agricultural Societies were entitled to appoint 1 delegate to the annual meeting for every 10 of their members, and none ever sent more than 5.[43] But this deficit did not unduly trouble free-trade enthusiasts, who seem to have envisaged the societies as platforms for leading public opinion. "Our own Society, the Agricultural Lens of our County invites her Members to become the Radii of Attraction for all the Agricultural Light within its Sphere: for the purpose, first of concentrating and giving it 'a form and substance,' and then diffusing it," explained George Blow, secretary of the Sussex Agricultural Society.[44] His attitude, which applied just as well to his campaign against the tariff as to agricultural reform, was that "if the change was effected in our most intelligent citizens—the example would soon be followed by the less enlightened."[45]

No single individual defined the antitariff movement in Virginia to the extent that Carey dominated protectionism in Pennsylvania, but a few are worthy of particular mention. Taylor invented many of the arguments that were endlessly recycled against an increase in import duties, although his advanced age limited his participation in other respects.[46] Edmund Ruffin, the fire-eating secessionist best known to history for firing the first shot of the Civil War, made his earliest appearance on the political stage as a founding member of the United Agricultural Societies and author of three petitions to Congress remonstrating against the protective policy.[47] And James Mercer Garnett, whose brother Robert Selden Garnett represented Virginia in the House of Representatives during this period, served simultaneously as president of the Fredericksburg Agricultural Society and vice president of the Virginia Society and wielded the most prolific pen among opponents of protection.[48]

All three of these men shared with Carey a profound disenchantment with political parties. "Nations are always enslaved by the ingenuity of creating a blind confidence with party prejudices," observed Taylor in one of his weighty tracts against the tariff. "A reigning party never censures itself, and the people have been tutored to vote under two senseless standards, gaudily painted over with the two words 'Federalist and Republican,' repeated, and repeated, without having any meaning, or conveying any information."[49] Garnett, like Taylor, had served his political apprenticeship in the Republican ranks but became disillusioned by the party's conduct once installed in government following Thomas Jefferson's election to the White House in 1800. "The whole 'Republican Party' (God save the mark) in commotion to determine which out of 5 or 6 men shall rule over them," he complained during the presidential campaign of 1824, "& at the same time this Party are—to all appearances, utterly indifferent to the great, vital Interests of the Nation."[50] As for Ruffin, his attitude is succinctly expressed by a Fourth of July toast that he gave in 1819: "A political party; a few knaves leading a great many fools."[51]

The prospect of an act to increase import duties passing the Sixteenth Congress spurred the free traders into action. Because of extended debate over the admission of Missouri, the House did not take up for discussion the tariff bill reported by Baldwin in his capacity as chairman of the Committee on Manufactures until April 1820. Remonstrances against the proposal to raise existing rates were received from several Virginia agricultural societies, along with merchant groups in Massachusetts and Pennsylvania, but these were easily outnumbered by petitions in its favor.[52] Yet despite this advantage, the protectionists were to be disappointed. The Baldwin bill eased through the House by 91 votes to 78, but with the end of the session approaching, its opponents in the Senate succeeded in postponing consideration of the measure in a close vote of 22 to 21, effectively killing it.

The free traders emerged victorious from this skirmish, but the war was far from won. Both sides had recognized the need to organize their forces in order to project their voices into the corridors of power, but it was the protariff men who organized faster and further. Although their objects were diametrically opposed, the two movements adopted similar strategies, employing nonpartisan voluntary associations well-suited to the task of shaping policymaking in Washington. These groups provided a focal point and stimulus for public expressions of support in the shape of pledges, meetings, and petitions. Unlike party organizations, which effectively went into hibernation between election seasons, protectionist and agricultural societies could keep up a constant pressure on Congress throughout each session. As a public body, each could credibly claim to be more than the sum of its parts, no mere collection of individuals but the representative of a broader constituency, whether it be farmers in Virginia or friends to manufacturing in Pennsylvania. And the ease with which the associational template could be replicated from one locality to the next facilitated the fusion of these scattered constituencies in a single cause. As the protectionist network continued to expand, the free traders knew that the Senate's decision marked only a temporary cessation of hostilities. "The advocates of the manufacturers are foiled, but are not defeated," warned Ritchie in the *Enquirer*. "They will be busily engaged during this summer in recruiting their troops to take to the field next winter."[53]

❖ The protectionist and free-trade organizations described thus far, like those of the anticonventionists in Illinois or the Middling Interest in Massachusetts, were local in nature, albeit conceived for the purpose of influencing federal policy. But as the campaign progressed, both sides also took steps to coordinate their efforts on a national scale. As early as November 1819 the Pennsylvania Society had issued a public call for "the manufacturers of the United States, who are interested in the modification of the tariff of duties, to send delegates to [a] general convention to be held in the city of New York."[54] This proposal was disseminated through the press and circular letters addressed to known supporters in other states. No instruction was given on how delegates should be selected, with the result that some were deputed by local societies, some were put forward by public meetings, and others simply chose to attend on their own account. When the meeting took place on 29 November 1819, those present adopted a petition to Congress, recommended "to the manufacturers and their fellow citizens in the different states to form societies for the encouragement of domestic industry," and made plans for another national convention in January of the new year.[55]

At the second convention it was agreed that a permanent national protectionist organization should be formed. A committee was chosen to draft a constitution and raise funds, and a temporary board of managers was appointed to serve until the society could be properly established. The latter were entrusted with the task of publicizing the endeavor, which they did by sending copies of their proceedings to each of the state legislatures and every member of Congress.[56] Then in June 1820, just one month after the defeat of the Baldwin bill, protectionist delegates gathered in New York once again to formally inaugurate the National Institution for the Promotion of Industry.

The stated objects of the society were "to call the public attention to the subject of National Industry; to diffuse information in reference to the policy of protecting those branches of it which may be injured by foreign competition; . . . [and] to promote the formation of Associations in all parts of the country, for the encouragement of industry." The organization was headed by the usual set of officers, who would also serve as part of a twenty-five-strong Board of Managers, which included men from nine different states. The board was empowered to appoint a Committee of Correspondence, to "communicate with such societies throughout the Union as have objects congenial with those of this Institution, and use their best endeavors to effect the establishment of such Societies," and a Committee of Publication, to "determine what Books and Pamphlets it may be proper for the Institution to publish, and adopt suitable measures to ensure their circulation." The only significant difference from the Pennsylvania Society model was the subscription rate, which was set at a relatively high five dollars, suggesting that the National Institution envisioned itself as a coordinating body for the state and local societies rather than a mass-membership organization in its own right.[57]

The free-trade response also originated in Pennsylvania, but this time with the Philadelphia Chamber of Commerce. This group had been established by the city's mercantile community in 1801, and like the agricultural societies of Virginia, it combined political and nonpolitical functions, mediating in business disputes between members and campaigning for laws advantageous to their interests.[58] It was in the latter capacity that on 14 June 1820, one week after the third protectionist meeting opened in New York, the chamber appointed a committee to "take the most early and effectual measures to prevent the proposed alteration [in the tariff]." This committee in turn concluded that "the sentiments of the merchants, and others connected with commerce, may be most effectually collected and embodied, and a system of uniform and general action be best matured, by a convention of delegates, from as many of our mercantile towns and cities as can conveniently send them."[59]

The Philadelphia Chamber of Commerce advertised this plan to sister organizations and prominent merchants all along the Eastern Seaboard, from Belfast, Maine, to New Orleans, Louisiana.[60] The response was mixed. One correspondent questioned whether "if the doings of a body thus assembled is solely to be relied upon to influence Congress . . . as much effect would be produced upon that body, as by a petition emanating from each commercial town," while others praised the scheme but regretted that the time frame involved precluded them from participating.[61] Nonetheless, several towns did select representatives to the convention, either through their own chambers of commerce or in public meetings. In Virginia, the citizens of Norfolk and Portsmouth signaled their approval by adopting a series of antitariff resolutions, while their counterparts in Richmond approved a petition to the same end, although both declined to depute anyone to attend the convention itself.[62] In Fredericksburg, where "numbers of agriculturalists came from the adjacent counties, and united in sentiment with our most intelligent merchants," Taylor penned a remonstrance against any change to the existing rates, and when he professed himself unable to travel to Philadelphia personally, Garnett was chosen as his replacement.[63]

The free-trade convention sat for four days, from 1 to 4 November 1820, adopted a number of resolutions against protection, and approved a petition to Congress that Garnett was credited with drafting.[64] The contribution of the latter notwithstanding, there appears to have been no concerted effort to forge an alliance between the interests of commerce and agriculture, and no plans were made to establish a permanent institutional presence like that of their opponents. The whole project was widely ridiculed in the protectionist press. "What has become of the members of the convention of merchants, who made such a distinguished figure last fall?" taunted the *Pittsburgh Gazette* six months later. "Have they exhausted all their powers in one poor *anonymous* memorial?"[65]

In some respects the National Institution also proved a disappointment to the protectionist cause. It expended much effort publishing addresses and petitioning, but its exertions were marred by infighting among the principals. Carey was elected as an officer of the new society but almost immediately fell out with other members over the tactics it should employ, even refusing to put his name to their productions.[66] Perhaps for this reason, the National Institution seems to have exerted little direction over the activities of the state societies. The constitution promised that any associations "which co-operate and correspond with this Institution, and contribute to its funds, shall receive its publications; [and] their Presidents shall be considered Members," but there is no evidence that this offer was widely taken up.[67] This failure is particularly striking in comparison with the success of the American Bible Society and the American Tract Society in establishing a network of local auxiliaries that made substantial contributions to their parent bodies.[68]

Nonetheless, the efforts of both sides to organize on a national scale involved real innovation. The first protectionist convention, in November 1819, brought together delegates from nine different states, while eight were represented at the free-trade convention one year later. In an era when very few organizations crossed state borders, it would be another decade before any political party replicated this feat.[69] And the National Institution too, though it failed to realize its full potential, suggested the possibilities for national political association on a federal model, an example that would subsequently be followed by more famous reform movements, such as abolitionism and temperance.[70]

Activists on the tariff question were also pioneers in the establishment of a nonpartisan press, which would become a staple of antebellum reformers. One of the first acts of the National Institution was to establish its own biweekly newspaper, the *Patron of Industry*.[71] The *Patron* published reports of protectionist meetings, extracts from pamphlets and congressional speeches relating to the tariff, and correspondence on the subject. "Very strong evidences have been presented of the necessity of a paper devoted to the interests of National Industry," the editor explained, because existing publications "are characteristically political [i.e., partisan] or commercial, [and therefore] their principal influence cannot be expected to be felt in this direction." For himself, he disclaimed "all party and local purposes; being satisfied that the policy in question should be discussed and supported upon those broad principles which belong to the subject abstractly, and those general considerations which are applicable to the whole commonwealth."[72] Initial prospects for the paper appeared promising, and plans were even made to mail free copies to all members of Congress. But despite attracting a nationwide audience, the *Patron* made a loss in its first year, and publication was discontinued.[73]

The free traders enjoyed better fortune with the press. Despite possessing the support of influential papers like the *Enquirer,* many Virginia planters still yearned for a national periodical "devoted principally to the Interests of agriculture."[74] Their wish was fulfilled in 1819 with the foundation of the

American Farmer by John Skinner, a Maryland lawyer and postmaster. Skinner conceived of his new periodical as "a sort of common register, where each should be invited to record for the benefit of the agricultural community, whatever might have a tendency to enlighten and improve them in the *practice* of their calling," but he was adamant that "this Register should be at the same time a zealous advocate to explain and defend the political rights of Husbandmen." Since most existing newspapers looked to urban centers for their main sources of revenue, the editor claimed, "these papers circulate through, without depending upon, the country—hence the Farmer is not only uninformed, but often misinformed and deluded, as to *his* true interest!"[75] And just like his counterpart at the *Patron*, Skinner was determined that "not a word of party politics will ever be allowed to enter [the *Farmer's*] columns." "The *professed* objects of the paper, *Agriculture* and *Domestic Economy*, are its *real* objects," he insisted: "these are of no sect or party."[76] The *Farmer* soon claimed more than fifteen hundred subscribers across the Union, a healthy base for any contemporary newspaper, and provided an important forum for agricultural societies to communicate with one another, advertise their proceedings, and expound on their objections to protection.[77]

National organization in New York and Philadelphia may have dominated the headlines between the two sessions of the Sixteenth Congress, but local efforts also proceeded apace. As the protectionist petition drives continued, "A Citizen—but no merchant" directed opponents of tariff reform to "the example of the Agricultural Societies of Virginia." "How long will you suffer the manufacturing interest to predominate over the public mind?" he demanded. "You must fight them with their own weapons. *You* too must hold meetings. *You* must address the public. *You* must memorialize Congress."[78] This call was duly answered, as a new wave of public meetings were held across Virginia to protest against any increase in duties and further remonstrances were adopted by several agricultural societies.[79] Reviewing these measures, Ritchie reported that "the friends of manufactures had nearly the whole of last year to themselves, to make good their cause before the public. This year, a strong current seems setting against *them*."[80] His confidence proved well founded, for the new tariff bill drafted by the Committee on Manufactures failed even to come to a final vote during the second session of the Sixteenth Congress. The advocates of free trade were victorious once again.

❖ By far the most common mode through which both sides sought to shape federal tariff policy was petitioning. Like its close relative instruction, the petition was introduced to America by the earliest colonists from Britain. Petitions differed from instructions in that they were addressed to the whole legislature rather than to the representative of a single district and traditionally solicited action in the manner of a subordinate rather than commanding it in the manner of an employer directing his agent. While voting rights were restricted to only a small minority of the population, petitions were the primary medium of communication between the people, including the disenfranchised, and their representatives in government. The right of the people "to petition the Government for a redress of grievances" was enshrined in the First Amendment to the United States Constitution, and most states made similar provisions. Even before the advent of near-universal white male suffrage and mass political parties, the act of petitioning provided a practical expression of the republican principle of popular sovereignty and allowed large numbers of Americans to participate in the policy-making process. The historian Raymond Bailey has calculated that in eighteenth-century Virginia more legislation originated from petitions than from any other source, and other scholars have confirmed that this was no isolated case.[81]

Congress was flooded with petitions on the tariff. According to the economist Jonathan Pincus, in the fifteen years following the War of 1812 no other subject, not even slavery, received more public attention.[82] Many of these memorials were produced by organizations already described in this chapter. Others originated with ephemeral public meetings or brought together individuals involved in a branch of industry that would feel the impact of tariff reform. So, for example, petitions from the inhabitants of New Bedford and Nantucket asking for an additional duty on tallow to protect their involvement in the fishing industry were quickly followed by a remonstrance from the tallow chandlers of Boston.[83] Given the difficulties associated with long-distance communication during this period, it is no surprise that almost all memorials came from groups of people gathered in a single place, either through residency, occupation, or membership in an association. Yet logistical obstacles did not prevent some from attracting hundreds or even thousands of subscribers, and meetings frequently appointed committees to continue soliciting signatures for several days after they dispersed. Carey estimated that more than thirty thousand individuals signaled their support for the Baldwin bill in this manner, a number that represents approximately 3 percent of the national electorate, a not inconsiderable sum at a time the names had to be collected by hand.[84]

Like the wooden-buildings episode in Boston and the convention question in Illinois, congressional debates over tariff policy also provoked broader discussion about the role of the people in government. In this instance, the catalyst was a report delivered to the House by Henry Baldwin in November 1820, in which he declared that certain antitariff petitions referred to the Committee on Manufactures, including one from a public meeting in Virginia, contained passages "inconsistent with the respect due to the Representatives of the nation." These memorials variously alleged that the proposed increase in import duties was deliberately designed "to assail our commerce in the most vital manner, and eventually to destroy it." Such language, Baldwin claimed, "prevents the fair and legitimate action of public opinion, [and] deceives and misleads the people, by directing their attention from what is really proposed to be adopted to phantoms which exist only in the fears and ignorance of those who raise them." "By abusing," he concluded, "it may impair, the sacred right of petition and remonstrance, to either ignorantly or wilfully misrepresent the proceedings of any branch of the government."[85]

Although Baldwin had been careful to affirm the right of citizens to petition Congress, the tone of his report nevertheless triggered a storm of protest. "There is no excuse for so elaborate a *tirade*," ranted Ritchie in the *Enquirer*. "The memorialists meant no disrespect to Congress; though they spoke freely, as freemen ought to speak."[86] "A Repentant Citizen" was equally caustic. Addressing his remarks to the signatories of the petition, he sneered, "You thought yourselves entitled to state your ideas, like freemen, to your representatives, . . . [but] it seems, that you have arrogated a right which did not belong to you; and that you have committed an unpardonable sin against the sovereignty of their High Mightinesses." "All that you can do now," the author added sarcastically, "is to express your humble contrition for the liberty you have used and prostrate yourselves in dust and ashes at the feet of the Committee of Manufactures."[87] Discussion of the import of Baldwin's remarks would continue for some time in the press, and Ritchie took great pleasure in reprinting critical extracts from across the nation.

Within Congress, responsibility for replying to Baldwin fell on the future president John Tyler, then just a junior member of the House, who had presented the offending memorial on behalf of his Richmond constituents. Like "A Repentant Citizen," Tyler ridiculed the notion that the petitioners should "have presented themselves before you [i.e., Congress] as humble suppliants . . . trembling in your presence." "They have exercised a Constitutional right in a manly manner," he proclaimed. "They have approached you, not as their masters, but as the servants of the people." "The committee [of Manufactures] suggest that the right of petition will be brought into disrepute if the House was to sanction the language used in the memorial," Tyler continued, but in his view it was Baldwin's report that seemed "calculated to destroy the exercise of that right." "Will the people of this country condescend to approach you, if they are to subject themselves to your reproaches?" he demanded. "They have a right to speak to you in the language of authority. Who are you, that you should thus elevate yourselves above them?"[88]

The chief protagonists in this dispute voiced two very different conceptions of the relationship between the people and their representatives. Baldwin insisted that the petitioners respect the authority of government or else their pleas would not be heard, an attitude that would have been considered entirely proper prior to the Revolution. In the decades since Americans founded their new nation on the principle that the people must rule, however, the balance of power had shifted, and now it was the people who expected their authority to be respected. Tyler was widely praised for his defense of the right to petition, while Baldwin, suitably chastened, adopted a more deferential manner toward the memorials that continued to arrive in opposition to the protective policy.[89]

It is difficult to assess precisely the impact that petitioning had on the tariff debates in Congress. Certainly the fate of the Baldwin bill proves that even when a majority of the memorials presented were in favor of a measure its success was far from assured, an outcome that prompted one satirist to comment that "the surest way to prevent a law being passed was to get half the nation to petition for it."[90] The apparent ease with which legislators could evade the obligations placed on them by petitions if so inclined is illustrated by the case of Samuel Smith, a senator from Maryland, who voted against protection when the issue resurfaced in 1824. On the floor of the Senate, Smith acknowledged that his conduct placed him "in opposition to [a] memorial from Baltimore" that had been "unfurled triumphantly" by the tariff bill's supporters "as if to deter me from [my] course." He admitted that the signers of that petition were "highly respectable"; indeed, "some of them [are] my relations—most of them my friends." He then proceeded to summarily dismiss their arguments in favor of protection and claim that the proposed bill would lay an unwarranted tax upon the people, concluding by blithely announcing that "I feel almost confident that, if that had been known to be the effect of the memorial, it would have had few subscribers."[91] In this instance, Smith's conduct hardly implies a respect for petitioning as an instrument of popular sovereignty.

Yet other sources suggest that a more positive assessment may be in order. There are clear cases of members of Congress reluctantly supporting an increase in duties contrary to their personal preference. Senator Jonathan Roberts of Pennsylvania believed the Baldwin bill to be "most wild & extravagant without any admitted object or ascertained effect" and called Carey a "mad man," but when it came to the crucial vote, he took the side favored by his overwhelmingly protectionist state.[92] And none other than Samuel Smith, still representing Maryland in the House in 1820, reportedly notified a friend that he too would support the measure, because "a great portion of his constituents had petitioned congress on the subject of manufactures . . . [and] no remonstrance . . . had been sent to him or his colleague; nor had he received a single letter, *disapproving*—he must, therefore, conclude it was agreeable to the wishes of his constituents."[93] Those with most at stake in the debates certainly believed that petitions could have an impact. "I think it most important to present memorials," one Washington correspondent informed Carey in April 1820. ". . . I wish a thousand might arrive the coming week."[94]

Petitions served several functions for those competing to shape federal tariff policy. They played to the deliberative function of Congress, providing detailed arguments, often supported by reams of statistics, in order to persuade vacillating legislators. The Pennsylvania Society in particular took considerable care to engage with the case for free trade put forward by the memorials of their opponents and to refute their conclusions point by point.[95] Unlike elections, petitions also provided a guide to popular sentiment on specific issues, which made them an invaluable resource in an era lacking in sophisticated polling methods. And by uniting their voices in petition, individuals who were insignificant in isolation could transform themselves into plausible representatives of that all-powerful body "the people," whether in the guise of "inhabitants of the city of Philadelphia," "citizens of Pennsylvania," or a general convention of "the friends of national industry."[96]

❖ In addition to harnessing the weight of public opinion through petitions, both sides also sent delegates to personally apply pressure to members of Congress. Examples of individuals seeking to influence their elected representatives through face-to-face meetings may be found as far back as the First Congress. Even if defined more strictly as "paid agents representing mobilized special interest groups," this lobbying became increasingly widespread in the decades following the War of 1812, reflecting the transition toward an interest-based conception of politics.[97] According to the historian Jeffrey Pasley, the term *lobby* was popularized by a New York pamphleteer who used it in 1819 to describe a "class of men . . . whose profession and trade it is to attend . . . during the sessions of the Legislature, with a view of soliciting or opposing the passing of bills, banks, insurance companies, &c."[98]

Just days after the Sixteenth Congress opened in December 1819, a New York confidant advised Carey that "we shall send an agent from here to Washington to support our Memorial & the cause of the Manufacturers" and suggested that "a suitable person ought to be sent from all the Principal towns North of Virginia."[99] This grand scheme was never realized, but the Pennsylvania Society did dispatch one of its members, the state legislator Condy Raguet, to the national capital.[100] Raguet reported that he had "spent a good deal of time with Mr. Baldwin," and "conversed also with a number of members from different States" during his week-long stay, which was paid for by the society. He recommended to Carey that "a confidential well informed individual should be deputed here to continue for some weeks to whom application might be made by the Chairman of the committee [on Manufactures] for information as to details &c., and who could be ready to procure some such particularly respecting the various branches of manufacture, as might be required on the draft of a bill." "Such an individual should be a private and not a publickly declared agent," he cautioned, for "if there is room for the exercise of individual persuasion, *that* can only be effectual where the instructing party appears as a voluntary *amateur*."[101] Raguet's reference to "the exercise of individual persuasion" suggests that the private politicking that inevitably accompanied the formulation of public policy, while far removed from popular oversight through elections, was not an activity limited solely to members of the legislature.[102]

When Raguet returned to his official duties, he was swiftly replaced by the Philadelphia physician John Harrison. Shortly after his arrival, the latter recorded that he had "already had several private conferences with members who are friendly to our views, & I find it is the best policy to feel my way, before I make my appeal to those who are either doubtful or notoriously opposed." Following Raguet's advice, the doctor obtained permission to use the dining room of his boardinghouse as an office in order to "see without interruptions & in a reputable way such persons as the nature of my business may require me to consult with." This decision may also have been influenced by the limited resources at his disposal. The ad hoc character of the mission is revealed by Harrison's complaint that "I have not received one line from the Board of Manufactures not *even my Instructions,* or answers to enquiries on particular points, or the letter of introduction to a Gentleman from New York who is here on the same subjects to enable me to consult with him upon the cause that ought to be pursued."[103]

The "Gentleman from New York" was Eleazar Lord, acting on behalf of the grandly named American Society for the Encouragement of Domestic Manufactures, and it was he who would continue to work closely with Baldwin after Harrison was forced to return home prematurely by the death of his child.[104] Lord remained in Washington for several months and was intimately involved in the preparation of the bill that failed to pass the first session of the Sixteenth Congress. "I am set to work drafting a schedule of a new tariff," he informed Carey in January 1820. "Material alterations & additions can be made if adequate information & statements can be furnished. Please give me such hints, & observations as will be of use in this view."[105] Another of his duties, it appears, was to sustain Baldwin, whom Lord found to be "in a very uncomfortable state of mind" by the end of February. The representative from Pittsburgh had voted with the South to admit Missouri as a slave state in order to bring that episode to a conclusion, and he was worried by the hostile reaction to his conduct in many northern newspapers. "As he evidently esteems you, I pray you to conciliate him as far as possible," Lord advised Carey. "Let it appear that no personal disrespect or diminution of confidence has taken place in regard to him."[106] As the tariff debates reached their climax, the New Yorker was a constant presence in the congressional galleries, writing almost daily reports on the proceedings.[107]

The efforts of protectionist lobbyists would not go unnoticed. "Emissaries, agents and borers have haunted the doors of the House, like the ghost of the murdered Banquo; as if determined by the certainty of their appearance to destroy the peace of its occupants, till they granted their request," testified "Marcus" in the *Philadelphia Aurora*.[108] Yet the free traders were not above engaging in similar activity. Daniel Webster, for example, was a frequent recipient of what he called "subscriptions," "gifts," and "sweeteners" from the Boston Associates, a collection of entrepreneurs who favored low import duties.[109] During the Sixteenth Congress it was an open secret that "Mr. Webster was retained by the Boston importers to advocate the unconstitutionality of the new Tariff" to his friends in the national legislature.[110] And after Webster was himself elected to the House of Representatives in 1822, "protection of the Boston Associates' interests became [his] congressional speciality."[111]

When tariff reform resurfaced in 1824, Webster transmitted to his benefactors copies of the proposed measure, along with a note acknowledging that "something is expected from me."[112] Thomas Handasyd Perkins, fresh from seeing off the Middling Interest, replied that plans were afoot among Boston merchants to "send a deputation to Washington, of some of their practical men."[113] Nathan Appleton, another Associate, was accordingly dispatched, and he was soon able to report that Webster's opinion of the tariff "meets my own views."[114] The latter's speeches in favor of free trade were well received, although they would come back to haunt him later when the shifting business interests of the Associates compelled him to switch to the side of protection. Indeed, it is particularly ironic that Webster's most famous utterance—"Liberty and Union, now and forever, one and inseparable"—was made in 1830 in response to South Carolina's bid to declare the principle of protection unconstitutional, a claim this staunch supporter of federal power had himself been one of the first to make ten years earlier.[115]

Lobbying occupies an ambiguous position in the politics of the early United States.[116] Legislators were expected to work for the common good, and contemporaries clearly recognized the potential for corruption where they were exposed to the solicitations of privately deputed individuals. Yet elected representatives were far from being experts on many of the issues they were required to make policy on, and party leaders generally offered little guidance. Lobbyists, then, like petitions, could perform a useful service by bringing public concerns to the attention of government and helping to craft a solution, a role that Lord certainly seems to have played in the drafting of the Baldwin bill. The presence of agents in the national capital also allowed the protectionists to identify wavering legislators on whom pressure might fruitfully be brought to bear; of twelve members of the Sixteenth Congress targeted for special attention, ten ultimately voted in favor of the defeated measure.[117] Although his efforts ended in failure on this occasion, Lord was subsequently presented with a silver pitcher by the "friends of National Industry in Philadelphia" in approbation of "the Zeal, talents, and intelligence he displayed at Washington, in support of American Manufacturers, during the first session of the sixteenth Congress."[118]

❖ The ballot box offered another potential avenue for shaping federal policy, but elections posed a dilemma for protectionists and free traders alike. As the Middling Interest had discovered, partisan loyalties remained a powerful force to contend with. If those on either side chose to promote their cause at the polls, they would have to challenge the existing parties' claims to the sympathies of the electorate without appearing to sacrifice their principles for the pursuit of public office.

One prime target for the Virginia free traders' attention appeared to be Thomas Newton, the only member of the state's twenty-three-strong delegation in the House of Representatives to vote for the Baldwin bill in April 1820. He had voted for the bill despite his position as chairman of the Committee on Commerce, which left contemporaries mystified. "Virginius," addressing the congressman in the columns of the *Enquirer,* sarcastically observed, "You could gain nothing [by supporting the bill], and have most liberally surrendered the best interests of your district, state and nation.—Your independence of popular favor commands my admiration."[119] In Prince George County attendees at a Fourth of July celebration toasted *"The Hon. Messrs. Newton and Baldwin, chairmen of the committees of Commerce and Manufactures*—May they have the benefit of a new course of political economy, with a teacher more sane than Mathew Cary [*sic*]."[120] Newton's home district of Norfolk was decidedly mercantile in its proclivities, and an antitariff meeting held there in September pointedly resolved to transmit a copy of its proceedings to their representative "as the deliberate sense of this portion of his constituents."[121] "With your private virtues, sir, I am perfectly unacquainted," gloated "Virginius," "but they must be as remarkable as your good fortune has hitherto been, if you continue to possess the confidence of your constituents."[122]

Yet when Newton stood for reelection in April 1821, he was unopposed and won all but a scattering of votes.[123] Newton's survival may be explained by the fact that he was one of the longest-serving members of the House and personally popular in his district. At least one of his colleagues was not so fortunate: The *Patron of Industry* reported that Benjamin Adams, a representative from Massachusetts, was defeated in his bid to return to the Seventeenth Congress "on the ground of his having voted last winter for the measures recommended by the committee on manufactures." However, the article continued, "this, we believe, is the only instance of opposition upon the same ground."[124] Adams, a Federalist, seems to have fallen victim to an opportunistic Republican challenger who took advantage of the shifting partisan balance in that state and seized on the tariff as a convenient campaign issue. There is no evidence that the free traders, in Virginia or elsewhere, made a systematic effort to punish at the polls those members of Congress who voted for an increase in duties contrary to the sentiments of their constituents.

Their protectionist opponents, in contrast, appeared keenly aware of the value of the vote. "I am entirely persuaded that our hopes rest on *alarming* those in power for their *popularity*," a friend from New York wrote to Carey early in 1820. "Not one individual of talents is found in Congress, who has the *courage* to propose any measure, however salutary, until he is impelled by the popular voice—until he has well ascertained that *it will be popular*."[125] One year later another New York correspondent echoed this assessment. "Our last Congress have disgraced the Country & themselves," he declared, "but how we are to remedy the evil I know not, unless it is at the Polls. I shall use every exertion to put in Men from this Place in the next Congress, that be efficient friends to the protection of Domestic Industry."[126]

Rather than nominating their own men for office, the protectionists initially sought to influence the existing parties by promising to vote only for candidates who pledged to support an increase in duties. John Forbert, a Delaware manufacturer, set out the details of this plan in relation to that state's gubernatorial election in 1819. At a recent public meeting held to form a local protectionist association, he reported to a member of the Philadelphia Society, "a resolution was passed to support none but such as are favorable to National Industry." Immediately thereafter, "a call to know the sentiments of Mr. Bull one of the Candidates for Governor" was published in the press, and Forbert expected that "a similar one will be made . . . to Mr. Molleston the opposition candidate." "If both come out favorable the[y] will as it regards their standing be on a footing and we shall consider we have done much in making them declare in favor," he explained. However, "if it is ascertained that one is favorable & the other not every man should be expected to elect the one that is, let him be on what side he may as to party politicks."[127]

Carey advocated the same strategy on a national scale. Following the setback suffered by the protectionists in the first session of the Sixteenth Congress, he prepared a mammoth pamphlet entitled *The New Olive Branch*, a name chosen to emphasize the nonpartisan nature of the cause. In a specially prepared "Prefatory Address" he urged his intended readers to "associate yourselves throughout the nation, wherever there are a dozen of you together," and "resolve to vote for no man who is unfriendly to domestic manufactures." Carey hoped that through the act of association voters would acquire a public identity that would supersede their partisan affiliation and thus guide their choice at the polls. He even pushed this argument to its extreme, claiming that he would rather support a member of "the Hartford Convention, [with] all its deeds of darkness" than support "my nearest and dearest friend," if the former would show himself "a friend to American manufactures."[128] But such sentiments proved too radical for his associates, and Carey later recalled that *The New Olive Branch* was published without the "Prefatory Address" "at the request of some of my friends, who thought it rather too violent, and likely to offend."[129]

Carey's decision to suppress the "Prefatory Address" reflected the uncertainty among the protectionist ranks as to how much they should involve themselves in elections. Forbert's experiment in Delaware was hardly proving an unqualified success; when the protariff men inquired about the opinions of one of the state's two congressmen, he responded that he had "no notion of being ruled or directed by *a mob*."[130] In contemporary discourse, "a mob" was the inverse of "the people," an unorganized and unruly body of individuals who had no legitimate role in the political process, so this was a damning judgment on the protectionist societies. Many tariff activists were reluctant to invite more of the same criticism. Following the failure of the Baldwin bill, "An Injured Manufacturer" received a lukewarm response when he inquired of the editor of the *Aurora,* "Would it not be advisable to have *town* and *country meetings* called to declare their approbation, or disapprove of the conduct of such as have voted against it?"[131] William Duane, himself a member of the Pennsylvania Society, replied that although "every individual who suffers, has the right to exercise the freedom he enjoys to reject bad men and select good," it is "the *sense of the wrongs of one man*" that should provide "the impulse by which he is moved to obtain redress." "If meetings are to be called, let it be as in the town meeting called for the purpose of protecting domestic industry," he continued, adding that "these meetings should not mix the politics of elections with the policy of manufactures."[132]

Two years later, however, the continued failure of the protectionist cause persuaded Carey and his Philadelphia-based allies of the need to run their own slate of candidates in the state and congressional elections to be held in October 1822. This movement originated in a public meeting held on 26 September, after the local Federalist and Republican parties had made their own nominations, which resolved that "the tickets now before the public not having been formed with a due regard for the several interests of the city do not meet with our approbation and cannot obtain our support." Carey chaired the meeting, and several other members of the Pennsylvania Society were appointed to the committee tasked with drawing up an alternative list of candidates. Like the anticonventionists in Illinois, the protectionists presumably chose to make their nominations in this manner rather than through their existing associations to insulate themselves from charges of self-interest. To this end, members of the committee were also instructed "not to place themselves on the ticket which they report."[133]

The new list, made up of men from both major parties, was presented at a second public meeting convened a few days later. Five thousand copies were ordered to be printed, and arrangements made "to procure a house at which these tickets can be had on the day of the election; [and] to have printed in large characters, and placed in the front of the house, '*The Manufacturers' and Mechanics' Ticket may be had here.*'" Those present also adopted a public address in which they set out their case to the electorate. "It is believed, from an enquiry into the subject, that a majority of the people of this city depend upon the promotion of manufactures, and with this belief, we do not think it unreasonable to ask the votes of our fellow citizens for such persons as we think will pay due attention to this grand object," the message proclaimed. "We have no political object in view," avowed the authors, again implying a separation between the making of policy and the election of men to office. "We protest against any prejudice or partiality for either of the parties, that have selected tickets; and we trust that the impartiality of our selections will secure credit to our declarations." "We ask you to do what we are ourselves prepared to do," the address concluded, "sacrifice political and party feelings to keep our shuttles, and our hammers, our adzes and our spinning machines in motion."[134]

Responsibility for championing the movement in the press fell to William J. Duane, who had taken over editorship of the *Aurora* from his father and now stood atop the protectionist ticket for Congress. In a style reminiscent of Joseph Buckingham, Duane acknowledged "that parties are at times unavoidable, and that they are sometimes useful," but demanded to know "*upon* WHAT *are the* PEOPLE *now separated?*" "The true secret of *present* distinctions is this," the editor explained: "there are a number of persons on all sides, who want to serve in public stations, some for the honor, and some for the emolument; but without some other merit than their own, they know perfectly well that their hopes are idle." "No wonder, then," he concluded, "that *party* is the watch-word, and that adherence to its candidates, whether good or bad, is said to be the only countersign that can gain admission to the political camp!"[135]

Duane's description of the methods parties used to control the electoral process in Philadelphia mirrors the complaints of opponents of party in Massachusetts and Illinois. Any citizen who approached the polls was immediately confronted by an agent, the editor wrote, and if he maintained his right to choose which candidates to support he was told that "*you have no right to choose,* you are bound by what the *party* have done, and if you vote any other ticket but this you are an apostate." Yet the prospective voter would have no say in the composition of the ticket thrust upon him, for party insiders "select from themselves the candidates for nearly all offices" and the rank and file were expected "like sheep to follow the leaders." In contrast to this practice, Duane emphasized, the protectionist ticket "was formed at a general meeting of all the citizens of Philadelphia, without distinction, who chose to attend—it was openly proposed—[and] every man had a right to give his opinion upon it."[136] Yet even the editor was pessimistic about its chances, admitting that "although it might puzzle sensible men of all sections, to explain the present meaning of party words—*the charm* prevails, and some men of sense, as well as blockheads, believe that, it is unsafe to vote independently of party."[137]

These expectations proved well founded. The protectionist slate finished a distant third, behind those of the major parties, garnering just 218 votes for Congress compared with 2,268 for the victorious Federalist candidate.[138] In defense of this disappointing showing, Duane noted that "nothing less than a miracle could secure the success of a ticket, formed within four days of the election, and opposed by the two contending political parties, whose plans were already laid, and whose passions were already excited."[139] Poor preparation was certainly a factor in the defeat. Several of the original nominees declined a place on a ticket, and a split in the protectionist ranks over how to respond saw two different lists of names circulated at the polls.[140] As the Middling Interest also found to their cost, individuals of different partisan persuasions proved able to cooperate when principles were at stake, but once they turned their attention to the election of men to office, old prejudices soon resurfaced. And this problem was not confined to the protectionist camp in Philadelphia, for a similar bid to unseat a prominent free trader in New York also failed because of a delay in putting up an opposition candidate and the absence of "systematic arrangements . . . in his behalf."[141]

The parallels with contemporaneous events in Massachusetts were made plain in Duane's analysis of the election result. Noting that a Boston paper sympathetic toward the insurgency there had praised "the bone and muscle of the population of Philadelphia" for likewise challenging the established parties, the editor of the *Aurora* observed that given their numerical advantage, "'the bone and muscle of the population of Philadelphia,' if disposed to unite their energies to the accomplishment of any purpose, could obviously effect it with ease." The protectionists had hoped that "the condition of the country, and the state of this district especially in relation to domestic manufactures" would produce such a common accord. But this outcome "did not suit the views of the aristocracy of the democrats any more than it did the aristocracy of the federalists, and therefore every art was used to put out of existence, what had scarcely given any symptoms of vitality."[142] Opponents of party in Boston and Philadelphia alike were convinced that so long as the mass of the people lacked a political weight proportionate to their numbers because of their failure to organize effectively, they would be robbed of their sovereignty by a few party insiders intent on dividing the electorate for their own selfish ends.

The result in Philadelphia signaled a real nadir for the protectionist movement. The Seventeenth Congress, which served from December 1821 until March 1823, offered no relief. With the election of Philip P. Barbour of Virginia to the Speaker's chair the free traders controlled the appointment of House committees, and consequently few observers were surprised when the Committee on Manufactures deemed it inexpedient to proceed with a revision of import duties during the first session. "Mr. Baldwin seems to have relinquished his visionary schemes of 'national wealth' & 'national prosperity' by means of tariffs," gloated one opponent of protection; "he being outvoted . . . in his own committee."[143] During the second session a new tariff bill was debated briefly on the floor of the House, but it never reached a third reading. The United Agricultural Societies were so emboldened by this turn of events that they actually petitioned Congress to request a reduction, rather than simply a freeze, in existing rates, but this proposal was not acted on either.[144]

❖ The Eighteenth Congress, which opened in December 1823, presented a much improved prospect for the protectionists. With Clay returned to the Speaker's chair, sympathetic appointments to the Committee on Manufactures were assured. States in favor of increased duties also gained in the decennial reapportionment of seats in the House, although the fact that the protectionists' majority on the final vote would actually fall from thirteen in 1820 to just five in 1824 indicates that this shift alone was insufficient to guarantee victory. Another factor to consider was the forthcoming presidential election. Pennsylvania had no favorite son of her own in the race, and free traders feared that the friends of each aspirant in Congress would compete to show their support for protection with the aim of securing the state's substantial electoral vote. "We may imagine the genius of this great state, in the sober guise of a Dutch or Quaker manufacturer, standing before the candidates for the Presidency, and offering to them Mr. Baldwin's bill, in one hand, and a blank ticket in the other," lamented "An Inhabitant of the South." "Thus is Pennsylvania, thus are the United States, offered for sale to the highest bidder of votes for the tariff."[145]

The tariff bill introduced in the first session of the Eighteenth Congress by John Tod of Pennsylvania, who had taken over Baldwin's duties as chairman of the Committee on Manufactures, provoked remarkably little response in Virginia. Garnett was the exception, using his annual address to the Fredericksburg Agricultural Society to urge farmers throughout the Union to protest against the measure.[146] Writing in the *American Farmer* under the pseudonym "Ruris Consultus," he even suggested "a non-consumption agreement solemnly entered into among ourselves; and inviolably observed, as was done in the Boston tea affair, which the new Tariff Bill strictly resembles in principle, as it does in all its chief bearings." The proposed remedy, Garnett acknowledged, was "a desperate one," but "it appears the only legitimate means left to us. Reason and argument, dissuasion, petition, remonstrance,—all have been tried, but I fear, in vain."[147] Yet these proposals received little support, and public reaction to the bill was confined to meetings in a few major towns, where the usual remonstrances against protection were adopted.[148]

A likely reason for the apathy displayed by the Old Dominion on this occasion was the absence of the agricultural societies that had carried on the struggle so successfully during the Sixteenth Congress. Not a single petition from this source is recorded in the *Annals of Congress,* and the columns of the *Farmer* suggest that this silence reflected a general decline in associational activity. A decade later, "An Ex-Member" recalled that "from 1819 to 1822 there was a *rage* for forming agricultural societies in Virginia. Nearly all ran the same course, and in a few years ceased to be heard of." The writer attributed their disappearance to failures in organization. "When the formation of an agricultural society is first proposed, there are plenty of members to be obtained," he explained. "Each is willing to give his name to support the scheme; and he is willing also to add a little of his time, and a small contribution in money. But very few think of becoming *working members.*" This problem was exacerbated by the tendency of societies to choose for their officers "the most aged, respectable, intelligent and popular members" rather than those with "zeal and energy" for the cause.[149] The exception to this rule was the Fredericksburg Agricultural Society, which consistently reelected Garnett as president and survived into the 1830s.

The fortunes of the protectionist associations in Pennsylvania were more mixed. The activities of the Philadelphia Society terminated in acrimony after little more than a year when several members refused to pay for a series of pamphlets that Carey had written without their sanction. "In a fit of scorn and indignation," Carey subsequently recalled, "I withdrew from the society—justly considering that if I had to write, and print, and publish, and pay the expense of paper and printing, I had no need of a society." Like its agricultural counterparts in Virginia, the Philadelphia Society proved overly reliant on the contribution of its leading actor. "The society never published a line afterwards," Carey recorded, "and very soon died a natural death."[150] In contrast, the Pennsylvania Society, with its large Board of Manufactures, proved much more stable. The president of the organization, William Tilghman, was presumably chosen for the prestige associated with his position as the chief justice of Pennsylvania, for his surviving papers suggest that he spent little time fretting about the tariff.[151] Yet the managers continued to meet frequently, and the society played an active part in the protectionist campaign in 1824.[152]

The organization-building of the protariff forces left them well placed to promote Tod's bill. The first session of the Eighteenth Congress received an unprecedented number of petitions on the subject; more than one hundred had been counted two months before the final vote was taken.[153] Lobbyists too were much in evidence. Representative James Hamilton Jr. claimed on the floor of the House that there had been "more outdoor than indoor legislation, in regard to the measure. . . . All sorts of pilgrims had travelled to the room of the Committee on Manufactures, from the sturdy iron master down to the poor manufacturer of whetstones."[154] Even so, the final roll calls were extremely close. Only two representatives were absent, and several members "were brought in upon their sick couches," as the bill squeaked through the House on 16 April by a vote of 107 to 102.[155] After more impassioned debate the Senate added their assent on 13 May by a vote of 25 to 21.[156] Nine days later President Monroe, a Virginian, signed the new tariff bill into law. Credit for this result must go in large part to the public crusade begun by Mathew Carey five years previously. In the judgment of a disappointed Daniel Webster, the measure would never have passed "if there were not so many members who would vote on the judgement of their constituents, not on their own."[157]

❖ In the struggle over federal tariff policy from 1819 to 1824, Americans confronted the challenge of translating the interests of a diverse electorate into a coherent program of governance. Modern scholars have suggested that political parties were very effective in performing this function. Yet contemporaries on both sides of the tariff debate rejected this conclusion; they found instead, as the historian Samuel Hays writes, that "the party's need to appeal to diverse groups within given geographical areas, while giving single-minded expression to none, was a limited and confining method of political expression to those who wished to give more concentrated support to specialized objectives."[158] For this reason, protectionists and free traders alike preferred an alternative organizational strategy centered on nonpartisan voluntary societies.

Spurred on by the Panic of 1819, protectionists heeded the advice of Mathew Carey to "associate yourselves throughout the nation."[159] In Carey's home state the Philadelphia Society and the Pennsylvania Society illustrate the dual nature of their operation; the former served to concentrate the resources of wealthy, well-connected individuals in order to shape public opinion, while the latter sought to give expression to that opinion and channel it to the points where it would have most impact. The free traders, determined to "oppose combination with combination," responded through the agricultural societies of Virginia and chambers of commerce all along the Eastern Seaboard.[160] Both sides held interstate conventions a decade before political parties would make such occasions a regular occurrence. And in the National Institution and the *American Farmer* they pioneered methods of campaigning that would be replicated by future reform movements.

"This is a government of opinion," observed Carey after the defeat of the Baldwin bill in 1820. "It is not, it cannot be, supported by physical force against that public opinion."[161] To understand the role public opinion played in the outcome of the struggle over the tariff, it is also necessary to take a more holistic view of popular participation in politics than is common among historians. Election results provide little clue to ultimate triumph of the protectionists with the passage of the tariff of 1824; the protariff men conspicuously failed to elect their own candidates on the few occasions when they attempted to do so. Yet by judicious use of petitioning and lobbying, the former bringing the weight of both numbers and argument to bear on

Congress as a whole and the latter targeting the conversion of individual members, the advocates of increased duties nonetheless succeeded in their crusade. Through these devices, then, and through membership in the organizations that employed them, Americans demonstrated their determination to play an active part in policymaking outside of parties and between elections.

4

"YOU MUST ORGANIZE
AGAINST ORGANIZATION"
The Presidential Election of 1824

Written during the canvass by John C. Calhoun, himself a candidate for the White House, the following appraisal of the presidential election of 1824 presents a stark contrast to the standard celebratory narrative, which paints political parties as agents of democracy:

> It cannot be doubted that a party has grown up in our country, who aspire to the government of the Union, not th[r]ough the confidence and attachment of the people, but by a dextrous use of what is called party machinery. The great object of the party has been to enlist in its cause political leaders, who were supposed to possess a control over the machinery and in this it has succeed[ed] to a great extent. They are now struggling to give to this machinery the highest possible force.[1]

In the eyes of most modern scholars, the emergence of mass parties signaled the dawning of the Age of the Common Man. To Calhoun, however, the rise of party portended something else entirely: government of the politicians, by the politicians, for the politicians.

The object of Calhoun's ire was William H. Crawford. Crawford and those that backed his bid for the presidency sought to make the campaign a referendum on the proper role of party in a republican polity. In their hands, they contended, party would be an organ of good government, facilitating the rule of the majority and restraining the improper ambition of individuals. But this vision did not go unchallenged. Crawford's rivals united to condemn his version of party as a tool for self-serving politicians, while defending their own right to organize in opposition. In this chapter, then, as in chapter 1, we see that neither partisanship nor antipartisanship is as monolithic as they sometimes appear.

The 1824 election also provides a lesson in the motives of these early party builders. Scholars have suggested that parties were created to serve three main functions: to engage and mobilize a mass electorate; to translate popular preferences into legislative outcomes; and to regulate access to public office.[2] In chapter 2 the opponents of slavery demonstrated that nonpartisan organizations were capable of performing the first of these functions, and in chapter 3 activists on both sides of the tariff issue performed the second. In the race for the White House, however, it was the third function that took precedence; campaign practices and policy agendas were dictated by the need to win votes, as the friends of each candidate forsook national consistency in order to shape their message to local circumstances. This episode underlines the remarkable diversity of political life in the United States during the early 1820s and the real differences in how contemporaries interpreted the promise of popular sovereignty.

❖ While Republicans rejoiced in "the great depression of the Federal party" following the War of 1812, the more prescient among them also recognized that their triumph would "relax the bonds by which the Republican party has been hitherto kept together."[3] Respect for James Monroe ensured that his reelection in 1820 was effectively unopposed, but five main contenders emerged from the Republican ranks to challenge for the presidency at the end of his second term.

William H. Crawford displayed no hesitation in staking a claim to the White House based primarily on his devotion to party. The supporters of the secretary of the treasury styled him as "*the* Republican candidate," ready to repel any threat from a resurgent Federalism.[4] They maintained that he had "established a peculiar claim to the esteem of the republican party" by declining to challenge Monroe for the nomination when urged by many to do so in 1816.[5] Their confidence had merit, for friends and enemies alike conceded that "Crawford is the favorite of a majority of Congress," and custom dictated that the Republican members of that body would choose the party's official candidate.[6] "He intends to rest on a single ground," recorded Calhoun, "that of being a thorough partisan."[7]

In contrast, the candidacy of John Quincy Adams much more closely approximated the conventional republican model, at least on the surface.[8] The secretary of state was the most eligible aspirant when measured by public character and length of service, but he was also a former Federalist, and his allies alleged that "the attempt to revive the distinctions and animosities of *party* . . . has been got up only as a counterpoise to the superior qualifications and pretensions of John Quincy Adams."[9] To his private journal the candidate confided, "Upon the foundation of public service alone must I stand; and when the nation shall be called to judge of that, by the result, whatever it may be, I must abide."[10] Adams was certainly fluent in the language of republicanism, but his flowery words did not always accord with his conduct during the canvass.

Junior to their rivals in age and experience, neither Secretary of War John C. Calhoun nor Speaker of the House Henry Clay could expect to succeed on a past record of party loyalty or public service alone. Instead, each chose to construct his campaign around the promise of future policies. Clay was acclaimed as the architect of the "American System," a scheme that included a protective tariff for domestic industry, federal aid for internal improvements, and a national banking system. Likewise, Calhoun was an enthusiastic supporter of a strong central government, epitomized by his call for Congress to "bind the Republic together, with a perfect system of roads and canals. Let us conquer space."[11] Advocates of both men argued that these measures were "of the last importance to the welfare and prosperity of our country, and the[ir] successful and vigorous prosecution . . . must depend upon the elevation of a statesman who is identified with them."[12]

The final contender for the presidency was Andrew Jackson. Aside from his celebrated victory over the British in 1815, the Hero of New Orleans appeared entirely unqualified for the White House. He had retired from public life, and his previous spells in civil office had done little to enhance his reputation. Jackson's supporters turned these apparent obstacles to his advantage, however, by arguing that "in contra-distinction to all the other candidates he is unconnected with party politics, local feelings or sectional jealousies, and of course the only one among them who can go into the Presidential chair unpledged to any thing but the interests of his country."[13] Though he was an avowed Republican, the General's military career had insulated him from the dirty work of partisan politicking. "No one believes he would be a party man," wrote one admirer. "In fact, he is known to despise most cordially the petty Bucktail interest of New York," a reference to Martin Van Buren's well-drilled political organization.[14] Jackson's campaign would attract many citizens who had become disillusioned with the state of politics. "They vote for Andrew Jackson," explained one public meeting, "because he will root out corruption and purify the polluted atmosphere of the city of Washington."[15]

❖ Crawford was a natural party leader, far more comfortable in that role than Jackson would ever be. In 1820 the secretary of the treasury arranged for his supporters in Congress to push through the first Tenure of Office Act, which made all federal officeholders, with the exception of judges, subject to reappointment every four years. Officially these appointments were made by the president, but in practice the measure granted enormous powers of patronage to the department heads. Unsurprisingly, the main beneficiary was Crawford. "One thousand persons scattered through the United States . . . who for the tenure of their offices are compelled to rest upon the smiles and the approbation of the secretary of the treasury, present a phalanx and an influence, at once to be seen, dreaded, and felt," complained one critic.[16] Eight years before "King Andrew the First" entered the White House, Crawford was already pioneering his own version of rotation in office.[17]

Crawford's personal papers were destroyed in a fire, so it is difficult to piece together a full account of his efforts to make himself president. There can be no doubt, though, that he abused his official position. In one much-publicized incident he appointed Jesse B. Thomas to inspect the federal land offices in several western states simply so that the Illinois senator could conduct an electioneering tour on Crawford's behalf.[18] This act, which violated the spirit if not the letter of the Constitution, was condemned by Thomas's rival Ninian Edwards as "a species of Walpoole [sic] management, that it is to be hoped our country is not yet ripe for," a reference to former British prime minister Robert Walpole's liberal distribution of political favors to sustain his administration.[19]

The secretary also bought the support of influential editors with Treasury Department printing contracts. More than two years before the country went to the polls, Adams recorded that "the organization of newspaper support for Mr. Crawford throughout the Union is very extensive, and is managed with much address."[20] Crawford was not the only candidate to take such steps, but the scale of his efforts was unprecedented and made him the early favorite for the presidency. "His Chance is the best," declared the well-respected South Carolina congressman William Lowndes, another potential contender until his premature death in 1822, because "he [is] the only Candidate who ha[s] an *Organised Party.*"[21]

If Crawford was skilled as a party organizer, Van Buren was supreme. The Little Magician had risen to prominence through the tangled web of New York politics by welding his faction of the state Republican Party into a formidable political machine. According to Van Buren, the sole function of party was to facilitate the exercise of popular sovereignty. "The majority of the People, the sovereign power in our Government, had again and again, . . . decided . . . in favor of the Republican creed," he later wrote in his memoirs. "That creed required only that unity amongst its friends should be preserved to make it the ark of their political safety."[22] From this perspective, party discipline was nothing more or less than obedience to the dictates of the people.[23]

Following his election to the United States Senate in 1821, Van Buren shifted his party-building ambitions to the national stage. To replicate his achievements in New York, he would need an ally in the White House willing to place the vast reserves of presidential patronage at his disposal. With this object in view, the Little Magician chose to back Crawford in 1824, a decision he attributed to his impression that the secretary's supporters were "more anxious to preserve the unity of the Republican party" than those of the other aspirants.[24] Also a factor in his calculations, no doubt, was the fact that Crawford was the preferred candidate of political leaders in the Old Dominion, and a New York–Virginia axis had provided the foundation for past Republican successes. When the treasury secretary suffered a paralytic stroke in September 1823, rendering him convalescent virtually up until the election, Van Buren effectively became his campaign manager.[25]

While Van Buren toiled tirelessly behind the scenes, others provided the Crawford campaign with its public face. Chief among these was Senator Benjamin Ruggles of Ohio, who chaired the congressional caucus that formally nominated the treasury secretary for the presidency in February 1824. In an accompanying address, Ruggles firmly set out his candidate's claim to the White House in the language of party. After admitting that the exertions of the Federalists had weakened of late, the senator nonetheless warned that "our adversaries have not lost their disposition to avail themselves" of "pending divisions in the republican party." "It is not to be doubted that it was by union and concert of action that the strength of the republican party was consolidated, and its success in the decisive controversy *effected*," he declared. "It is as little to be doubted, that it is by adherence to the same principle and policy of action that its unbroken force and continued ascendancy can be preserved." The good of the party, then, required all true Republicans to abide by the decision of the caucus or else precipitate the "break up [of] the entire system of conventions for the nomination of candidates, in reference to state as well as federal elections . . . and with it the securities of the republican ascendancy." For this reason, Ruggles concluded, the choice of president involved nothing less than "*the dismemberment or preservation of the party*."[26]

Newspapers sympathetic to Crawford echoed this message. "The Federalists and their allies the *No-Party men,* combined with a few *apostates from the good cause,* are now vigilantly watching for some quarrel between Republicans on the Presidential question," cautioned "A Republican" in Connecticut.[27] "This is a struggle of THE PEOPLE to regain their rights, and of THE REPUBLICANS for their *existence* as a party," agreed a commentator writing under the same pseudonym in South Carolina.[28] The fact that no Federalist candidate was even in the running did not dim the ardor of the Crawfordites, especially as Adams, son of the last Federalist president and a former member of the party himself, provided a ready-made surrogate for their fire.

The private correspondence of Crawford's supporters sheds more light on their conception of party. Following the announcement of his nomination as the caucus choice for vice president on the Crawford ticket, the venerable Albert Gallatin, who had served in the Jefferson and Madison administrations, explained to an ally his own reasons for wishing a revival of two-party competition in federal politics. Only in passing did he mention the "trite" opinion that opposing parties "watch one another and are one of the best safeguards against illegal or oppressive measures." Instead, he stressed the danger posed by "the disordinate ambition of individuals, especially of disappointed individuals," suggesting that "these are and will be more effectually kept in check and controlled by the force of party and by the bond resulting therefore than by any other means whatever." For Gallatin, devices like the Congressional caucus were necessary to "select men for [office] . . . whose political opinions are not discordant" with the doctrines of the Republican Party, as defined by the men who controlled the party machinery.[29]

Gallatin and Ruggles were political veterans, but the Crawford campaign also attracted a younger generation who shared their vision of party. Typical of these was Elias Kent Kane, a rising star in Illinois and therefore well versed in the effect that a lack of party regulation could have on politics. In a letter to his patron, Senator Thomas, before the congressional caucus made its pronouncement, Kane pondered "what singular operation of nature has turned republicans into partisans." "One great cause for the present divisions may be traced to the fears that the republican party is now so numerous that expectants can not all be provided for," he surmised. The fault, then, lay with "the Calhounites, Adamsites &c," that is, men who attached themselves to the cause of a favored candidate in the hope of future reward.[30] Once again, access to office was at the crux of this argument. And the language in which Kane expressed himself neatly captures the ambiguous position of party in contemporary discourse. In the course of a single paragraph he employs the terms "republican" and "republican party" almost interchangeably as synonyms for those who believed the people should rule, but he also criticizes the conduct of "partisans," using the latter word in the traditional republican sense to mean those who pursue their private interests at the expense of the public good. Although confusing to the modern eye, this position would have appeared perfectly consistent to the author: if "the republican party" and "the people" were one and the same, after all, then no one could be both a "partisan" and a good party man.

The notion that the Republican Party represented the embodiment of the people was hardly controversial, except in Federalist circles. Yet what distinguished Van Buren and his fellow Crawfordites was their resolve to take this doctrine to its logical conclusion: that the will of the party, expressed in congressional caucus, was as sovereign as the will of the people themselves. Undoubtedly there was an element of personal calculation involved in this. As Kane confided to Thomas, his determination "to support the regularly nominated *democratic* [i.e., Republican] candidate was formed and expressed under the full expectation that Mr. Crawford would be that man." Nonetheless, should these hopes not be realized, he would support whoever received the caucus nod, because "without a nomination" the Republicans "must all go . . . to the devil."[31] This attitude was shared by Jonathan Roberts, a former U.S. senator from Pennsylvania. While he too favored Crawford, he informed his brother that "I have gone upon the ground that nominated be who may I am for a caucus & will abide its decision," for if the Republicans failed to unite on a single candidate, the party "will be dispersed before the winds & federalism will make the election not of [presidential] Electors only but members of Congress & assembly &c."[32]

For Roberts, Kane, Gallatin, and many others, the 1824 election was primarily about access to public office. This is not to say that each of these men was concerned exclusively for his own advancement; indeed, Gallatin actually withdrew from contention for the vice presidency when he concluded that his presence on the ticket was hurting Crawford's chances.[33] Instead, what united them was the understanding that patronage, not shared principles or a commitment to certain policies, was the glue that held the Republican Party together. From this perspective, the prospect of losing control of the presidency, the ultimate font of federal appointments, to a candidate who was hostile to their views on party and perhaps even a closet Federalist, was unthinkable. What would be the effect, Kane fretted, "if the sleeping monster who has for eight years been veiled by the tapestry of 'amalgamation' and 'good feelings' should rise in the majesty of his strength and working through the openings formed by these divisions seize upon the sovereignty of the country?"[34] These sentiments are remarkably similar to those expressed by John Lowell when he warned that the "very existence" of the Federalist leaders in Massachusetts "as publick men" depended "on the *power* of the *party*."[35] The language of party regularity was finding expression in many parts of the Union, by men at both ends of the political spectrum.[36]

❖ The other presidential candidates faced a dilemma: how to criticize the Crawford wing of the party, known as the Radicals, without distancing themselves from the Republican name, without which no contender for the White House could succeed.[37] The solution, as Calhoun succinctly articulated, was to make the contest a choice between "the *discipline* and the *principles* of the party."[38] "We adhere to sound democratical principles, that is, that every thing should be by and for the people," he explained to one correspondent, whereas "the Radicals make a partnership against the people and for themselves, and expect to direct the latter to their purpose by what is called the machinery of party."[39] "The old doctrines of our party, founded on the great principles of the Revolution, is [sic] with them no longer the test of Republicanism," he complained to another. "No; adhesion to the dicesion [sic] of a caucus is in the eye of this degenerate party the only test of pure Republicanism."[40] Calhoun's antipartisanship was far from absolute; he accepted that "no reasonable objection" could be made to "a previous understanding among those who think and act alike as to principles or policy," but he considered the absolute obedience to party demanded by the Crawfordites to be "unnatural and in a great degree indefensible."[41]

While Crawford's supporters claimed that they were continuing the old struggle against Federalism, Calhoun argued that they had in fact taken up the mantle of their former adversaries. "I have no doubt, that the Radical party is in its nature essentially anti-Democratical, as much as the old Federalist party," he informed Lewis Cass, governor of the Michigan Territory and a future presidential candidate himself. "If Federalism favored the few against the many, the few wealthy and well born against the body of the people, so does Radicalism favor the cause of the few, not indeed the same class, but the few intrigue[r]s and managers against the people."[42] To Calhoun, the Federalists and the Radicals were less differentiated by their policies than they were united by their single-minded pursuit of political place and their disregard for the public will.

The advocates of the other candidates also took care to distinguish between their commitment to the doctrines espoused by the Republican Party and their refusal to be bound by its dictates. "Although of that party, [Clay] is not a partisan," declared the *Cincinnati Gazette*, "he has sailed with the squadron on the political voyage, but received orders from no commodore. Principle has been his guide, but that principle has kept him within the regions of purest republicanism."[43] As for Adams, no one could doubt that he "*now* belongs to the republican party," claimed "Tell," but his earlier defection from the Federalists was proof that "*consistency of principle*, and uninterrupted *attachment to party*, are utterly incompatible with each other." "And surely," the author added, "he who looks at a question with the expansive and liberal views of a national legislator, is more fit to be entrusted with the management of a *nation's* concerns, than he who either believes that *his party* can never be wrong, or blindly follows it whether right or wrong."[44]

Most effective at pushing this message, however, were the Jackson men.

One of the first newspapers to adopt the General's standard was the *Aurora* in Philadelphia. "It is time that the ultra Federalism, which lately prevailed in the New England states . . . and on the other hand, the radical democracy [i.e., Republicanism], which is shouted forth in anathemas by certain bigotted *Caucusites,* should descend to the Tomb of the Capulets," proclaimed William J. Duane, "for the reasonable class of all parties, turn with aversion from the one, and will not tolerate the violence of the other." "There are thousands of young men, who now for the first time, come forward to exercise their right of suffrage—who . . . feel little interest in the worn out dispute between Democracy and Federalism," the editor averred, echoing Joseph Buckingham in Boston. "The election of the Hero of New Orleans, will give rise to a *purely American* party, and become a rallying point for those who have retired from the political ranks, disgusted with party zeal."[45] Once again, the word *party* is employed twice in the same passage, with different connotations; an "*American* party" unites the people, whereas "party zeal" divides them.

The same themes were hammered home repeatedly in the "Letters of Wyoming," which one biographer has called "a blueprint of the ideological intentions of the developing Jacksonian movement."[46] The "Letters" were originally serialized in the Philadelphia *Columbian Observer,* then widely circulated in the press and as a pamphlet. According to the author, the presidential contest came down to one question: "*who shall govern this nation, the People or the Leading Men?*" Of the five candidates, all but Jackson were "at the City of Washington electioneering, and striving to win upon those who are termed the LEADING MEN of the COUNTRY."[47] Meanwhile, the people were "carried along by caucus management . . . and cajoled to the belief that they are sovereign, at the very moment when their dearest rights are undermining." The only way to preserve the republic was to elect Jackson. "He alone, remains the people's candidate," proclaimed "Wyoming," and "those lazy drones who hang on office, sucking in the sustenance of the country, will in vain seek for favor and approbation from such a man."[48]

Clay, in one of his frequent moments of levity, compared the presidency to a kiss: "not to be sought, and not to be *declined.*"[49] This remark played upon the conventional expectation that "a contest for individual advancement . . . proves, that the man who can resort to it, must act alone from motive—from selfish considerations, and be wanting in those honorable feelings which qualify for the possession of office."[50] Indeed, given all their paeans to the popular will, one might assume that Crawford's opponents wanted nothing more than to allow voters a free choice among the candidates. But in truth, none was so naïve as to trust the sovereign people to pick their own president.

One way around the proscription on personal campaigning was for a candidate to have others take steps on his behalf. Jackson liked to tell inquirers that he intended to "leave the people free to adopt such course as they may think proper, & elect whom they choose, to fill the Presidential chair, without any influence of mine exercised by me."[51] This was a convenient choice of words, for the Hero of New Orleans was surrounded by a circle of acolytes who were determined to do everything they could to hoist him into the White House. Chief among these was fellow Tennessean John H. Eaton, who fully recognized the importance of organization. "Intrigue is worming itself easily along," he remarked early in the canvass, "and unless the friends of Jackson shall do something more than *pray for him,* the busy ones will keep his road a rough & troublesome one."[52] Eaton managed the General's campaign right down to the minutiae of drafting his correspondence, so much so in fact that Adams could casually refer to "Jackson, or rather Eaton, who rules him."[53] This U.S. senator was also the anonymous author of the "Letters of Wyoming," with all their fulminations against the influence of the "leading men."

Clay devoted much time to corresponding with supporters in various states, offering not simply encouragement but specific instructions and financial contributions.[54] After the first session of the Eighteenth Congress concluded in May 1824 and propriety forced the Kentuckian to sit out the final months of the campaign on his plantation, he too engaged a political manager to oversee operations in the eastern states. Senator Josiah S. Johnston of Louisiana traveled extensively where Clay could not, browbeating local contacts and buying up newspaper support.[55] Like Eaton, Johnston placed great value on organization. Just one month before the polls opened, he wrote to Clay of his struggle to "keep alive your Cause which sank every where under the want of direction & management.—I had myself no Idea until the adjournment of Congress of the total want of Interest or Zeal or arrangement among your friends."[56]

Ironically, given that to many historians he would become a figurehead for the forces of reaction they imagine arrayed against Jacksonian Democracy four years later, it is Adams who is often identified as most reluctant to interfere with the people's choice in 1824.[57] Early in the campaign, a supporter from Pennsylvania contacted Adams's wife to protest against the secretary of state's apparent determination to pursue "the Macbeth policy—'if chance will make me king, why chance may crown me.'" "[This policy] will not answer where little is left to chance or merit, but kings are made by politicians and newspapers; and the man who sits down waiting to be crowned, either by chance or just right, will go bareheaded all his life," argued the letter writer. The embargo on campaigning should be interpreted flexibly, he suggested, advising that Adams "might communicate much information to be usefully employed in repelling attacks upon him, or in exhibiting his claims to advantage." Of course "we would not have him make corrupt bargains," the correspondent was quick to assure her, another irony given the course that the election would ultimately take.[58]

In response, Adams was resolute that he would not promote his own presidential pretensions nor solicit such aid from others. "He who asks or accepts the offer of friendly service contracts the obligation of meeting it with a suitable return," he explained. This relationship could not but be "essentially and vitally corrupt" for a statesman, who should concern himself solely with the public good. In any case, the secretary added, all efforts to influence the election would inevitably prove futile. A president could only be chosen by "an unequivocal manifestation of a public sentiment," and "if that feeling does not exist, and in a force which no effort of intrigue can suppress or restrain, it would be a useless, and perhaps worse than useless, thing for a few personal friends of mine to attempt to produce it." "If your watch has no main-spring," he concluded, "you will not keep time by turning round the minute-hand."[59]

Yet Adams's conduct belies the claim implicit in this passage that he believed campaigning would have no impact upon the outcome of the election. Under the cover of his official duties he met frequently with old political allies, and on the advice of his wife he sought to make new ones by holding regular balls throughout the Washington season.[60] Adams's power to appoint the printers of federal laws in each state also gave him enormous influence over the nation's press. In his diary the upstanding candidate pledged that he would never "purchase the services of any printer, either with public money or my own."[61] Yet in the summer of 1824 he transferred all State Department printing work to the *National Journal,* a newspaper recently established in the capital to promote none other than John Quincy Adams for president.[62] And it was Adams, alone among the candidates, who broke with protocol by publishing several pamphlets under his own name that detailed his long record of public service. Each of these ventures was occasioned by a specific attack upon his character, and Adams was quick to rationalize that "surely to parry the daggers of assassins is not to canvass votes for the Presidency."[63] Unsurprisingly, many contemporaries remained unconvinced.

Calhoun was also busy coordinating his campaign from behind the scenes, and he too believed that circumstances justified this departure from tradition. "In a good cause activity is a virtue. Ours is the cause of the people and the country," he assured his close friend Virgil Maxcy, adding that "we must not rely on a good cause and trust that it will take care of itself. All we can ask is that active virtue shall be superior to active vice."[64] Writing to an ally in New York, he warned that "the enemy is bus[y]ing; and we must remember, that truth is only stronger than error, when maintained with equal energy and activity."[65] And in a letter to another supporter in Van Buren's home state he was even more succinct: "You must organize against organization."[66]

Eaton's determination to defeat "intrigue," Adams's desire to "parry the daggers of assassins," and Calhoun's direction that his friends "organize against organization" were all typical of the way in which contemporaries defended political activities that might otherwise be denounced as illegitimate interference with the people's will. We have already witnessed similar statements, whether Thomas Ritchie's counsel that the free traders "oppose combination with combination" or Edward Coles's caution during the convention contest that "when bad men conspire, good men should be watchful."[67] In the case of the 1824 election, the Crawfordites rationalized their employment of party machinery as nothing more than an attempt to embody the popular will. The supporters of the other candidates, in turn, countered that this scheme to monopolize political office made their own organizational efforts necessary if the sovereignty of the people was to be preserved. And so the building of new parties proceeded under the banner of antipartisanship.[68]

❖ The congressional caucus loomed large over the 1824 presidential campaign. Beginning with the election of 1800, it had become customary for a meeting of the Republican members of Congress to choose the party's candidate. The caucus served the function of concentrating the Republican

vote in the face of Federalist competition, but from its inception the practice provoked criticism that it took the choice away from the people. With
no obvious obstacle to Monroe's reelection in 1820, attendance had been so
lackluster that the caucus broke up without actually making a nomination.
Nonetheless, four years later it was widely assumed that a meeting would
be held and that Crawford would be the beneficiary. This fact alone made
the latter the automatic front-runner in the race for the White House, for
no Republican presidential candidate selected in this manner had ever been
defeated.[69]

Crawfordites argued that the congressional caucus facilitated the exercise
of popular sovereignty by assisting voters to make an informed decision at
the ballot box. "It is impossible that the mass of the nation, who, besides their
want of personal knowledge of the candidates, are engaged in agriculture
and other pursuits, can enjoy a full opportunity of investigating satisfactorily
the comparative merits of those distinguished individuals," asserted "Virginius." "To whom therefore, can they look with a better prospect of obtaining
the desired information, than to the representatives of the nation in Congress?"[70] Similarly, a gathering of New York legislators, acting at the behest
of Van Buren, resolved that "assembled as [the Republican members of Con-
gress] are from the different quarters of the union; coming from the various
classes of the community; elected during the pendency and discussion of the
question, and, in a great degree, with reference to it; they bring into one body
as perfect a representation as can be expected of the interests and wishes of
all and of each."[71]

However, recognizing that each on his own could not challenge Crawford for the nomination, the other candidates united in condemnation of the
caucus. Pragmatism, not principles, dictated this course of action. Midway
through the campaign, Adams had observed that although "strong objections
against this mode of designating a candidate for the Presidency have lately
arisen ... I consider it as one of the least obnoxious modes of intrigue."[72]
Only later, after he had become "satisfied there was at this time a majority
of the whole people of the United States, and a majority of the States, utterly averse to a nomination by Congressional caucus," did he declare that
he "would not now accept a Congressional caucus nomination, even for the
Presidency."[73] Clay and Calhoun likewise held off censuring the practice until they were convinced that they had no chance of success.[74] Jackson was at

least consistent in his denunciations of the caucus, but then he could well afford to be, for as a Washington outsider he never had any prospect of receiving the nomination.[75]

The most hostile critics denied the validity of a congressional caucus under any circumstances. "It is time to put an end to *Caucuses*," Daniel Webster wrote to his brother, conveniently forgetting the foundations of Federalist ascendancy in Massachusetts. "They make great men little, & little men great. *The true source of power is the People.*"[76] Condemnation on principle was fine for Federalists with no stake in the presidential contest, but the friends of the other candidates, many of whom had supported such nominations in the past, had to be more careful. Some pointed to the changed political context. "A South-Carolinean," for example, contended that in 1824 a caucus was "not warranted even by those dangerous party times, which gave rise to other meetings of the same kind, and utterly precluded the idea of any thing like a fair expression of the public will."[77] Others argued that the Radicals had perverted the original purpose of the caucus. Jackson supporters in Pennsylvania labeled the meeting "a flagrant departure from the established usages of the republican party" because it was called not "with a view to promote the harmony of the party by uniting upon the most deserving for the office of President, but with a single view to promote the interest and success of William H. Crawford."[78] All the beleaguered Crawfordites could do in response was state the obvious. "All the candidates, with probably the exception of Jackson, and many of their friends had formerly attended a caucus," protested Ritchie in the *Richmond Enquirer*. "Why did they withdraw on this occasion? . . . Was it because they expected to be out numbered?"[79]

Lacking any constitutional sanction, the caucus depended upon popular sympathy to give force to its edicts, and with four of the five presidential candidates in opposition such sentiment was in short supply. Newspaper columns overflowed with pieces denouncing the practice, and the legislatures of Maryland and Tennessee actually ordered their congressional delegations not to attend. When a notice advertising the meeting finally appeared in the Washington press over the signatures of eleven members of Congress, it was accompanied by a statement that "of two hundred and sixty-one, the whole number of Members composing the present Congress, there are ONE HUNDRED AND EIGHTY-ONE who deem it inexpedient, under existing circumstances, to meet in Caucus."[80] In the event, only sixty-six of those eligible actually dared to assemble on 14 February 1824 and duly endorse Crawford for the presidency. "Never was any political measure quite so unpopular in the United States," commented *Niles' Weekly Register*, that "the *mere fact* of such a nomination . . . must inevitably destroy all his prospects."[81] No congressional caucus would ever again nominate a candidate for president.

Crawford's competitors may have succeeded in neutralizing the congressional caucus, but they still needed to have their own names brought before the public by some body that might plausibly claim to represent the popular will. One option was recommendation by a state legislature, either in its official capacity or, more usually, through an informal meeting of the members, that is, a caucus. During the campaign every one of the contenders received nominations made in this manner, producing much derision among commentators. As Buckingham, no fan of Crawford but ever willing to expose the hypocrisy of career politicians, observed in the *New-England Galaxy*, "It seems to savor a little of inconsistency, when the friends of . . . those candidates, who are holding caucuses in every state legislature, in every city, in every village, and in every steamboat, where there is a majority of passengers in his favor, condemn, in the most pointed terms, the holding of a congressional caucus."[82]

As Buckingham's remark suggests, the other alternative for Crawford's rivals was to seek nominations directly from the people, either in simple public meetings or through a convention of delegates elected for that purpose. Advocates of the latter method naturally claimed that such gatherings were of a completely different character from the caucus that backed the treasury secretary. "Belthazar," writing in the *Baltimore Patriot*, explained that "a caucus is a self-created body" and since "the people do not authorize them to assemble, consequently they usurp the prerogative of the people." A convention, in contrast, "is a body of men delegated by the people for some special purpose," and so "a convention in fact is the people themselves."[83] Likewise, the *Washington Republican*, Calhoun's newspaper organ in the capital, maintained that a convention "appears to be the only true and legitimate mode of concentrating the public voice," for "a Caucus may express an opinion against that of the people . . . as it consists of members of legislative bodies, who are chosen long before-hand, and are subject to the arts and wiles of corrupt politicians."[84]

Other contemporaries, however, were more skeptical. "The proportion of [voters] who sanction those conventions, and who concur in the election of delegates, is not perhaps one fourth or one fifth," complained one observer. "The nominations . . . may be carried by clamor, party invocations, intrigues, &c., but they are not the work, nor the genuine free will of the sound majority."[85] "The people have about as much exercise of the freedom of choice, as sheep have in following their leader over a stone wall," concurred another, "since many are afraid to do otherwise, than as their leaders suggest or hint to them, whether they like it or not."[86] Significantly, the most vocal support for replacing the congressional caucus with a single national nominating convention came not from Crawford's opponents but from Ritchie's *Enquirer,* a lynchpin of Van Buren's plan to revive the power of party in federal politics. The editor presumably believed that such a convention might just as easily be bent to the will of party leaders as might the caucus. But supporters of the other candidates also suspected this and so dismissed the plan as impractical, notwithstanding the fact that both sides in the tariff struggle had already held comparable gatherings.[87] The transition from caucuses to conventions in U.S. politics, of which the 1824 election was an important catalyst, demonstrates that party builders recognized the need to appear more receptive to popular participation in the nominating process, but this does not necessarily mean that most citizens actually enjoyed any more influence over the outcome than they had possessed under the old system.[88]

❖ With so many viable contenders, it was clear to all concerned that "preparations were making for a violent canvass for the Presidential election of 1824."[89] The past two decades had seen the franchise extended, for presidential and congressional elections at least, to include almost all adult white males outside of Louisiana, Rhode Island, and Virginia. Methods of choosing presidential electors remained diverse, however; twelve states employed a single statewide popular vote, six opted for popular voting by district, and six retained selection by the legislature. This fact, along with restrictions on the personal involvement of the candidates and the limited communication facilities of the era, ensured that the nature of the campaign in each state would be primarily determined by local, not national, circumstances, as a brief survey of the four states that have featured in previous chapters, plus Van Buren's home state of New York, illustrates.

In Massachusetts, native son John Quincy Adams was acknowledged by all sides as the favorite. Nonetheless, the Bay State had changed its mode of choosing electors several times in the past, and Adams's opponents harbored hopes that if the district method were employed on this occasion a few votes might still be siphoned off from his column. These expectations were dashed in the summer of 1824, when the legislature, dominated by Adams supporters, mandated that electors must be selected on a single statewide ticket. A majority of the Republican members subsequently met in caucus to nominate a slate of candidates pledged to the secretary of state and establish a central committee to promote his cause.[90] Thereafter, the friends of Adams attempted little in the way of public organization until a few weeks prior to the election, when they held meetings to energize his support base and appoint ballot distributors to attend on polling day.[91]

The implementation of the general-ticket method, an ill-disguised maneuver by the legislative majority to ensure an undivided vote for their preferred candidate, provided an issue around which those hostile to Adams could rally. "We came to the Understanding, that in opposition to Q. [i.e., John Quincy Adams] we could unite, . . . [and] after the passage of the [electoral] Law we took the resolution of getting up an Opposition Ticket without reference to Candidates, but merely to resist the Law," a local correspondent explained to Clay.[92] As we shall see, when one candidate was particularly strong in a state it was quite common for the friends of the others to unite on a single opposition ticket, with the understanding that they would share the electoral votes if it were successful. In this case, the "unpledged ticket" was commenced with the nomination of a single elector by a district convention in Berkshire and completed in like manner by a series of meetings across the state.[93]

The main tactic of Adams's opponents was to attack the manner in which his ticket was put forward by members of the legislature. "The will of the people was not consulted or regarded in the nomination," maintained one electioneering broadside, whereas "the list of Electors . . . which was nominated by the people assembled in most of the Congressional Districts, was selected in a manner consistent with our Republican institutions."[94] In response, sources sympathetic to the secretary claimed that the protests were no reflection of real popular sentiment. "The noise created by about a score of young men in this town may be called, with great justice, a *paper opposition* to Mr. Adams," declared the *Boston Patriot*, adding that the same individuals were turning up at separate meetings for Jackson, Clay, and Crawford in order to swell the appearance of support for the unpledged ticket.⁹⁵ These allegations were seemingly corroborated on election day, when the Adams ticket triumphed with 82 percent of the vote.⁹⁶

The campaign in Massachusetts reveals how far removed presidential politics had become from old party conflicts. Adams was conscious that a Federalist show of support might rebound to his disadvantage and advised his friends that "if a legislative opinion should ... be taken in Massachusetts, I should wish it might be confined to the Republican party."⁹⁷ Adams's Federalist allies acquiesced to his request and kept a low profile during the campaign, trusting its management to the same Republicans whom they continued to castigate mercilessly in the arena of state politics. "The Federalists have got our *Asses* in the Legislature to nominate Adams—But if he gets the vote of Mass, it must be by Federalists," one correspondent remarked to Clay. "They dare not nominate him—but may vote him. It looks a little quer [*sic*], to see Adams a Candidate for P. & Otis for Govr.—but so the game goes—no Party at Washington, but Party enough at home."⁹⁸

It swiftly became clear, however, that what remained of the Federalist Party in Massachusetts and elsewhere was hopelessly divided between advocates of Adams and those who refused to forgive his apostasy. In Boston, a Federalist meeting called to consider the presidential question dissolved in disarray, leaving the *Columbian Centinel* to report that "the federalists individually, [are] left to act, or decline acting, as they might think expedient."⁹⁹ Separate gatherings of Federalists were subsequently held in support of and in opposition to the pledged electoral ticket. In the realm of print, the Federalist *Centinel* joined the Republican *Patriot* in pressing Adams's claims, their respective partisan counterparts the *Commercial Gazette* and the *Statesman* came out for Crawford, while the *Galaxy* maintained that its inflexible opposition to caucuses meant that it could support neither of those candidates.¹⁰⁰ For some observers, the willingness of certain Massachusetts Federalists to collude with the Crawfordites provided yet more evidence that a lust for power was all that motivated those at both ends of the political spectrum. "The Ultras [i.e., ultra-Federalists] will join the Radicals," wrote Johnston to Clay, "—the extremes meet."¹⁰¹

In truth, all of the presidential candidates solicited Federalist support in private, however strongly they distanced themselves from the disgraced party in public. James Hamilton, son of the Federalist luminary Alexander, found himself courted by Calhoun, who praised his father's fiscal measures as "the only true policy for the country."[102] Jackson's friends pointed to a letter he had written in 1816 advising Monroe to elevate a Federalist to his cabinet as evidence that the General would pay no heed to party distinctions in making appointments to office.[103] Even Crawford, "*the* Republican candidate," somehow acquired two of the three electoral votes at the disposal of the Delaware legislature, the only such body in the country still under Federalist control.[104] Events "have very much mixed up Federalists with some or other of the parties," mused Webster, "and tho' it is true that some men make great efforts to keep up old distinctions, they find it difficult."[105] A Jackson activist in Pennsylvania provided a simple explanation for the changed political landscape: "the contest is not, nor never was, between Federal and Democrat,—but between those in office—and them who want their places."[106]

❖ Virginia was central to Van Buren's strategy to elevate Crawford to the White House. The politics of the state were dominated by a shadowy group known as the Richmond Junto, with *Enquirer* editor Thomas Ritchie at its center.[107] "Th[r]ough the 'Richmond party' the Radicals calculated to govern your state. New York was to be governed by what is called the Albany Regency," Calhoun explained to a friend in the Old Dominion. "The joint efforts of these two great States were to control the caucus at Washington; and thus a President be given to the people by the cooperation of the two Juntos."[108]

Virginia chose its presidential electors by statewide popular vote. Customarily, the Republican members of the legislature would caucus to agree on a ticket in order to avoid splitting the party's support. On this occasion, Crawford's friends were decidedly in the majority, and electors pledged to their favorite were nominated at a meeting held in February 1824. The caucus also appointed committees to promote the treasury secretary's cause in every county under the auspices of a Central Corresponding Committee.[109] The Central Committee spent the months until the election in November issuing periodic addresses praising its candidate's presidential qualifications and arranging for the printing of electoral tickets for distribution by the county committees.[110] These in turn were charged with employing "their energy in promoting the cause of W. H. Crawford—in prevailing upon the people to turn out, and giving a strong vote on the pending election."[111]

The Virginia campaign was decisively shaped by the belief of Clay, who had been born in the state, that he would reap the benefit if Crawford's continued illness forced him to retire from the race. In neighboring North Carolina the nomination of the treasury secretary by members of the legislature prompted his opponents to unite behind an unpledged "People's Ticket."[112] In Virginia, however, Clay's friends rejected similar overtures for fear of alienating the Crawfordites.[113] Instead, a handful of Clay supporters in the assembly held their own caucus, adopted a virtual replica of the Crawford organization, and thereafter effectively ceased operations.[114] As late as two weeks before the election, the Speaker's chief ally in the state reported that "your friends here have forbourn to manifest their Strenth [sic], because they are under the impression that it would be useless untill Mr C[rawford] is out of the way."[115]

Lacking any substantial strength in the legislature, the followers of Adams and Jackson turned to public meetings to promote their respective favorites.[116] These meetings followed an established pattern: a notice would be published in the local press inviting the supporters of a particular candidate to assemble, the attendees would pass resolutions declaring their preference on the presidential question, and a committee might be appointed to correspond with sympathizers elsewhere. Advocates emphasized the potential for popular participation, which was noticeably absent from the Crawford and Clay campaigns. Jackson leaders claimed that "*they could* immediately form a Ticket composed of some of the most respectable and enlightened citizens of the state; but they deem it best to lay before a convention all the information they have received, and by concert form such a ticket as may emphatically be denominated the 'People's Ticket.'"[117] This convention duly met in July, although the *Enquirer* cast doubt on its claim to represent public opinion, pointing out that "the proceedings do not state the names of the deputies present nor do they state how many counties were represented."[118] One month later the Adams men reported that their own electoral ticket was also nearing completion, adding that the remaining vacancies "could long since have been filled, had the committee chosen to make a selection; but they preferred, in every instance, to receive nominations from others, and, where practicable from public meetings of the citizens themselves."[119]

Over the course of the campaign, the historian Joseph Clifft has calculated, forty-one public meetings were held in Virginia, of which thirty-seven were for either Adams or Jackson.[120] Instead of attempting to outdo their opponents, the Crawfordites simply dismissed these efforts, claiming that the gatherings were attended by few persons, and even fewer who were actually qualified to vote. "Crawford's friends have rested so confident of success, that like Clay's friends in Kentucky, they have not held a single meeting of the people," explained the *Enquirer*.[121] "These meetings are mere bubbles, which can have no serious effect in lessening the confidence of the great mass of voters . . . in the nomination at Richmond by the members of the Assembly," echoed "A Looker-On."[122] This confidence would prove well founded, for Crawford took Virginia with 55 percent of the vote, followed by Adams with 23 percent, Jackson with 19 percent, and Clay with 3 percent.

Crawford's reputation for championing strict constitutionalism and states' rights served him well in Virginia, but to the north and the west, where voters favored more active national government, his friends did not hesitate to declare him favorable to protection for manufactures and federally sponsored internal improvements. This cynical strategy did not go unnoticed. "Many of the states are directly opposed to many other states, in the views of policy which will influence them in the choice of a president," observed "Roanoke," "yet, it seems to be Mr. Crawford's singular good fortune, to be urged in each particular state on precisely the grounds the most popular therein."[123] Yet the other candidates were also culpable of obfuscating their opinions on important public issues, thus allowing their supporters free reign to shape their message according to local predilections.[124] This conduct enraged those who thought elections should be about more than the pursuit of office. James M. Garnett was disgusted to find Crawford's friends in Virginia "trying to convince me that Citizen C. is no Tariff man; but 'only recommends as Secretary of the Treasury what he disapproves as a private man!!!'" As far as Garnett was concerned, "they (the Candidates) are all nearly as much Tariff-men, as Mathew Carey himself."[125]

❖ In Pennsylvania the presidential electors would also be selected by state-wide popular vote. Unlike their caucusing counterparts in Massachusetts and Virginia, however, the state's Republicans had embraced the practice of holding conventions of elected delegates to decide on candidates for office. Calhoun was the early front-runner, enjoying the support of many prominent politicians, and his backers seemed content to run a low-key campaign similar to that of the Crawfordites in Virginia. When Jackson entered the race late in 1822, however, popular sentiment in his favor grew at a speed that astounded observers. The General's promoters worked with "unceasing perseverance" to organize public meetings and advocate his cause in the press.[126] They also established some of the earliest Hickory Clubs, a prominent feature of subsequent presidential campaigns. These organizations, composed of "young men ... disposed to promote the Election of *General Andrew Jackson*," targeted in particular first-time voters unencumbered by old party loyalties.[127] Calhoun's allies became alarmed. As the date for the Pennsylvania nominating convention approached, one Philadelphian warned that although the "great mass of the leading and reflecting Democrats of this section of the State are decidedly for Mr. Calhoun, ... I should not be surprised if we were out generalled."[128]

At the elections for delegates to the convention, the Jacksonians ran rampant. "A new set, either wholly unknown or known only for their obliquities and disaffection, supplied the places which have generally been filled by our most respected names," marveled one onlooker.[129] Calhoun supporters deserted in droves, and when the convention assembled in Harrisburg in March 1824 its proceedings were a formality. Jackson was endorsed by a vote of 124 to 1, an electoral ticket was nominated, and committees were appointed to ensure its success.[130] From that point the course of Pennsylvania was settled. "All opposition is worthless at least at the present," recorded Jonathan Roberts, the lone Crawfordite holdout at Harrisburg. "There is nothing to make an opposition of."[131] Crawford's friends did hold their own convention in August, but with delegates from less than one-quarter of the counties it was a pale shadow of the convention that backed Jackson.[132] The Adams and Clay forces relied on public meetings to make their arrangements, but both struggled even to name full electoral tickets.[133] The Harrisburg convention had dealt Calhoun's campaign a mortal blow, and he soon withdrew from the race entirely to focus his efforts on securing the vice presidency. In the final vote, Jackson swept the state with 76 percent of the vote, compared with 11 percent for Adams, 9 percent for Crawford, and only 4 percent for Clay.

Jackson's victory at Harrisburg transformed him from an outside chance into a genuine presidential contender. The tireless efforts of those who organized on his behalf were undoubtedly a factor in the General's success, and the antipartisan tone of his campaign seems to have had greater resonance in

Pennsylvania, which had a long history of struggles against party regularity, than in Massachusetts and Virginia, where party rule was more firmly entrenched. Jackson also proved adept at straddling the tricky issue of protection, on which, as Van Buren later recalled, he "assumed a position . . . more equivocal than any he had ever occupied on any public question."[134] When a member of the Pennsylvania Society sent the Hero of New Orleans a bonnet of domestic manufacture for his wife, the gift giver received the guarded response that no one could "feel more sensitively" than Jackson "the necessity of encouraging" American industry.[135] After this statement was circulated in the press, the General was contacted by a concerned supporter from North Carolina who inquired whether he intended by his remarks to indicate a support for increased import duties. In reply, Jackson reassured the well-wisher that his preference was merely for "a careful and judicious Tariff."[136] This studiously ambiguous answer reportedly provoked Clay to exclaim "well, by——, I am in favor of an *in*judicious tariff."[137]

Jackson's success would prove to be no laughing matter for Clay, however. The Kentuckian, alone among the candidates, placed support for protection at the forefront of his campaign. This proved to be a fatal miscalculation. Advocates of increased duties were wary of tying their cause to the fortunes of a single candidate, no doubt sharing Van Buren's opinion that if they "suffered their interests to become identified with a political party (any one), they would share the fate of that party, and go down with it whenever it sunk."[138] Such was Mathew Carey's reluctance to mix policy with presidential politics that when an associate suggested that a public dinner organized by the former to thank Clay for his efforts on the tariff might also be used to endorse the latter's bid for the White House, the Philadelphia penman threatened to withdraw from the proceedings.[139] Only on the eve of the election, after incessant pleading from Clay supporters elsewhere, did Carey come out in his favor.[140]

Even then, Clay was far from uniting the protectionist camp. Henry Baldwin was one of Jackson's earliest promoters in Pennsylvania, and at least two members of the Philadelphia Society followed his lead.[141] "The great misfortune is that Jackson is supported by exactly that school of politicians who would otherwise have been decidedly & unanimously for you," a local devotee informed the disappointed Speaker.[142] Meanwhile, his support for increased duties hurt him badly in the Old Dominion, where one observer reported that the public "look on Mr. Clay as a deserter from the *good old Virginia politicks*."[143] As Clay watched his presidential chances crumble, he lamented to Johnston that "it is a little remarkable that my support of the Tariff has excited against me in the South, a degree of opposition, which is by no means counter-balanced by any espousal of my cause in Pennsa. and other quarters, where the Tariff was so much desired."[144] The Speaker would have been better served had he heeded the advice of a Jackson supporter: "A man who is determined to be a successful Candidate, must be all things to all men, never express his opinion freely & learn the nack of geting round every subject that presents it self."[145]

❖ Illinois differs from the states considered thus far because its electors were chosen individually by district. This fact, combined with local politicians' limited experience in partisan organizing and the overwhelming distraction of the convention question, ensured that the contest would be highly fragmented. The most active campaigning occurred in the Third District, where Alexander P. Field, a state legislator, arranged a series of public meetings for Jackson and announced himself as a candidate for elector.[146] In the Second District Henry Eddy, the editor of the *Illinois Gazette,* also enthusiastically promoted the General and was rewarded with an endorsement for elector by a gathering of local citizens.[147] Both men, however, faced opposition from several self-nominated Jacksonites who threatened to divide the vote. Eddy ran advertisements in his paper naming Field and himself as the regular candidates and appealed for the others to withdraw, although even he did not pretend to choose between the two contenders who put themselves forward as Jackson electors in the First District.[148] These efforts brought limited success; only in the Third District was the Jackson vote concentrated on a single individual come polling day.

The First District was the site of Adams's greatest strength, and a few events were held there in support of him as the election approached.[149] His main competition came from a candidate ostensibly pledged to vote for either Jackson or Clay, whichever had the better chance of success, although this was denounced in the press as a plot to steal a vote for Crawford. The suspect individual was put forward by a meeting of "Democratic Republican Delegates" from "several counties in the first Electoral District," which was the most sophisticated piece of political apparatus employed by any side in the state.[150] There is no indication that Adams's friends made use of any public nominating mechanism, but some combination of private communication and basic common sense at least ensured that he was the only presidential contender to be represented by a single candidate for elector in each district. Neither Crawford's nor Clay's supporters did much in the way of overt organizing, and in the end Jackson took two of Illinois's electoral votes to Adams's one, although none of the victorious electors proved able to secure an outright majority in their district.

The presidential contest in Illinois apparently bore little relation to the long-running convention saga, which was settled only three months before the choice of electors. At the height of the debate over slavery, Hooper Warren had observed that "the non-conventionists, as a party, have never expressed an opinion on the Presidential question, or any thing connected with it. They, like the conventionists, are divided on the subject."[151] This was certainly true of the state's leading politicians, as antislavery governor Edward Coles's preference for Crawford placed him in the same camp as several prominent advocates of a convention.[152] If any candidate seemed likely to benefit from the anticonventionist victory it was Adams, since he was the only nonslaveholder in the race. Yet Warren, who championed both in the *Spectator,* never explicitly connected the two. In Madison County a toast was drunk to Adams at a public dinner to celebrate the defeat of the convention, and a few members of the Madison Association participated in a meeting to promote the secretary of state's pretensions in the First District.[153] On election day, however, the suspected Crawfordite elector actually outpolled his pro-Adams opponent in the town of Edwardsville, though the latter narrowly prevailed across the county as a whole.[154]

Outside of Illinois the subject of slavery also seems to have played no major part in the election. The Missouri Crisis was still fresh in the public consciousness, but in a contest for national office no candidate yet saw any profit in positioning himself as the champion of an exclusively sectional interest. Undoubtedly there were voters who, like Senator Rufus King of New York, an ardent opponent of Missouri's admission as a slave state, acted on the view that Adams "is the only northern Candidate; and as between him and black [i.e., slave state] Candidates, I prefer him."[155] But more typical, it seems, was the young William Lloyd Garrison, future abolitionist but for now just a devoted Federalist whose abhorrence of Adams overrode any antislavery sentiments he may have harbored and prompted him to support the plantation-owning Crawford.[156] In the final count, slaveholding candidates secured 69 of the 147 electoral votes on offer in the free states, while Adams won one in every four popular ballots cast in Virginia, one in three in Mississippi, and close to one in two in Maryland.

❖ As the largest state in the Union and one of the last to declare its preference, New York had a pivotal role in the election. Van Buren hoped to deliver the state to Crawford, but the treasury secretary's cause found little favor with the public. "The zeal & pertinacity with which Van Buren & his friends have pushed Mr Crawford (who has no substantial popularity here) without any other argument in his favor than the necessity of *party discipline,* have disgusted the Republicans of this state, & produced great dissatisfaction & division in our ranks," reported one observer.[157] Fortunately for the Little Magician, however, the legislature had always selected the state's electors in previous contests, so the Bucktails might still secure victory for their preferred candidate without the inconvenience of a popular vote. Realizing this, the supporters of the other contenders united to form the People's Party, which called for a reform of the electoral law and denounced their opponents' use of the caucus as "a dark and foul *aristocracy* in disguise."[158] "The people claim their Constitutional right of choosing electors; the political managers, who have suc[c]eeded in wielding what is called party discipline will use every effort to evade or defeat their right," Calhoun observed. "One or the other must yield."[159] Rejoicing in the difficulties of the man who would later become his most loyal ally, Jackson likewise predicted that "Mr. Vanburen [*sic*] can not *manage* New York."[160]

Even if the People's Party triumphed in the state elections of October 1824, however, it would be the lame-duck lawmakers who designated the state's presidential electors the following month. In desperation, Crawford's opponents persuaded the governor to call a special session of the legislature to pass a bill transferring the power to choose electors to the people. "It was an awkward affair for a party which prided itself on being most in favor of employing the direct agency of the People in the conduct of public affairs, to refuse such an application when there was yet time enough to accede to it and to carry it into effect," Van Buren blithely remarked in his memoirs thirty years later.[161] Yet refuse the application they did, as a small cabal of Regency stalwarts in the state senate blocked the move on procedural grounds, sacrificing all claim to popular favor in the name of loyalty to party. Even the result of the subsequent elections, in which Van Buren's followers were "completely routed," could not sway their leader from his mission.[162] By their blatant disregard for the basic principles of democracy, the Bucktails appeared to have snatched victory from the grasp of the majority.

But the contest was not yet over. Supporters of Adams and Clay possessed sufficient combined strength in the legislature to block the Crawfordites' initial efforts to nominate a slate of electors, and the possibility arose that New York's votes might simply be thrown away. Into this deadlock stepped Thurlow Weed, a young man on his first visit to the state capital to lobby for a bank charter, who would go on to rival Van Buren in his effectiveness as a manager for the Whig Party. Favoring Adams for the presidency, Weed took it upon himself to arrange a complicated deal with the Clay forces by which New York's electoral votes would be split between those two candidates, cutting Crawford out almost entirely.[163] The Little Magician had been outmaneuvered, and as he would later recall, "I left Albany for Washington as completely broken down a politician as my bitterest enemies could desire."[164]

Events in New York should give pause to those historians who celebrate the rise of party for facilitating the rule of the people. Pursuit of office was the guiding principle of the 1824 presidential campaign. In Virginia the Crawfordites relied on their strength among the state's established politicians, while the Adams campaign appealed directly to popular sympathies, whereas in Massachusetts these roles were reversed. Calhoun ran under the banner of "the People's candidate" in North Carolina while relying on the efforts of a few well-connected individuals to secure him Pennsylvania.[165] Clay deplored backroom bargaining when it robbed him of the electoral votes of Louisiana but turned a blind eye when it served his cause in New York.[166] Jackson supporters railed constantly against the influence of "the leading men," ignoring the efforts of Eaton and other high-ranking Tennessee politicians on his behalf. And the friends of the contenders proved none too choosy about who they would collaborate with when the circumstances suited either, whether it be Adams and Clay in New York; Adams, Calhoun, and Jackson in North Carolina; or everyone against Adams across much of New England. Consistency, it seems, mattered little when compared with success.

❖ The presidential election played out over October and November 1824, as polling days differed considerably from state to state. When all the popular votes were in, Jackson led the way with 151,287, followed by Adams with 111,811, Clay with 47,707, and finally Crawford with 47,417. With so many candidates, however, none was able to secure the necessary majority in the Electoral College. Jackson and Adams were the clear front-runners, with 99 and 84 votes, respectively, but it was Crawford who edged into third place ahead of Clay, by 41 to 37. This development would prove to be of utmost significance because the Constitution mandated that in the event of no candidate's achieving an absolute majority the House of Representatives must choose between the three highest candidates, with each state casting a single vote. In the House election, held on 9 February 1825, the eliminated Clay threw his support to Adams, who was elected on the first ballot by the bare minimum of thirteen states despite having trailed Jackson in both the popular vote and the Electoral College. Jackson supporters immediately charged that a "Corrupt Bargain" had been struck, an accusation that appeared to be corroborated when Adams appointed Clay as his secretary of state.[167] The consequences for the future of U.S. politics would be profound.

Voter turnout in the 1824 presidential election averaged just 29 percent, ranging from a low of 15 percent in Connecticut, where Adams took four out of every five ballots cast, to a high of 54 percent in Maryland, where Jackson outpolled Adams by less than one hundred votes.[168] Only in two states, New Jersey and Connecticut, did turnout equal or exceed the average for congressional and gubernatorial elections between 1820 and 1825, and in the latter case at least that clearly says more about how low participation rates were generally than it does about popular enthusiasm for the presidential contest. This outcome illustrates how little the race for the White House impacted upon the lives of most Americans; it did not directly affect their political rights, as did the struggle of the Middling Interest in Boston, or their consciences, as did the battle over slavery in Illinois, or even their pocketbooks, as did the efforts to shape tariff policy. Not until the party builders succeeded in reconnecting with real issues of popular concern would turnout begin to rise, first to 58 percent in 1828 and then to 80 percent in 1840. In 1824, however, the competition for the presidency remained first and foremost about access to office, a subject on which, as John Taylor had discovered, "partisans are zealous, and a great majority of the people indifferent."[169]

The fate of each of the candidates in the presidential election of 1824 tells us something about party development in the early United States. The enthusiasm that greeted Andrew Jackson's first bid for the White House suggests the extent to which many Americans had become disenchanted with the established parties and politicians. As early as 1820 Calhoun had commented on "a general mass of disaffection to the Government, not concentrated in any particular direction, but ready to seize upon any event and looking out anywhere for a leader."[170] The Hero of New Orleans offered that leadership, and his success in the popular vote allowed his supporters to claim that the people had been robbed of their preferred choice by Adams and Clay with the connivance of Congress.[171] Ironically, though, the main beneficiary in the Corrupt Bargain saga was the concept of party. As the historian Gerald Leonard argues, had Jackson secured the presidency in 1824 after a campaign waged against partyism, "that result might have destroyed Van Buren's cause for a generation" by "confirm[ing] for the people that their will could and must be made effective without the mechanism of party."[172] Instead, Van Buren abandoned the crippled Crawford and allied himself to the General's rising star, proclaiming that only through organizing could the people overcome the aristocratic pretensions of Adams and carry their champion into the White House.[173] And so Democracy became the name of a political party.

Jackson's fortunes contrasted markedly with those of John C. Calhoun and Henry Clay. It is no coincidence that these two men, whose candidacies were most closely identified with questions of policy, fared worst in the contest. To build an electoral coalition broad enough to encompass pro- and antislavery activists in Illinois, or Pennsylvania protectionists and Virginia free traders, or the hundreds of other constituencies that made up the national electorate required a campaign couched in vague generalities and empty platitudes.[174] Jackson set a precedent in this regard, and over the following decades parties would turn time and again to mediocre candidates like William Henry Harrison, Zachary Taylor, and Franklin Pierce, whose campaigns were based on military exploits and little else.[175] Neither Clay nor Calhoun learned this lesson. The Kentuckian's response to defeat was simply to redouble his commitment to the American System, while the new vice president abandoned his earlier support for a strong federal government in favor of the extreme states'-rights views of his native South Carolina. As a result, neither of these political giants would ever attain the presidential chair, to which both so fervently aspired.

While the careers of Clay and Calhoun would end in disappointment, John Quincy Adams's misfortunes began the moment he was elected president by the House of Representatives. It was long assumed that Adams's activist agenda failed because it was widely unpopular, but recent studies have suggested that a majority of Americans actually favored policies such as protection for manufactures and federal support for internal improvements.[176] Once again, however, party conflict proved an obstacle to the translation of popular opinion into government programs. Jacksonian congressmen from Pennsylvania, Ohio, and a host of other states that naturally would have favored Adams's developmental vision put their partisan identity first and voted down administration bills.[177] Thanks to the efforts of his opponents, Adams will always be remembered for his ill-judged appeal to Congress not to be "palsied by the will of our constituents."[178] Few now recall that he actually celebrated "representative democracy" in his inaugural address, the first president to do so, and identified "collisions of party spirit" as one of the main threats to the nation's future.[179]

Surely the most tragic figure of the presidential election, however, was William H. Crawford. One of the most powerful politicians of his day, he is now virtually unknown except to a handful of historians, and their accounts have hardly been sympathetic. Yet the case for party put forward by the Crawford campaign in 1824 was almost exactly the same as the one scholars would praise when adopted by the followers of Jackson four years later. The career politician, preferred candidate of both Jefferson and Madison, made a far more natural party leader than the General, whose partisan credentials even Van Buren considered somewhat suspect.[180] But the Hero of New Orleans enjoyed a popularity with ordinary citizens that the treasury secretary never did. And unlike Calhoun and Clay, Van Buren had learned an important lesson from the presidential election of 1824: the effectiveness of party machinery depended upon its identification with the only true arbiter of political legitimacy in a republican regime, the sovereignty of the people.

CONCLUSION

In his inaugural address, in March 1825, John Quincy Adams expressed the hope that the "baneful weed of party strife" might be finally eradicated from the nation's politics.

> Ten years of peace, at home and abroad, have assuaged the animosities of political contention and blended into harmony the most discordant elements of public opinion. There still remains one effort of magnanimity, one sacrifice of prejudice and passion, to be made by the individuals throughout the nation who have heretofore followed the standards of political party. It is that of discarding every remnant of rancor against each other, of embracing as countrymen and friends, and of yielding to talents and virtue alone that confidence which in times of contention for principle was bestowed only upon those who bore the badge of party communion.[1]

But, the new president was to be bitterly disappointed. Over the next fifteen years partisan conflict would spread to the four corners of the Union, and Adams would be one of its most prominent casualties as his bid for reelection in 1828 went down to defeat at the hands of Andrew Jackson and the emerging Democratic Party.

If Adams's foresight was suspect, his recollection was also far from accurate. The decade that preceded his inauguration had hardly been one of peace and harmony. True, the Republicans faced no obvious challenge to their ascendancy in Washington after the collapse of Federalist opposition. But in other respects the country remained a checkerboard of political contention. At every level of the federal system candidates continued to compete for public office, and citizens looked to government to solve problems arising from the Panic of 1819, western expansion, and a multitude of other sources. Politics did not cease simply because there were no longer two clearly defined parties to contest presidential elections.

This reading of the decade following the War of 1812 has not, for the most part, found favor with historians. Where Adams saw peace and harmony, they see indifference and apathy. The overarching celebratory narrative of U.S. politics between the Revolution and the Civil War identifies political parties as the driving agents of democratization, and since partisan competition waned during the early 1820s, subscribers to this interpretation assume, most citizens must simply have lost interest in politics. But the episodes explored in the previous chapters have shown the so-called Era of No Feelings to be a myth. Although election turnout did fall in some states, many Americans continued to participate in political life with unconcealed enthusiasm and extraordinary creativity. Their experiences suggest the potential for rethinking several components of the celebratory narrative.

As numerous scholars have shown, political parties played an important role in stimulating and maintaining unprecedented levels of election turnout in the early United States. It does not follow from this, however, that the presence of two-party competition was alone enough to ensure popular engagement. In Massachusetts, conflict between Federalist and Republican parties continued to dominate public life into the early 1820s, as it had for two decades previously. Yet this highly organized and hotly contested environment failed to produce high rates of participation at the polls. Instead, it spawned the Middling Interest, a protest movement born of the conviction that despite near-universal adult male suffrage the people were denied a real political voice. The established parties, these rebels argued, controlled the electoral process in Boston from beginning to end and exercised that control in the 1822 mayoral contest to frustrate the popular will. Likewise, the dispute over wooden buildings demonstrated party leaders' disregard for efforts to make them accountable to their constituents through the practice of instruction. Viewed from this contemporary perspective, parties were hardly the agents of democracy that they are often portrayed to have been today.[2]

Taking a broader view, newly available data suggest that throughout the Union from 1820 to 1825 election turnout was strongest where parties were weakest. Of course, this classification is somewhat arbitrary. The unprecedented 80 percent turnout in the Illinois convention referendum of 1824 was the product of a contest that, though conducted in the absence of established parties, assumed many of the characteristics commonly associated with a two-party system: intense competition, sustained organization, and "binary symmetry" on the question at stake.[3] Yet the four-way gubernatorial race of 1822, in which candidates openly boasted of their lack of organiza-tional backing and offered no consistent response to a confusing melee of issues, had still brought 67 percent of the electorate to the polls, a figure that compares favorably with the turnouts for party-driven contests in Delaware, Massachusetts, and New York that same year. Over in Kentucky, consecutive turnouts of 70 percent plus in 1820 and 1824 may be attributed to competi-tion between distinct "Relief" and "Anti-Relief" groupings generated by the Panic of 1819, but it is worth noting that these were achieved without any of the formal party machinery common in the eastern states. In Alabama and Mississippi, meanwhile, similar rates of participation were achieved in the absence of any discernible form of political organization.[4] Such cases once again illustrate the diversity of political practices during this period, but the overall trend is sufficiently clear to suggest that Massachusetts was not the only state in which entrenched political parties had a dampening effect on participation in elections during the early 1820s.

This pattern reflects a widespread disillusionment with the disintegrating Federalist-Republican system following the War of 1812. "A continuation of party names, of democrats and federalists, after the differences in principles which they were used to designate, has ceased to exist, is injurious to the best interests of the community," concluded a meeting of Philadelphians in 1822.[5] Party leaders are "indifferent" to the concerns of the people "provided their friends and favorites are kept in power," echoed a newspaper correspondent in Boston.[6] It was attitudes like these to which John C. Calhoun referred when he commented to John Quincy Adams on the existence of "a general mass of disaffection to the Government." "The disease is apparent, the rem-edy not discernible," the secretary of state concurred.[7] For some citizens the remedy was simply to withdraw from politics entirely, which explains why participation rates in contests where candidates continued to do battle un-der old party labels, whether as Federalists versus Republicans or as factions within a dominant Republican Party, were generally lower than in those un-regulated by partisan organization. Competition between parties does bring voters to the polls, as the celebratory narrative suggests, but only when the electorate is convinced that something meaningful is at stake; in the absence of important issues, the reliance of party leaders on tired slogans and stage-managed conventions is likely to depress, rather than raise, turnout.[8]

Many Americans, however, did not abandon politics during the early

1820s. Some, like the Federalist grandees of Boston or the backers of William H. Crawford's presidential campaign, remained resolute defenders of party. Others manifested feelings that might conveniently be labeled "antipartisan" but were more varied and complex than that simple term allows.[9] The Middling Interest accepted the "principle" of party organization but not the "exclusive and one-sided policy" by which a few political leaders monopolized public office.[10] In Illinois, in contrast, opponents of slavery took on the challenge of mobilizing a mass electorate in the absence of established parties. For protectionists and free traders, the "miserable spirit of party" that prevailed at polling places across the nation and on the floor of Congress was an obstacle to their efforts to shape federal tariff policy.[11] In the race for the White House, conversely, Crawford's competitors pledged their continued fealty to the Republican standard, reserving their condemnation for those who demanded obedience to "the machinery of party."[12] What these different strains of antipartisanship shared was a commitment, whether real or professed, to majority rule; in their judgment, the existing parties deserved censure not because they made politics too democratic, as some elitist critics continued to argue, but because they did not make politics democratic enough.

The protagonists in these campaigns were not marginalized figures out of touch with reality but astute political operators who recognized the power of numbers in a polity founded on the principle of popular sovereignty. "United we stand, divided we fall," proclaimed the Middling Interest ticket in the mayoral election of 1822, and the insurgents effectively entered Boston politics as a third party, deliberately mirroring the structure of their Federalist opponents.[13] Likewise, while four of the five main candidates in the 1824 presidential election clamored against party machinery, their disciples made use of caucuses, conventions, and a host of other methods to rally support. In Illinois, where such devices had previously been unknown, the anticonventionists placed their faith in the ingenuity of activists working at the local level. The result was a network of voluntary societies designed to disseminate their message to the people and a public nominating system to concentrate their strength at the polls. Those involved in the tariff struggle, meanwhile, adopted a similar nonpartisan associational strategy in their bid to fuse scattered constituencies in a single national cause, establishing important precedents in their use of interstate conferences, a federal template for organizing, and a specialist press. Following their example, anti- and nonpartisan movements would continue to play a central role in politics in the decades before the Civil War, providing a vehicle for popular engagement in disputes over Sabbatarianism, Indian removal, slavery, temperance, immigration, and many other issues that the major parties failed to address.[14]

If the episodes explored here show that there was more to early nineteenth-century politics than parties, they also show that there was more to popular participation than elections. The celebratory narrative prioritizes the importance of voting because it was at the polls that parties competed for access to office, and historians' use of turnout figures as a proxy for measuring democratization in turn reinforces the centrality of party competition to that process.[15] But while elections certainly are a potent symbol of popular sovereignty, their role in translating public preferences into a coherent program of governance is more difficult to define. As Glenn Altschuler and Stuart Blumin remind us, "The success of the parties' efforts relied on many things—from heroic candidates to election-day drinks—that had little to do with public policy."[16] Nonetheless, it remains true that for some contemporaries the ballot box marked the beginning and the end of the people's role in politics. This view was encapsulated by President Monroe in his second inaugural address, when he declared that according to the "representative principle" the power of the people is transferred "to persons elected by themselves, in the full extent necessary for all the purposes of free, enlightened and efficient government."[17]

There were large numbers of Americans, however, who embraced a more expansive vision of popular sovereignty. The right of constituents to instruct their representatives was championed by the Middling Interest in Boston and also featured one thousand miles away in the Illinois convention contest. In the national struggle over import duties, protectionists and free traders turned to petitioning and lobbying to circumvent party control of the polling place. To these three widely practiced forms of participation more unusual ones could also be added: the nonconsumption agreement proposed by James Mercer Garnett in protest against a protective tariff; the proslavery mob that sought "to intimidate, and crush all opposition" to the convention scheme; and the spate of effigy burnings that greeted John Quincy Adams's elevation to the White House.[18] Disputes over municipal building codes, the legalization of slavery, federal tariff policy, and the choice of a new president all touched, directly or indirectly, on what the *Defence of the Exposition of the Middling Interest* called "a question on the fundamental principles of our government; whether the power of the State resides in the people; or is vested at every election beyond their controul in the representatives elected."[19] Elections are a vital part of any democracy, but to focus on them exclusively is to neglect those citizens who declined to let their participation be bound by the ballot box.[20]

Indeed, even the stories recounted here fail to capture the full diversity of American political practices during the early republic in one important respect. The characters appearing in these pages have been almost exclusively white males, that is, the section of the population that the vast majority of contemporaries referred to when they talked of politics and "the people." The fact that all women and most persons of color were barred from running for office, voting in elections, and engaging in partisan activities on equal terms with their white male counterparts offers another important caveat to the celebratory narrative of democratization, one that has received well-merited attention elsewhere.[21] Yet a number of historians have also shown that these groups, though formally disenfranchised, were nonetheless frequently able to exercise an influence on politics by experimenting with their own, often informal modes of participation and organization.[22]

Viewed in the light of this growing literature, what is most striking about the four episodes explored in the preceding chapters is the continued marginalization of women and persons of color. Where women do appear as agents, it is typically from the shadows of the private sphere, and their involvement was almost invariably accompanied by critical commentary. Speculating on Josiah Quincy's motive for accepting the Middling Interest mayoral nomination in 1822, for example, one correspondent remarked that "there are some who apologize for him by saying that he would have been quiet had there been no ladies in his parlor, or rather one at the head of his household."[23] In public, women as agents are almost invisible in these episodes. No mention is made of their participation in either the Middling Interest or the established parties in Boston during the early 1820s, and there is also no evidence that their contribution was sought to the antislavery societies in Illinois; most likely, the latter implicitly subscribed to the same gendered expectations that the Morganian Society explicitly expressed in its constitutional requirement that "no person shall be admitted a member of this society, unless *he* has attained the age of eighteen years, is averse to slavery, and is a citizen of this county."[24] On the few occasions when women did engage in overt political activity, such as when the Ladies of the County of Cortland, in New York, "formed a society for the encouragement of manufactures" or when women in Pennsylvania, Kentucky, and Indiana assembled to register their support for Andrew Jackson's presidential campaign, the novelty of such occurrences was much remarked upon in the press.[25]

Similar observations may be made about the participation of persons of color. Massachusetts was one of the few states to permit African Americans to vote during this period, but there is no record of what this constituency made of the Middling Interest insurgency in Boston. In Illinois, the same session of the legislature that passed the convention resolution refused to act on a petition calling for the enfranchisement of the state's free black population, and there is little to suggest that this community was permitted any further input in the eighteen-month debate over slavery that followed. Instead, their political voice was apparently appropriated by others with more sinister motives; "M" alleged in the *Edwardsville Spectator* that "convention letter factories" were producing forgeries for dissemination through the press, including "a letter purporting to have been written from 'a free negro of Ohio' ... to induce a belief that if our state remains free, it will be filled up with free negroes, from Ohio and elsewhere."[26] The female political voice was also subject to this form of misappropriation in the service of reiterating gendered expectations of behavior. "Fidelia Flimsey" complained in the *Spectator* that "my husband has turned *Politician*" after a visit from "Mr. Office-hunter" and concluded with the wish that "some method could be devised to allay the passions, and smooth the asperities of party feeling, and restore my husband to his senses and the bosom of his family." Regardless of whether the writer was in fact male or female, this was hardly a recipe for women's political activism; on the subject of the convention itself, "Fidelia Flimsey" observed only that "should this political question terminate either way, the sun will continue to shine, except in cloudy weather, and the usual phenomena of nature continue as heretofore."[27] These examples, then, stand as testaments to the continued obstacles that faced the many women and persons of color who were engaged in efforts to influence the course of American politics, obstacles that make those efforts all the more meaningful.

At the core of the celebratory narrative lies the rise of a new national two-party system following the presidential election of 1824. Gerald Leonard has suggested that the tendency of historians to neglect the origins of this system in favor of the "substantive issues" that separated Whigs and Democrats in subsequent decades leaves the impression that "the party politician and his machinery were thrown up almost spontaneously by preexisting social divisions."[28] A study of the 1824 campaign confirms that political organizations did not arise organically from a polarization of the electorate over issues of policy but were deliberately constructed by ambitious politicians in search of public office. Though Adams's triumph appeared to represent a defeat for the cause of party, the manner in which it was achieved gave credence to Martin Van Buren's claim that without some form of organization the majority could never prevail against a privileged minority. The most important legacy of the 1824 election, then, was not some fundamental point of principle that would divide the emerging parties in years to come but a shared discourse of "partisan antipartisanship" through which the organization building of each side was legitimated by their opponents' supposed determination to subvert the will of the people.[29]

There can be no doubt that the advent of competitive two-party politics across the nation promoted mass participation in elections; the extraordinary turnout figures of the Party Period testify to that. But the meaning of that participation is more problematic. The difficulty of connecting results at the polls to policymaking in the state and national legislatures has already been discussed, and the chorus of complaints we have witnessed from Massachusetts, Illinois, Pennsylvania, and Virginia also suggest widespread dissatisfaction with the degree to which parties controlled the electoral process. Advocates of party from both ends of the political spectrum, Federalists in Boston and Radical Republicans in the 1824 presidential campaign, sought to regulate access to public office, not open it to all. The fact that a new generation of politicians, typified by Van Buren, tended to come from humble backgrounds that contrasted with the gentrified origins of their predecessors should not be misread as proof that any man could forge a successful political career during this period. Instead it demonstrates that "the badge of party communion," as Adams put it in his inaugural address, had replaced social standing as the most important criterion for political advancement, a qualification that in different ways was just as exclusionary.[30] Party, as John Brooke observes, could serve the purposes of those who wished "to restore traditional oligarchical power" as much as it could facilitate "popular resistance" to their efforts.[31]

So is democracy, as one modern scholar claims, simply "*unworkable save in terms of parties*"?[32] The celebratory narrative would suggest so. Yet throughout the early 1820s countless Americans proved otherwise, as they associated together to engage with their fellow countrymen, to mobilize their support, and to secure government policies that met their expectations. Contrary to the intentions of the Founding Fathers, these energetic citizens refused to confine their political presence to the polling place, pushing the definition of popular sovereignty to its limits. Over time, it could be said, these limits have actually narrowed in some respects; instruction is no longer practiced, lobbying has become the preserve of special interests, and petitions occupy only a subsidiary role beside the ballot box. The nature of political organization has also been transformed. A transition "from membership to management," from encouraging grassroots activism to advocating on behalf of passive constituents, concludes the political scientist Theda Skocpol, has left us living "in a much less participatory and more oligarchicly managed civic world."[33] But none of this was foreordained in the Era of Experimentation, as Americans debated the very meaning of "We the People" and sought new ways to make the extraordinary promise contained in those words a reality.

1 : U.S. ELECTION TURNOUT, 1820–1825

To calculate the size of the electorate in each state I used data from the U.S. federal censuses of 1820 and 1830 and from state censuses where appropriate. For some states the electorate included all adult males; for some it included only white adult males; and for some it included only a proportion of white adult males determined by a landholding and/or taxpaying requirement.

To calculate the number of votes cast in each election I used data from the database A New Nation Votes; from the private collection of Phil Lampi; and from Michael Dubin's *United States Congressional Elections, United States Gubernatorial Elections,* and *United States Presidential Elections.*

My methodology is modeled on that employed by Walter Dean Burnham, in "Those High Nineteenth-Century American Voter Turnouts," and Jeffrey Pasley, in "Cheese and the Words," in order to facilitate comparison with their figures. I recognize that certain criticisms have been leveled at this methodology, perhaps the most important of which is the general consensus among recent studies of the subject that nineteenth-century censuses undercounted eligible voters by a rate of roughly 10 percent (see Winkle, "The U.S. Census as a Source in Political History"). I make no claim, therefore, that my figures are accurate right down to the last voter, but they do provide a frame of reference for comparisons between states and for comparing the early 1820s as a whole with other periods in American history. Or to put it another way, I acknowledge that any flaws in the model pioneered by Burnham apply equally to my calculations, but I consider this to be a strength as well as a weakness of this approach.

For a more detailed breakdown of election turnout during this period, which includes a full methodology for every state, please contact the author.

TABLE A.1.1. *Turnout in presidential elections, 1820 and 1824, by state*

State	1820 Size of electorate	Vote	Turnout (%)	1824 Size of electorate	Vote	Turnout (%)
Alabama	Electors appointed by legislature			26,911	13,535	50
Connecticut	60,362	4,246	7	63,901	9,818	15
Delaware	Electors appointed by legislature			Electors appointed by legislature		
Georgia	Electors appointed by legislature			Electors appointed by legislature		
Illinois	11,508	1,445	13	14,444	4,708	33
Indiana	Electors appointed by legislature			35,252	15,833	45
Kentucky	83,978	5,853[a]	7	92,028	24,205	26
Louisiana	Electors appointed by legislature			Electors appointed by legislature		
Maine	61,402	5,454	9	71,555	13,572	19
Maryland	58,078	5,371	9	61,871	33,214	54
Massachusetts	119,661	23,014	19	130,423	38,660	30
Mississippi	9,686	775	8	11,101	5,119	46
Missouri	Electors appointed by legislature			14,300	3,434	24
New Hampshire	52,937	9,530	18	56,033	10,209	18
New Jersey	55,275	4,102	7	59,839	18,768	31
New York	Electors appointed by legislature			Electors appointed by legislature		
North Carolina	84,453	3,340	4	89,525	36,028	40
Ohio	114,562	7,164	6	129,936	49,994	38
Pennsylvania	220,097	32,206	15	249,375	47,185	19
Rhode Island	7,295	724	10	7,611	2,344	31
South Carolina	Electors appointed by legislature			Electors appointed by legislature		
Tennessee	62,256	2,062[a]	3	76,278	20,737[b]	27
Vermont	Electors appointed by legislature			Electors appointed by legislature		
Virginia	61,395[b]	5,247	9	64,992[b]	15,473	24
United States	1,062,945	110,533	10	1,255,375	362,836	29

[a] Data incomplete (20% or more of the returns missing).

[b] Estimate.

TABLE A.1.2. *Turnout in congressional elections, 1820/21, 1822/23, and 1824/25, by state*

	1820/21 Size of electorate	Vote	Turnout (%)	1822/23 Size of electorate
Alabama	20,061	17,029	85	Data unavailable
Connecticut	61,246	7,062	12	63,016
Delaware	11,628	7,502	65	11,772
Georgia	38,476	11,832	31	42,076
Illinois	11,508	7,685	67	12,976
Indiana	28,352	17,954	63	31,802
Kentucky	Data unavailable			Data unavailable
Louisiana	8,994	4,599	51	9,511
Maine	61,402	9,958	16	69,017
Maryland	58,078	33,868	58	59,975
Massachusetts	119,661	26,592	22	125,042
Mississippi	9,686	3,910	40	10,393
Missouri	Data unavailable			13,550
New Hampshire	52,937	10,826	20	54,485
New Jersey	55,275	4,777	9	Data unavailable
New York	202,510	145,471	72	259,387
North Carolina	Data unavailable			Data unavailable
Ohio	Data unavailable			Data unavailable
Pennsylvania	220,097	131,353	60	234,736
Rhode Island	7,295	5,663	78	7,295
South Carolina	Data unavailable			49,376
Tennessee	Data unavailable			72,772
Vermont	50,513	21,282	42	53,071
Virginia	Data unavailable			Data unavailable
United States			46	

Note: Congressional elections were held in different years in different states. Those listed for 1820/21 were for the Seventeenth Congress; those for 1822/23, for the Eighteenth Congress; and those for 1824/25, for the Nineteenth Congress.

Vote	Turnout (%)	1824/25 Size of electorate	Vote	Turnout (%)	Average turnout (%)
		Data unavailable			85
5,486	9	64,785	6,639	10	10
7,587	64	11,916	6,650	56	62
19,371	46	—	—	—	38
8,569	66	14,444	12,021	83	72
20,649	65	35,252	26,888	76	68
		Data unavailable			Data unavailable
5,037	53	Data unavailable			52
26,509	38	71,555	17,060	24	26
30,614	51	61,871	44,443	72	60
25,592	20	130,423	36,277	28	24
7,470	72	11,101	5,962	54	55
9,906	73	14,300	10,684	75	74
12,604	23	56,033	12,429	22	22
		59,839	17,706	30	19
128,348	49	283,884	183,398	65	62
		90,793	56,881	63	63
		129,936	63,675	49	49
103,412	44	249,375	94,114	38	47
1,447	20	7,769	5,278	68	55
8,145	37	Data unavailable			37
56,240	77	79,783	58,331	73	75
18,513	35	55,629	22,056	40	39
		Data unavailable			Data unavailable
	47			51	50

TABLE A.1.3. *Turnout in gubernatorial elections, 1820–1825, by state*

State	1820 Size of electorate	Vote	Turnout (%)	1821 Size of electorate
Alabama	—	—	—	20,061
Connecticut	60,362	20,568	34	61,246
Delaware	11,628	7,488	64	—
Georgia	—	—	—	Appointed by legislature
Illinois	—	—	—	—
Indiana	—	—	—	—
Kentucky	83,978	62,546	74	—
Louisiana	8,994	4,752	53	—
Maine	61,402	22,114	36	63,940
Maryland	Appointed by legislature			Appointed by legislature
Massachusetts	119,661	53,924	45	122,352
Mississippi	—	—	—	10,040
Missouri	12,800	9,228	72	—
New Hampshire	52,937	26,454	50	53,711
New Jersey	Appointed by legislature			Appointed by legislature
New York	195,272	94,322	48	—
North Carolina	Appointed by legislature			Appointed by legislature
Ohio	114,562	52,500	46	—
Pennsylvania	220,097	134,504	61	—
Rhode Island	7,295	1,981	27	7,455
South Carolina	—	—	—	Appointed by legislature
Tennessee	—	—	—	65,761
Vermont	50,513	14,086	28	51,792
Virginia	Appointed by legislature			Appointed by legislature

Note: Empty cells represent years in which there was no election.

Vote	Turnout (%)	1822 Size of electorate	Vote	Turnout (%)
17,115	85	—	—	—
11,551	19	62,131	9,950	16
—	—	11,772	7,546	64
—	—	—	—	—
—	—	12,976	8,683	67
—	—	31,802	18,342	58
—	—	—	—	—
—	—	—	—	—
24,388	38	66,479 Appointed by legislature	22,026	33
49,410	40	125,042	50,445	40
6,199	62	—	—	—
—	—	—	—	—
24,738	46	54,485 Appointed by legislature	25,462	47
—	—	259,387 Appointed by legislature	132,073	51
—	—	121,270	63,675	53
—	—	—	—	—
6,664	89	7,295	2,092	29
—	—	—	—	—
52,613	80	—	—	—
12,597	24	53,071 Appointed by legislature	11,687	22

(continued)

TABLE A.1.3. *continued*

State	1823 Size of electorate	Vote	Turnout (%)	1824 Size of electorate
Alabama	24,628	23,400	95	—
Connecticut	63,016	10,133	16	63,901
Delaware	11,844	8,399	71	—
Georgia	Appointed by legislature			
Illinois	—	—	—	—
Indiana	—	—	—	
Kentucky	—	—	—	92,028
Louisiana	—	—	—	10,156
Maine	69,017	19,400	28	71,555
Maryland	Appointed by legislature			Appointed by legislature
Massachusetts	127,733	65,910	52	130,423
Mississippi	10,747	8,493	79	—
Missouri	—	—	—	14,300
New Hampshire	55,259	30,748	56	56,033
New Jersey	Appointed by legislature			Appointed by legislature
New York	—	—	—	283,884
North Carolina	Appointed by legislature			Appointed by legislature
Ohio	—	—	—	129,936
Pennsylvania	242,056	154,147	64	—
Rhode Island	7,453	1,679	23	7,611
South Carolina	Appointed by legislature			—
Tennessee	Data unavailable			—
Vermont	54,350	13,408	25	55,629
Virginia	Appointed by legislature			Appointed by legislature

Vote	Turnout (%)	1825 Size of electorate	Vote	Turnout (%)
—	—	28,963	12,749	44
7,512	12	64,785	10,632	16
—	—	—	—	—
		48,081 .	40,667	85
—	—	—	—	—
		36,977	26,017	70
64,777	70	—	—	—
6,895	68	—	—	—
20,419	29	74,094	15,252	21
		Appointed by legislature		
74,174	57	133,114	37,426	28
—	—	11,455	9,345	82
10,801	76	—	—	—
30,677	55	56,808	30,780	54
		Appointed by legislature		
193,347	68	—	—	—
		Appointed by legislature		
76,527	59	—	—	—
—	—	—	—	—
2,751	36	7,769	1,731	22
—	—	Appointed by legislature		
—	—	Data unavailable		
15,781	28	56,908	12,851	23
		Appointed by legislature		

(continued)

TABLE A.1.3. *continued*

State	1820–1825 Average turnout (%)
Alabama	75
Connecticut	19
Delaware	66
Georgia	85
Illinois	67
Indiana	64
Kentucky	72
Louisiana	60
Maine	31
Maryland	n/a
Massachusetts	44
Mississippi	74
Missouri	74
New Hampshire	51
New Jersey	n/a
New York	56
North Carolina	n/a
Ohio	52
Pennsylvania	62
Rhode Island	38
South Carolina	n/a
Tennessee	80
Vermont	25
Virginia	n/a

TABLE A.1.4. Average and highest turnouts for gubernatorial and congressional elections, 1820–1825 (%)

State	Average gubernatorial turnout	Average congressional turnout	Average turnout	Highest turnout (election)
Alabama	75	85	80	95 (1823 gubernatorial)
Connecticut	19	10	15	34 (1820 gubernatorial)
Delaware	66	62	64	71 (1823 gubernatorial
Georgia	85	38	61	85 (1825 gubernatorial)
Illinois	67	72	69	83 (1824 congressional)
Indiana	64	68	66	76 (1824 congressional)
Kentucky	72	Data unavailable	72	74 (1820 gubernatorial)
Louisiana	60	52	56	68 (1824 gubernatorial)
Maine	31	26	28	38 (1823 congressional)
Maryland	Appointed by legislature	60	60	72 (1824 congressional)
Massachusetts	44	24	34	57 (1824 gubernatorial)
Mississippi	74	55	65	82 (1825 gubernatorial)
Missouri	74	74	74	76 (1824 gubernatorial)
New Hampshire	51	22	37	56 (1823 gubernatorial)
New Jersey	Appointed by legislature	19	19	31 (1824 presidential)
New York	56	62	59	72 (1821 congressional)
North Carolina	Appointed by legislature	63	63	63 (1825 congressional)
Ohio	52	49	51	59 (1824 gubernatorial)
Pennsylvania	62	47	55	64 (1823 gubernatorial)
Rhode Island	38	55	46	89 (1821 gubernatorial)
South Carolina	Appointed by legislature	37	37	37 (1823 congressional)
Tennessee	80	75	78	80 (1821 gubernatorial)
Vermont	25	39	32	42 (1820 congressional)
Virginia	Appointed by legislature	Data unavailable	n/a	Data unavailable

Note: Average turnout was calculated by adding the average gubernatorial turnout to the average congressional turnout and dividing by 2. This method, which gives an average of the two averages, was used to overcome the difficulty of comparing a state that had six gubernatorial elections during this period with another state that had only one. An alternative method would be to add together the turnout figures for every single congressional and gubernatorial election in a state during the period and divide by the total number of such elections. This would produce the following results: Alabama, 77%; Connecticut, 16%; Delaware, 64%; Georgia, 54%; Illinois, 71%; Indiana, 67%; Kentucky, 72%; Louisiana, 56%; Maine, 29%; Maryland, 60%; Massachusetts, 37%; Mississippi, 65%; Missouri, 74%; New Hampshire, 41%; New Jersey, 19%; New York, 59%; North Carolina, 63%; Ohio, 52%; Pennsylvania, 53%; Rhode Island, 44%; South Carolina, 37%; Tennessee, 77%; Vermont, 30%; and Virginia, no data.

2 : BOSTON ELECTION RESULTS, 1820–1824

The Boston election returns for 1820–24 are taken from the *Columbian Centinel* (Boston) and the *Boston Patriot & Daily Mercantile Advertiser*. On occasions where these two sources differ, I used the figures from the paper that gives the most detailed breakdown. In calculating the average vote for a party ticket I excluded any candidates on that ticket who were also on another ticket for the same election. For the sake of convenience, the label "Middling Interest" is used for any ticket put forward by a group other than the Federalist and Republican parties, even before the name was formally adopted by the insurgents.

TABLE A.2.1. *Boston election results, 1820–1824*

		Federalist	
Election	Total votes cast	Average vote	Average vote as % of total
Municipal 3/1820	4,168	1,883	45
Municipal(2nd ballot) 3/1820	4,840	2,065	43
State senate 4/1820	5,187	3,363	65
State representative 5/1820	2,464	1,537	62
U.S. Congress 10/1820	3,123	1,618	52
U.S. Congress (2nd ballot) 11/1820	3,622	2,187	60
Municipal 3/1821	2,443	187	8
State senate 4/1821	4,375	2,942	67
State representative 5/1821	1,610	1,036	64
State senate 4/1822	4,566	2,258	50
Municipal 4/1822	3,663	2,141	59
Mayoral 4/1822	3,700	1,384	37
Mayoral (2nd ballot) 4/1822[a]	2,650	—	—
State representative 5/1822	2,889	1,459	51
State representative (2nd ballot) 5/1822	3,826	1,722	45
U.S. Congress 11/1822	4,199	2,638	63
State senate 4/1823	5,659	2,875	51
Municipal 4/1823	4,777	2,519	53
Mayoral 4/1823	4,764	2,504	53
State representative 5/1823	4,334	2,211	51
State representative (2nd ballot) 5/1823	2,277	957	42
State senate 4/1824	6,392	3,289	51
Municipal 4/1824	4,176	2,436	58
Mayoral 4/1824	3,950	3,867	98
State representative 5/1824	3,406	1,690	50
State representative (2nd ballot) 5/1824	3,972	2,076	52
U.S. Congress 11/1824	3,672	3,669	100

Note: Empty cells indicate elections in which the given party did not field a candidate.

[a] John Phillips ran unopposed in this election as the compromise candidate of both the Federalists and the Middling Interest and received 2,500 of the 2,650 votes cast.

Republican		Middling Interest	
Average vote	Average vote as % of total	Average vote	Average vote as % of total
—	—	2,157	52
—	—	2,537	52
1,808	35	—	—
929	38	—	—
652	21	842	27
—	—	1,363	38
—	—	2,235	92
1,371	31	—	—
497	31	—	—
—	—	1,967	43
—	—	1,553	42
—	—	1,736	47
—	—	—	—
—	—	1,338	46
—	—	2,048	54
—	—	1,557	37
—	—	2,753	49
—	—	2,288	48
—	—	2,179	46
—	—	1,977	46
—	—	967	43
3,075	48	—	—
1,689	40	—	—
—	—	—	—
1,552	46	—	—
1,766	45	—	—
—	—	—	—

ABBREVIATIONS

AAS	American Antiquarian Society, Worcester, Massachusetts
ABE	American Broadsides and Ephemera
AHN	America's Historical Newspapers
ALPL	Abraham Lincoln Presidential Library, Springfield, Illinois
ASP	American State Papers, 1789–1838
ASSSCL	Albert and Shirley Small Special Collections Library, University of Virginia, Charlottesville
BA	Boston Athenaeum
BDUSC	Biographical Directory of the United States Congress, 1774–Present
BL	British Library, London
BPL	Boston Public Library
CHM	Chicago History Museum
EGSL	Earl Gregg Swem Library, College of William & Mary, Williamsburg, Virginia
EPL	Edwardsville Public Library, Illinois
HSP	Historical Society of Pennsylvania, Philadelphia
IHLC	Illinois History and Lincoln Collections, University of Illinois at Urbana-Champaign
LC	Library of Congress, Washington, DC
LCP	Library Company of Philadelphia
LV	Library of Virginia, Richmond
MHS	Massachusetts Historical Society, Boston
19CUSN	19th Century U.S. Newspapers
NNV	A New Nation Votes: American Election Returns, 1787–1825
NYHS	New York Historical Society
SA	Sabin Americana
UoD	University of Delaware Library, Newark
UoP	Rare Book and Manuscript Library, University of Pennsylvania, Philadelphia
VHS	Virginia Historical Society, Richmond

INTRODUCTION

1. "Virginius," *Richmond Enquirer,* 7 November 1820.

2. Ibid.; "From the Diary of William Plumer," 212. Federalist electors were chosen in Massachusetts, Delaware, and Maryland. I am grateful to Phil Lampi for this information.

3. "Era of Good Feelings," *Columbian Centinel* (Boston), 12 July 1817.

4. "No period is so misunderstood, and its significance for American party history so underestimated, as the laughably misnamed 'Era of Good Feelings.'" Ratcliffe, *Party Spirit,* 208.

5. Keller, *America's Three Regimes,* 72. For similar assessments see Altschuler and Blumin, *Rude Republic,* 14; and Schudson, *Good Citizen,* 112.

6. "Presidential Election," *Richmond Enquirer,* 7 November 1820.

7. *Western Carolinian* (Salisbury, NC), 8 June 1824, quoted in Newsome, *Presidential Election,* 140.

8. Taylor to John H. Bernard, 8 April 1824, Taylor Papers, LV.

9. These figures are from Burnham, "Changing Shape," 10.

10. R. L. McCormick, "Party Period," 281–83.

11. Silbey, *American Political Nation,* 9, 144.

12. Gienapp, "Politics Seem to Enter into Everything," 15. For a summary of the Party Period concept and some of the criticisms that have since been made of it see Formisano, "'Party Period' Revisited"; Voss-Hubbard "'Third Party Tradition' Reconsidered"; Holt "Primacy of Party Reasserted"; and Baker, "Midlife Crisis."

13. Ratcliffe, *Party Spirit,* 4. Several Party Period scholars deny that the Federalists and Republicans meet their definition of a political party; this debate is summarized in ibid., 2–5.

14. Pasley, "Cheese and the Words," 45. The scholars named here are all contributors to Pasley, Robertson, and Waldstreicher, *Beyond the Founders,* which places this interpretation at its core.

15. Pasley, "Cheese and the Words," 46. Limited work has been done on voter turnout prior to the 1830s, but two important exceptions are Pole, *Political Representation,* which includes data on several states from previous articles by the same author; and Ratcliffe, "Voter Turnout."

16. See Wilentz, *Rise of American Democracy;* and Wood, *Empire of Liberty.* Howe, *What Hath God Wrought,* is more ambivalent about the role of parties in promoting democratization. For an older but perceptive caution against the celebratory narrative see Formisano, "Deferential-Participant Politics," 473. And for a similar critique, from a political-science perspective, of what Selinger calls the "democratization" narrative, which suggests "that the second party system was without conditions and constraints—that it reflected the virtues of unfettered political competition," see Selinger, "Rethinking the Develop-

ment," 267. Selinger is building on the work of previous political scientists, such as Sorauf, "Political Parties."

17. Gienapp, "Politics Seem to Enter into Everything," 15.

18. Robertson, "Look on This Picture . . . ," 1280.

19. Turnout figures for all presidential, congressional, and gubernatorial elections occurring between 1820 and 1825 are presented in appendix 1. I am not the first historian to take note of these high levels of turnout. "Curiously," Ratcliffe remarks, "the decline in national party politics associated with the Era of Good Feelings had only a marginal impact" in Ohio, which actually experienced an "explosion of popular interest in electoral politics" during the early 1820s. "Voter Turnout," 245. Similarly, Silbey observes that "in the ten years after 1815, a national two-party system did not exist. Nearly everyone was Republican. But at the local level, political excitement increased in intensity, extent, and location." *American Political Nation,* 17. Critically, however, neither explores the implication of these findings for the prevailing consensus that party competition was the key variable that determined the extent of popular participation at the polls.

20. Any measure of partisan affiliation during this period of political flux is somewhat inexact, so it is impossible to give more precise figures. This analysis is based on data from BDUSC.

21. "Virginius," *Richmond Enquirer,* 7 November 1820

22. This and the following paragraph rely on R. P. McCormick, *Second American Party System,* supplemented by literature on individual states where necessary.

23. R. P. McCormick, *Second American Party System,* 151. Massachusetts politics provides the subject for chapter 1.

24. Formisano, *For the People,* 101.

25. See, for example, Shankman, *Crucible of American Democracy.*

26. Silbey, "Incomplete World"; Parsons, *Birth of Modern Politics.*

27. James Vernon, a historian of nineteenth-century Britain, suggests that the "invention of party can be seen as part of [a] closure of the public political sphere, a means of disciplining popular politics by securing it within certain limited and restrictive subjectivities and practices." Vernon, *Politics and the People,* 8–9. For similar reflections on the United States see Formisano, *For the People,* 198; Pasley, "Party Politics," 48; and Robertson, "1828."

28. See Fritz, *American Sovereigns;* and Hemberger, "Government Based on Representations."

29. See Altschuler and Blumin, *Rude Republic;* Bensel, *American Ballot Box;* and Pessen, "We Are All Jeffersonians."

30. See Carwardine, *Evangelicals and Politics;* Formisano, "Political Character"; Hofstadter, *Idea of a Party System;* and Silbey, *American Political Nation,* 18–22.

31. "The American Revolution [was] literally an enormous project in self-creation, the assertion of popular sovereignty." Brooke, "Ancient Lodges," 288.

32. For more on the role that secular and religious ideas played in the proliferation of voluntary associations, two good places to start are R. Brown, *Strength of a People;* and Howe, *What Hath God Wrought.*

33. John, "Governmental Institutions"; John, *Spreading the News;* Kielbowicz, *News in the Mail;* Skocpol, "Tocqueville Problem."

34. Tocqueville, *Democracy in America,* 215. Two modern studies that stress the importance of associational activity are Brooke, *Columbia Rising;* and R. Brown, "Emergence of Urban Society."

35. Koschnik, *"Let a Common Interest,"* 229.

36. R. Huston, "Popular Movements"; Voss-Hubbard, *Beyond Party.*

37. The notion that parties were actually "somewhat irrelevant" much of the time and that "individuals could carry out their demands upon government rather effectively without them" was suggested long ago by Samuel Hays but has found little traction in the literature. Hays, "Politics and Society," 50.

38. R. L. McCormick, "Party Period," 287. For variations on the same theme see Pasley, "Party Politics," 40–41; Robertson, "Look on This Picture . . . ," 1278; and Silbey, *American Political Nation,* 177.

39. Grob, "Political System," 10. For more recent restatements of the same problem see Bensel, *American Ballot Box,* 293; and Formisano, "'Party Period' Revisited," 102–7.

40. This point is discussed in Aldrich, *Why Parties?,* 97–125.

41. On the "interelection hibernation" of nineteenth-century parties see Ethington, *Public City,* 70–71; and Pasley, *"Tyranny of Printers,"* 10–11.

42. For evidence of this see Bowers, "From Logrolling to Corruption," 451; and Voss-Hubbard, *Beyond Party,* 141–77.

43. R. Brown, *Strength of a People,* 205. In "The Federalist No. 63" James Madison argued that America's representative system implied "*the total exclusion of the people in their collective capacity* from any share" in governance. Madison, "The Federalist, 63," in Hamilton, Madison, and Jay, *Federalist Papers,* 313.

44. These examples are taken from Pasley, Robertson, and Waldstreicher, *Beyond the Founders.*

45. Formisano, "Concept of Political Culture," 395.

1. "'WE THE PEOPLE' HAVE NO POLITICAL EXISTENCE"

1. "Advertisement," *New-England Galaxy* (Boston), 27 October 1820.

2. "The stability, durability, and balance of the parties in Massachusetts was, by contrast with other states, most extraordinary." R. P. McCormick, *Second American Party*

System, 40. See also Fischer, *Revolution of American Conservatism;* and Livermore, *Twilight of Federalism.*

3. Otis, Perkins, and Sullivan were selected as Massachusetts's commissioners to relay the proposals put forward by the Hartford Convention to the federal government.

4. J. Quincy Jr., *Figures of the Past,* 302–3.

5. Formisano, "Boston, 1800–1840," 41, 32.

6. "Federal Caucus, for the Nomination of City Officers," *Boston Commercial Gazette,* 8 April 1822. For more detail see also "Federal Caucuses," *Boston Daily Advertiser,* 18 May 1822.

7. With Boston's incorporation as a city in 1822 the municipal elections were moved from March to April but still held separately from the gubernatorial and senatorial elections.

8. "Odds between Maine and Massachusetts," *New-England Galaxy,* 23 March 1821. *Central Committee* was the old name for the General Committee, which the *Galaxy* continued to use.

9. Untitled notice, *Boston Patriot & Daily Mercantile Advertiser,* 26 October 1820; "Suffolk County Meeting," ibid., 28 March 1821; "Union List," ibid., 3 April 1820.

10. "Our Representative to Congress," *New-England Galaxy,* 3 November 1820. *Primary caucus* was the name given to the meeting of the Central Committee with delegates from the ward committees to nominate candidates.

11. Pasley, *"Tyranny of Printers,"* 15, 13. For more on the partisan press see Brooke, "To be 'Read.'"

12. Schudson, *Good Citizen,* 130.

13. Constitution of the Washington Benevolent Society, in Washington Benevolent Society, Journal, 1812–1824, Washington Benevolent Society Records, MHS.

14. "The 'Art' of Faction," *Independent Chronicle* (Boston), 6 May 1813, quoted in Crocker, *Magic of the Many,* 16. For more detail on the Washington Benevolent Societies and similar associations see Fischer, *Revolution of American Conservatism,* 110–28; and Koschnik, *"Let a Common Interest."*

15. Waldstreicher, *In the Midst,* 12.

16. *Historical View of the Public Celebrations,* iii.

17. "More Central Committee Dictation," *Boston Patriot & Daily Mercantile Advertiser,* 25 March 1820.

18. Ethington, *Public City,* 223.

19. "More Central Committee Dictation," *Boston Patriot & Daily Mercantile Advertiser,* 25 March 1820.

20. Otis to William Sullivan, 19 January 1822, reel 8, Otis Papers, MHS.

21. For a more detailed narrative of the events covered in this and the following paragraphs see Cayton, "Fragmentation"; and Crocker, *Magic of the Many.*

22. *Catalogue of the City Councils.*

23. The discord stirred up by sales at auction during this period is explored in Cohen, "Right to Purchase."

24. For election returns for this and all other Boston elections from 1820 to 1824 see appendix 2.

25. "Chaos is Come Again," *Boston Commercial Gazette,* 20 March 1820.

26. "Register of Deeds," *New-England Galaxy,* 17 March 1820.

27. "Era of Good Feelings," ibid., 20 October 1820.

28. Divisions over federal tariff policy are the subject of chapter 3.

29. Massachusetts law required that candidates be elected by an absolute majority of votes cast.

30. "Elections," *New-England Galaxy,* 10 November 1820.

31. "Mill Creek Wharf," ibid., 29 June 1821.

32. "Town Meeting," *Columbian Centinel,* 16 January 1822.

33. "Wooden Buildings," *New-England Galaxy,* 1 March 1822.

34. Otis to Sullivan, 21 March 1822, reel 8, Otis Papers, MHS. This represented a significant reversal for Otis since January, when he had written to Sullivan: "I see with dismay, the vote for wooden buildings—It seems incredible—Cannot you check it in the Legislature before, 'Ucalegon burns next.'" Otis to Sullivan, 19 January 1822, ibid.

35. *An Exposition,* 3–4.

36. *Middling Interest* ([March] 1822).

37. "Communication," *Boston Patriot & Daily Mercantile Advertiser,* 27 March 1822.

38. Very little has been written on the history of instruction in America. Two articles that deal specifically with the instruction of U.S. senators by their state legislatures are Eaton, "Southern Senators"; and Skeen, "Uncertain 'Right.'" For more general discussions of constituents instructing their elected representatives see Fritz, *American Sovereigns;* Morgan, *Inventing the People;* and Pole, *Political Representation.*

39. *Massachusetts Constitution,* 1780. Other states that enumerated the right of instruction in their constitution included Illinois, Indiana, Maine, New Hampshire, North Carolina, Ohio, Pennsylvania, Tennessee, and Vermont. An unsuccessful attempt was also made to enshrine it in the United States Constitution. Skeen, "Uncertain 'Right,'" 31–32.

40. [Sullivan], *Defence of the Exposition,* 12. George Sullivan, the reputed author of this document, was the brother of the Federalist leader William Sullivan.

41. "A Citizen," *Boston Daily Advertiser,* 19 January 1822.

42. "Communication," *Boston Patriot & Daily Mercantile Advertiser,* 27 March 1822.

43. "A Citizen," *Boston Daily Advertiser,* 19 January 1822.

44. "Wooden Buildings," *New-England Galaxy,* 8 March 1822.

45. [Sullivan], *Defence of the Exposition,* 13–15.

46. "Electioneering," *New-England Galaxy*, 22 March 1822.

47. *Middling Interest* ([March] 1822). In a letter written shortly after this meeting, Otis referred to the Middling Interest as "the advocates for wooden buildings or the Roulstone party or whoever they are," reflecting Federalist confusion over the meaning of the protest movement. Otis to Sullivan, 21 March 1822, reel 8, Otis Papers, MHS.

48. "Wooden Buildings," *Boston Commercial Gazette*, 1 April 1822.

49. "New List," ibid., 18 March 1822.

50. "One of the Remonstrants against any wooden houses," *Boston Daily Advertiser*, 6 March 1822. The value of deliberation as a component of democracy is the subject of Gustafson, *Imagining Deliberative Democracy*. Gustafson argues that efforts to promote deliberation often come into conflict with efforts to promote equality and participation, other key democratic values. The frequent debates over the right to instruct during this period provide a clear example of this. For the argument that the conduct of the wooden-buildings advocates was "anti-republican" because it was "fatal to free inquiry" see also "An Old Federalist," *Boston Daily Advertiser*, 30 March 1822.

51. *An Exposition*, 3.

52. [Sullivan], *Defence of the Exposition*, 4, 15. See also "A Middling Interest Man," *Bostonian & Mechanics' Journal*, 5 April 1823.

53. "Many Republican Petitioners," *Boston Patriot & Daily Mercantile Advertiser*, 6 April 1822.

54. For more detail on the incorporation process see Hubbard, "Boston's Last Town Meetings"; and McCaughey, "From Town to City."

55. "An Old Bostonian," *Columbian Centinel*, 8 December 1821. For an alternative take on incorporation that emphasizes the self-interested motives of the protagonists see [R. Webster], *Selections from the Chronicle*, 7–10.

56. Sullivan to Otis, 6 January 1822, and Fairbanks to Otis, 26 December 1821, both reel 8, Otis Papers, MHS.

57. *Full and Authentic Report*. See also the detailed reports in the *Boston Daily Advertiser*, 1–5 January 1822.

58. Mr. Adams, quoted in "Adjourned Town Meeting," *Boston Daily Advertiser*, 2 January 1822.

59. Otis to Sullivan, 19 January 1822, reel 8, Otis Papers, MHS.

60. Sullivan to Otis, 13 January 1822, ibid.

61. "The City Established," *Columbian Centinel*, 6 March 1822.

62. For scattered references to these negotiations see "City of Boston," *New-England Galaxy*, 22 March 1822; "General Committee's Report," *Boston Commercial Gazette*, 8 April 1822; and "Nominations," *Boston Patriot & Daily Mercantile Advertiser*, 8 April 1822.

63. Eliza Susan Quincy to Justin Winsor, 7 July 1880, reel 63, Quincy, Wendell, Holmes,

and Upham Family Papers, MHS. For confirmation see Sullivan to Otis, 6 January 1822, reel 8, Otis Papers, MHS.

64. The quotations in this paragraph are from "Federal Caucus," *New-England Galaxy,* 12 April 1822; and "Mr. Otis and the Middling Interest," ibid., 17 May 1822.

65. "Vox Populi," ibid., 17 March 1820.

66. "Our Representative to Congress," ibid., 3 November 1820.

67. "Who Shall be Mayor of the New City?," ibid., 29 March 1822.

68. Eliza Susan Quincy to Robert C. Winthrop, 29 October 1879, reel 63, Quincy, Wendell, Holmes, and Upham Family Papers, MHS. The identity of the carpenter is a mystery. No known Middling Interest organizers are listed in the *Boston Directory* as carpenters, although two, Augustus O. Barton and Rolun Hartshorn, are listed as "housewright."

69. Perkins to Otis, 5 April 1822, reel 8, Otis Papers, MHS.

70. "Middling Interest," *Boston Daily Advertiser,* 15 May 1822.

71. Eliza Susan Quincy to Winsor, 7 July 1880, reel 63, Quincy, Wendell, Holmes, and Upham Family Papers, MHS.

72. Eliza Susan Quincy to Winthrop, 30 June 1879, ibid.

73. Perkins to Otis, 5 April 1822, reel 8, Otis Papers, MHS.

74. Untitled editorial, *New-England Galaxy,* 12 April 1822. The charge that Otis had been unfairly nominated is also reported in a letter from the Federalist loyalist Leverett Saltonstall to William Minot, 9 April 1822, in Saltonstall, *Papers,* 1:97. For a partisan defense of the nominating process see "Ballot for Mayor," *Columbian Centinel,* 10 April 1822.

75. "Federal Caucus," *New-England Galaxy,* 12 April 1822.

76. Eliza Susan Quincy to Winsor, 7 July 1880, reel 63, Quincy, Wendell, Holmes, and Upham Family Papers, MHS.

77. [R. Webster], *Selections from the Chronicle,* 22.

78. Eliza Susan Quincy to Winthrop, 29 October 1879, reel 63, Quincy, Wendell, Holmes, and Upham Family Papers, MHS.

79. "Impartiality of Editors," *New-England Galaxy,* 12 April 1822.

80. "Mayor of Boston," *Boston Daily Advertiser,* 8 April 1822.

81. "Election of Mayor," *Boston Commercial Gazette,* 8 April 1822.

82. Van Buren to Rufus King, 31 May 1822, and Gore to King, 15 May 1822, in King, *Life and Correspondence,* 6:472–73 and 470, respectively.

83. See Altschuler and Blumin, *Rude Republic,* 47–86; Bensel, *American Ballot Box,* 26–85; and Ethington, *Public City,* 64–77.

84. "Municipal Elections," *New-England Galaxy,* 9 March 1821.

85. Ethington, *Public City,* 71.

86. Brooke, "To be 'Read,'" 116.

87. Saltonstall to Minot, 9 April 1822, in Saltonstall, *Papers,* 1:97.

88. Perkins to Otis, 5 April 1822, reel 8, Otis Papers, MHS.

89. This paragraph draws from Buckingham, *Annals;* Buckingham, *Personal Memoirs;* and Buckingham, *Specimens.* For more on Buckingham see Kornblith, "Becoming Joseph T. Buckingham."

90. The original title of the paper was *New-England Galaxy and Masonic Magazine,* shortened in October 1820.

91. For subscription figures see "The Budget Opened," *New-England Galaxy,* 2 January 1824.

92. "Mr. Otis and the Middling Interest," *New-England Galaxy,* 17 May 1822.

93. Cayton, "Fragmentation," 165.

94. *An Exposition,* 7. See also "A Middling Interest Man," *Bostonian & Mechanics' Journal,* 5 April 1823.

95. Popular discontent was fueled in January 1822 when a town meeting controlled by the Middling Interest voted to publish a statement of every resident's wealth from the municipal records to prove that taxes were not being assessed fairly. "This you may easily conceive," remarked one observer, "in a money getting town, where every one conceals his coppers, must be a very obnoxious measure." Ralph Waldo Emerson to John Boynton Hill, 11 May 1822, in Emerson, *Letters,* 1:111.

96. Here I differ from Ronald Formisano, who considers the movement "a genuine grass-roots protest against 'party.'" This conclusion is difficult to reconcile with Formisano's claim that the Federalists "did not need an organized political party." Formisano, "Boston, 1800–1840," 35, 32.

97. Emerson to Hill, 12 November 1822, in Emerson, *Letters,* 1:124.

98. "Election of Mayor," *Boston Commercial Gazette,* 22 April 1822. Christopher Gore estimated that the Federalist Party in Boston lost one-third of its supporters to the Middling Interest. Gore to King, 2 June 1822, in King, *Life and Correspondence,* 6:474.

99. "The Middling Interest," *New-England Galaxy,* 24 May 1822. Of the 51 candidates for public office nominated by the Middling Interest during the movement's lifetime, 23 were Federalists, 12 were Republicans, and the remaining 16 had no identifiable partisan affiliation.

100. "A Middling Interest Man," *Bostonian & Mechanics' Journal,* 5 April 1823.

101. "Electioneering," *New-England Galaxy,* 22 March 1822.

102. "Names," ibid., 24 May 1822.

103. "For the Bostonian," *Bostonian & Mechanics' Journal,* 17 May 1823.

104. *An Exposition,* 5, 7.

105. "Congressional Nomination," *Bostonian & Mechanics' Journal,* 2 November 1822.

106. "Federal Caucus," *New-England Galaxy,* 12 April 1822.

107. "Notice to Middling Interest," *Boston Daily Advertiser,* 27 April 1822. Similar notices also appeared in this and other papers around this time.

108. Emerson to Hill, 11 May 1822, in Emerson, *Letters*, 1:111.

109. *Constitution of the Middling Interest Association.*

110. Ibid.

111. "Federal Declension," *New-England Galaxy*, 9 May 1823. A glance at the roll call of officers of the Republican Institution suggests that this criticism may well have been applicable to that party too. Compare the lists in *Boston Patriot & Daily Mercantile Advertiser*, 15 March 1820, 13 March 1821, and 21 March 1822.

112. *Middling Interest* ([March] 1822).

113. The precise figures are: Middling Interest, 5 out of 28 (18%); Republicans, 10 out of 32 (31%); Federalists, 18 out of 41 (44%).

114. "Federalists Attend," *Boston Commercial Gazette*, 16 May 1822. See also "Federal Caucuses," *Boston Daily Advertiser*, 18 May 1822.

115. [Otis], "Speech before a Federalist Caucus, Spring of 1822," [12 May 1822], reel 8, Otis Papers, MHS. The rebels seemed to aggravate staunch Federalists in a way that their Republican counterparts never had. Leverett Saltonstall, for example, complained bitterly of having to board with one Middling Interest man on a visit to Boston, observing that "while he was a democrat [i.e., Republican] merely, he was not offensive." Saltonstall to James C. Merrill, [24 May 1822], in Saltonstall, *Papers*, 1:99.

116. "Mr. Otis and the Middling Interest," *New-England Galaxy*, 17 May 1822.

117. "Brutus," ibid., 29 September 1820.

118. Ibid.

119. "Electioneering," *New-England Galaxy*, 22 March 1822.

120. "The Mechanics' Journal, and Middling Interest Advocate," *Bostonian & Mechanics' Journal*, 28 June 1823. This quotation is actually taken from the prospectus for the paper's second year, but it applies equally to its first.

121. "The Press," ibid., 26 April 1823.

122. "H," *New-England Galaxy*, 3 November 1820.

123. "Many Republican Petitioners," *Boston Patriot & Daily Mercantile Advertiser*, 6 April 1822.

124. "H," *New-England Galaxy*, 3 November 1820.

125. Eliza Susan Quincy to Winthrop, 29 October 1879, reel 63, Quincy, Wendell, Holmes, and Upham Family Papers, MHS.

126. "Esprit De Parti," *New-England Galaxy*, 18 April 1823.

127. [Otis], "Speech before a Federalist Caucus, Spring of 1822," [12 May 1822], reel 8, Otis Papers, MHS. This speech proved prophetic in more ways than one: just three years later Federalist and Republican politicians would unite in nominating a single candidate for governor, finally ushering Massachusetts into its own long-delayed "Era of Good Feelings."

128. The classic text on this subject is Hofstadter, *Idea of a Party System*. See also Leonard, *Invention of Party Politics*.

129. "Mr. Otis and the Middling Interest," *New-England Galaxy*, 17 May 1822.

130. Lowell to Otis, 26 February 1823, reel 8, Otis Papers, MHS.

131. Formisano, *For the People*, 82. See also Cayton, "Fragmentation," 166; and Crocker, *Magic of the Many*, ix.

132. Eliza Susan Quincy to Winthrop, 29 October 1879, reel 63, Quincy, Wendell, Holmes, and Upham Family Papers, MHS.

133. Story, *Forging of an Aristocracy*, 4.

134. Pole, *Political Representation*, 545–48.

135. "Federal Declension," *New-England Galaxy*, 9 May 1823.

136. Untitled editorial, ibid., 9 April 1824.

137. "Names," ibid., 24 May 1822. The failure of the Federalists to recruit new members is suggested by the fact that the Washington Benevolent Society in Boston had been disbanded in 1821, ostensibly on the grounds that "the political purposes for which the Society was instituted had been fully accomplished." In light of subsequent events, this was either an act of incredible short-sightedness or a tacit admission that the society was no longer serving its intended function. Minutes of meeting of 8 February 1821, in Washington Benevolent Society, Minutes, 1812–1824, Washington Benevolent Society Records, MHS.

138. "The Constitution," *New-England Galaxy*, 6 October 1820.

139. Precisely because parties were so efficient, Glenn Altschuler and Stuart Blumin claim, nineteenth-century "Americans could, if they wished, leave the work [of politics] to the professionals, and go about their other business." Altschuler and Blumin, *Rude Republic*, 81.

140. *An Exposition*, 4.

141. Morgan, *Inventing the People*, 226. Morgan is actually discussing petitions when he uses this phrase, but it applies equally well to instructions.

2. "LET US UNITE LIKE ONE MAN"

1. John Reynolds, *My Own Times*, 155.

2. For an overview of Illinois politics during this period see Leichtle, "Rise of Jacksonian Politics."

3. "Rattlebrain," *Kaskaskia Republican*, 14 December 1824, quoted in Simeone, *Democracy and Slavery*, 70.

4. Horatio Newhall to J. & J. Newhall, 19 April 1822, folder 1, Horatio Newhall Letters and Journal, ALPL.

5. Nathanial Buckmaster to John Buckmaster, 14 April 1822, folder 3, box 1, Buckmaster-Curran Family Papers, ALPL.

6. "Zero," *Illinois Intelligencer* (Vandalia), 9 June 1819, and "A Republican," *Edwards-ville Spectator*, 5 June 1819, both quoted in Leonard, *Invention of Party Politics*, 58–60.

7. Horatio Newhall to J. & J. Newhall, 11 May 1822, folder 1, Newhall Letters and Journal, ALPL. Similarly, Nathanial Buckmaster reported that "the whole State is over whelmed by the sea of politics; all are deeply engaged from the hoary headed grandsire to the youth full striplings." Nathaniel Buckmaster to John Buckmaster, 14 April 1822, folder 3, box 1, Buckmaster-Curran Family Papers, ALPL.

8. Finkelman, "Evading the Ordinance," 41–49.

9. Horatio Newhall to unknown addressee, October 1821, folder 1, Newhall Letters and Journal, ALPL.

10. George Flower, "The history of the English Settlement in Edwards County, Illinois, from its commencement in 1817 and 1818" (MS), 185–88, Flower Family Papers, CHM.

11. For the absence of petitions see *Journal of the House of Representatives of the State of Illinois*. On the 1822 elections see Thomas Lippincott, "Early Days in Madison County," no. 30, *Alton Telegraph*, 10 March 1865. Coles, who had been open about his antislavery convictions but not about his determination to seek complete abolition, had eked out a narrow plurality of 33 percent for the governorship, but the combined vote of his two closest competitors, both suspected of proslavery sympathies, was 59 percent. Pease, *Illinois Election Returns*, 14–17.

12. One of these letters may be found in the Thomas Mather Papers, CHM.

13. Ford, *History of Illinois*, 53. Ford dates this disturbance to the night after the convention resolution passed, but other sources indicate that it actually took place the night prior to the passage of the resolution. See George Churchill, "Annotations, by G. Churchill, on Rev. Thomas Lippincott's 'Early Days in Madison County,'" no. 15, *Alton Telegraph*, 11 August 1865. Demonstrations such as this one, which "resembled the carnival, a form of folk celebration in which the normal rules of social interaction—hierarchical rank, privileges, prohibitions—are temporarily suspended or inverted," had a long history in America, and in Europe before that. See K. Smith, *Dominion of Voice*, 11–50, quotation from 22.

14. Lippincott, "Early Days in Madison County," no. 47, *Alton Telegraph*, 28 July 1865.

15. In a final twist to the story, Coles sought to compensate the unfortunate Hansen by securing him a federal appointment as an Indian agent, but this move was blocked by Secretary of War John C. Calhoun, most likely because of the governor's support for Secretary of the Treasury William H. Crawford, who was competing with Calhoun to succeed Monroe as president. See Calhoun to Coles, 1 September 1823, in Calhoun, *Papers*, 8:251. The presidential election of 1824 is covered in chapter 4.

16. Somewhat conflicting accounts of the proceedings within the legislature are provided in Simeone, *Democracy and Slavery*, 115–32; and Pease, *Centennial History of Illinois*,

2:76–80. Their respective versions may be compared with various contemporary reports in the state's newspapers.

17. Woods, *Two Years' Residence,* 245. The population figures are from Guasco, "Deadly Influence," 16; and Simeone, *Democracy and Slavery,* 60, 71.

18. Flower, *History of the English Settlement,* 199, 201.

19. Thomas Lippincott, "The Conflict of the Century" (MS), 10–11, Lippincott Papers, IHLC.

20. Lippincott, "Early Days in Madison County," no. 37, *Alton Telegraph,* 7 April 1865. A copy of this agreement, with the names of the subscribers, is reprinted in Hair, *Gazetteer of Madison County,* 68. Coles's name does not appear, and Lippincott did not recall his being present at the meeting.

21. W. H. Brown, "Historical Sketch," 25–26.

22. For background on the Illinois press in this period see Hooper, "Decade of Debate." There has been some disagreement over whether the *Illinois Gazette* was pro- or anticonventionist, but most participants in the campaign agreed that it was in the former camp, as would be expected give its proximity to the Salines. The *Illinois Intelligencer* did belatedly switch back to the anticonventionist camp after another change in management, orchestrated by Coles, in May 1824.

23. Lippincott, "Conflict of the Century," 12, Lippincott Papers, IHLC.

24. Birkbeck to Coles, 1 March 1823, reprinted in Washburne, "Sketch of Edward Coles," 142–43.

25. Coles to Birkbeck, 12 April 1823, reprinted in ibid., 144.

26. "Replication by Warren, 10 May 1855," in Alvord, *Governor Edward Coles,* 348–49.

27. "Communicated for the Spectator," *Edwardsville Spectator,* 12 April 1823.

28. "Address of the Monroe Society to the People of the State of Illinois," ibid., 31 May 1823. On the critical role of an informed citizenry in republican thought see R. Brown, *Strength of a People.*

29. Peck to Hooper Warren, 27 March 1855, in Alvord, *Governor Edward Coles,* 334.

30. Lippincott, "Early Days in Madison County," no. 45, *Alton Telegraph,* 14 July 1865.

31. Neem, *Nation of Joiners,* 81–113; Nord, "Evangelical Origins."

32. Beck, *Gazetteer,* 105.

33. *History of Madison County.*

34. "Communicated for the Spectator," *Edwardsville Spectator,* 12 July 1823.

35. Peck to Warren, 27 March 1855, in Alvord, *Governor Edward Coles,* 333–34.

36. These eighteen individuals are named in "Communicated for the Spectator," 12 July 1823, and "Madison Association," 6 January 1824, both in *Edwardsville Spectator.* Biographical information is taken from Lippincott, "Early Days in Madison County," nos. 1–47, *Alton Telegraph,* 26 August 1864–28 July 1865; Churchill, "Annotations," nos. 1–15,

24 March–11 August 1865; *History of Madison County;* Norton, *Centennial History;* various other newspapers articles; and the genealogy collection of the Edwardsville Public Library, Illinois.

37. Lippincott, "Early Days in Madison County," no. 41, *Alton Telegraph,* 12 May 1865.

38. On the importance of local opinion leaders in transient frontier communities see Bourke and DeBats, *Washington County;* and Doyle, *Social Order.*

39. Samuel D. Lockwood served in various high offices in the state before ending up as a justice of the state supreme court.

40. Eames, *Historic Morgan,* 12–14; Pease, *Illinois Election Returns,* 28.

41. Lippincott to Ninian B. Edwards, 16 February 1824, reprinted in Washburne, *Edwards Papers,* 220.

42. "Madison Association," *Edwardsville Spectator,* 6 January 1824.

43. "Communicated for the Spectator," ibid., 12 July 1823.

44. Lippincott, "Conflict of the Century," 15, Lippincott Papers, IHLC.

45. Coles to Lippincott, [1860], in "Edward Coles, Second Governor," 62; Coles to William Barry, 25 June 1858, in Alvord, *Governor Edward Coles,* 374.

46. "Madison Association," *Edwardsville Spectator,* 6 January 1824.

47. Correspondence between Coles, Nicholas Biddle, and Roberts Vaux, 1823–24, reprinted in Washburne, "Sketch of Edward Coles," 120–34.

48. Coles to Birkbeck, 29 January 1824, reprinted in ibid., 148. Coles is likely referring to Birkbeck's *Appeal to the People of Illinois,* which was serialized in the *Edwardsville Spectator* on 11, 18, and 25 October 1823.

49. The pamphlet referred to here is [Lippincott et al.], *To the People of Illinois.* The publication was reported by "No Partizan" in *Kaskaskia Republican,* 6 July 1824.

50. "A Friend to Religion," *Illinois Intelligencer,* 5 July 1823.

51. Horatio Newhall to J. & J. Newhall, 14 April 1824, folder 1, Newhall Letters and Journal, ALPL.

52. Lippincott, "Conflict of the Century," 13–14, Lippincott Papers, IHLC.

53. "The Edgar County Society to the Corresponding Committee of the anti-Conventionists in Lawrence County," folder 1, box 2, Williams-Woodbury Papers, IHLC. More correspondence between the societies is reported in "Madison Association," *Edwardsville Spectator,* 6 January 1824.

54. [Lippincott] to Vaux, 6 October 1823, folder 14, box 2, Vaux Family Papers, HSP.

55. "Madison Association," *Edwardsville Spectator,* 6 January 1824.

56. "Address of the Board Managers of the St. CLAIR SOCIETY to prevent the further introduction of Slavery in the state of Illinois," ibid., 12 April 1823.

57. Tocqueville, *Democracy in America,* 216.

58. Skocpol, Ganz, and Munson, "Nation of Organizers," 539.

59. Peck to Warren, 27 March 1855, in Alvord, *Governor Edward Coles,* 334.

60. Neem, *Nation of Joiners,* 3.

61. Madison, "The Federalist, 10," in Hamilton, Madison, and Jay, *Federalist Papers,* 49.

62. *Constitution of the Middling Interest Association,* 3.

63. Neem, *Nation of Joiners,* 18.

64. "Communicated for the Spectator," *Edwardsville Spectator,* 12 July 1823.

65. "Address of the Monroe Society to the People of the State of Illinois," ibid., 31 May 1823.

66. "Y. Z. Secretary," *Illinois Intelligencer,* 28 June 1823.

67. "Anti-Conventionists," *Edwardsville Spectator,* 16 August 1823.

68. Coles to Vaux, 11 December 1823, folder 14, box 2, Vaux Family Papers, HSP.

69. Coles to Birkbeck, 29 January 1824, reprinted in Washburne, "Sketch of Edward Coles," 149.

70. Untitled report, *Republican Advocate* (Kaskaskia), 8 January 1824; untitled report, *Illinois Intelligencer,* 13 February 1824.

71. "A Voter," *Illinois Intelligencer,* 20 February 1824.

72. Coles to Birkbeck, 29 January 1824, reprinted in Washburne, "Sketch of Edward Coles," 149.

73. When "several of the inhabitants of the United States . . . combine," Tocqueville noted, "from that moment they are no longer isolated men, but a power seen from afar, whose actions serve for an example and whose language is listened to." Tocqueville, *Democracy in America,* 218. For more on the debate over the legitimacy of self-created societies see Fritz, *American Sovereigns,* 175–83; and Koschnik, "Democratic Societies."

74. Horatio Newhall to J. & J. Newhall, 21 May 1823, folder 1, Newhall Letters and Journal, ALPL.

75. Coles to Biddle, 18 September 1823, reprinted in Washburne, "Sketch of Edward Coles," 131.

76. Untitled editorial, *Edwardsville Spectator,* 28 June 1823.

77. "Address of the Monroe Society to the People of the State of Illinois," ibid., 31 May 1823.

78. "Morgan County," ibid., 20 September 1823.

79. Untitled report, ibid., 20 January 1824.

80. "To the Non-Conventionists of Bond, Fayette, and Montgomery Counties," ibid., 27 January 1824.

81. *Edwardsville Spectator,* 10 February–30 March 1824.

82. "To the Voters of Madison," ibid., 13 April 1824.

83. Theophilus W. Smith, the proslavery state senator from Madison County, hinted at conventionist backing for Robinson in a letter to one of his associates. See Smith to Elias

Kent Kane, 28 June 1824, folder 4, box 1, Kane Papers, CHM. The candidacies of Todd and West were announced in the conventionist press. See untitled article, *Edwardsville Spectator*, 25 May 1824 (reprinted from *Illinois Republican* [Edwardsville]). Todd was the uncle of Mary Todd, Abraham Lincoln's future wife.

84. Pease, *Illinois Election Returns*, 198, 201, 211.

85. For other examples of organized nomination see "Communicated," *Illinois Intelligencer*, 13 February 1824 (Fayette, Bond, and Montgomery Counties); untitled editorial, *Edwardsville Spectator*, 13 April 1824 (Gallatin County); and untitled report, ibid., 27 April 1824 (St. Clair County). The Gallatin example appears to be a conventionist measure modeled on that of their opponents in Madison.

86. "St. Clair Anti-Convention Meeting," *Republican Advocate*, 2 March 1824.

87. "Address to the People of Illinois," *Illinois Intelligencer*, 5 March 1824.

88. "To the Non-Conventionists of Bond, Fayette, and Montgomery Counties," *Edwardsville Spectator*, 27 January 1824.

89. *Illinois Republican*, quoted in untitled editorial, *Edwardsville Spectator*, 6 April 1824. For similar examples see "To the Citizens of Fayette, Bond and Montgomery Counties," *Illinois Intelligencer*, 27 February 1824; and "Proscription," *Kaskaskia Republican*, 9 March 1824.

90. "Nathan," *Edwardsville Spectator*, 4 May 1824.

91. Untitled editorial, ibid., 23 March 1824.

92. Untitled editorial, ibid., 6 April 1824.

93. "A Madison Voter," ibid., 10 February 1824.

94. "Jack No Party," ibid., 10 February 1824.

95. "Junius," ibid. 6 July 1824.

96. "To the Non-Conventionists of Bond, Fayette, and Montgomery Counties," ibid., 27 January 1824.

97. "Meeting at Belleville," ibid., 17 February 1824.

98. Untitled editorial, ibid., 13 April 1824.

99. "Vive le Convention," *Kaskaskia Republican*, 13 July 1824.

100. "Junius," *Edwardsville Spectator*, 6 July 1824.

101. "Meeting at Belleville," ibid., 17 February 1824. For more on the practice of organized nominations in the early United States see A. Taylor, "Art of Hook & Snivey."

102. Lippincott, "Conflict of the Century," 35, Lippincott Papers, IHLC.

103. "Convention," *Illinois Intelligencer*, 5 April 1823.

104. "Truth," *Republican Advocate*, 27 February 1823.

105. Untitled editorial, *Edwardsville Spectator*, 9 March 1824.

106. David Blackwell, untitled editorial, *Illinois Intelligencer*, 23 July 1824.

107. "A Friend to ORDER," *Republican Advocate*, 8 March 1823.

108. "Freedom," *Edwardsville Spectator,* 7 June 1823.

109. Coles to Biddle, 18 September 1823, reprinted in Washburne, "Sketch of Edward Coles," 132.

110. As Peter Onuf has argued, both sides "accepted popular sovereignty as an operational premise." Onuf, *Statehood and Union,* 125. This point is obscured by accounts that portray the contest as a struggle between contending forces of aristocracy and democracy. See Guasco, "Deadly Influence"; and Simeone, *Democracy and Slavery.*

111. Lippincott, "Conflict of the Century," 36, Lippincott Papers, IHLC.

112. "Every Man to his tent, O! Israel!!!," *Illinois Republican,* 21 July 1824.

113. *History of Madison County,* 142.

114. Pease, *Illinois Election Returns,* 24–29, 207–16. The conservative estimate assumes that the size of the electorate increased by equal numbers each year between 1820 and 1825, but contemporary sources suggest that immigration virtually ceased for the duration of the campaign, only to explode thereafter. This would make the size of the electorate smaller in 1824 and the turnout correspondingly higher. There were also accusations that a number of anticonventionist votes were spuriously rejected by prejudiced counters, again having the effect of artificially reducing turnout. See Churchill, "Annotations," no. 14, *Alton Telegraph,* 14 July 1865. Other scholars have claimed that turnout was in the high eighties or even into the nineties. Simeone, *Democracy and Slavery,* 134, 245n3; Guasco, "Deadly Influence," 26.

115. Peck to Warren, 27 March 1855, in Alvord, *Governor Edward Coles,* 336–37.

116. Untitled report, *Edwardsville Spectator,* 31 August 1824. On the public functions of toasting see Pasley, "Cheese and the Words," 40–41.

117. Lippincott, "Conflict of the Century," 36–37, Lippincott Papers, IHLC.

118. See, for example, Ress, *Governor Edward Coles;* and Sutton, "Edward Coles." Studies of the rise of the Democrat-Whig party system, conversely, treat the convention contest as something of an aberration that "did not lend [itself] to normal political processes." See Leichtle, "Rise of Jacksonian Politics," quotation from 102; and Leonard, *Invention of Party Politics,* 60–65.

119. Coles, *History of the Ordinance,* 27.

120. Lippincott, "Early Days in Madison County," no. 39, *Alton Telegraph,* 21 April 1865. Lippincott later retreated from this claim somewhat. See Lippincott, "Early Days in Madison County," no. 46, ibid., 21 July 1865.

121. "Address of the Board Managers of the St. CLAIR SOCIETY . . . ," *Edwardsville Spectator,* 12 April 1823.

122. Lippincott, "Early Days in Madison County," no. 37, *Alton Telegraph,* 7 April 1865.

123. Neem, *Nation of Joiners,* 82.

124. Peck to D. L. Phillips, 6 June 1856, published in *Weekly Belleville Advocate,* 13 October 1858, quoted in Bridges, "John Mason Peck," 182.

3. "ASSOCIATE YOURSELVES THROUGHOUT THE NATION"

1. [Carey], *Prefatory Address.*

2. Eldred Simkins, representative from South Carolina, 32 Annals of Cong. 1732 (1818). For more on U.S. tariff policy during this period see Stanwood, *American Tariff Controversies;* and Taussig, *Tariff History.*

3. Rothbard, *Panic of 1819,* 1–23.

4. "Hamilton," "New Series [2nd ser.], No. V. Protection of Manufactures," 3 December 1822, 8, NYHS.

5. Clay, representative from Kentucky, 42 Annals of Cong. 1963 (1824).

6. Memorial of the American Society for the Encouragement of Domestic Manufactures, ASP, 16th Cong., 1st sess., no. 561.

7. Corbin to Littleton Waller Tazewell, 12 April 1820, folder 3, box 4, Tazewell Family Papers, LV.

8. Memorial of the Fredericksburg Agricultural Society, ASP, 16th Cong., 1st sess., no. 564.

9. Peskin, "How the Republicans Learned."

10. See, for example, Lewis, *American Union,* 133; and Forbes, *Missouri Compromise,* 122.

11. Madison to Richard Rush, 4 December 1820, in Madison, *Letters and Other Writings,* 3:195. The patchwork nature of pro- and antitariff sentiment during this period is best captured by Schoen, *Fragile Fabric,* 100–145, although his focus on the Cotton States means that he neglects Virginia's contribution to the campaign against protection.

12. "The Tariff," *Illinois Gazette* (Shawneetown), 10 January 1824.

13. A. Taylor, "Art of Hook & Snivey," 1376.

14. George Holcombe, representative from New Jersey, 42 Annals of Cong. 2382 (1824). The political legitimacy of these three interests was formally recognized by Congress with the separation of the House Committee on Commerce and Manufactures into its two component parts in December 1819 and the creation of the Committee on Agriculture in May 1820.

15. For more on protectionism in the early United States see Eiselen, *Rise of Pennsylvania Protectionism;* and Peskin, *Manufacturing Revolution.*

16. Carey, *Olive Branch,* 11.

17. Carey, *Auto Biographical Sketches;* Carter, "Birth of a Political Economist"; Carter, "Mathew Carey"; Rowe, *Mathew Carey.*

18. Carey, *Auto Biographical Sketches,* 48.

19. Ibid., 46–54; Receipt Book for the Philadelphia Society for the Promotion of

National Industry, Young Family Papers, HSP. Unfortunately, Carey's diary for this period skips from "debated the project of a Society for Promoting national industry" (2 January 1819) to "read Address No. 1 to the Society" (27 March 1819). Diary of Mathew Carey, vol. 27, Gardiner Collection, HSP.

20. "American Manufactures," *Aurora General Advertiser* (Philadelphia), 7 September 1819.

21. The formation and early life of the Pennsylvania Society may be followed in the *Aurora General Advertiser*, August–December 1819, esp. "Public Meeting without Distinction of Party," 21 August; "Public Meeting," 23 August; "American Manufactures," 7 September; "American Manufactures," 8 September; and "National Industry," 26 October. See also Diary of Mathew Carey, vol. 26, Gardiner Collection, HSP.

22. Carey, *Auto Biographical Sketches*, 53–54.

23. Receipt Book for the Philadelphia Society, Young Family Papers, HSP.

24. "Public Meeting without Distinction of Party," *Aurora General Advertiser*, 21 August 1819; untitled notice, ibid., 17 August 1819.

25. Members of the board are listed in "National Industry," ibid., 26 October 1819. Occupations are from Desilver, *Philadelphia Directory*; Oberholtzer, *Philadelphia*; and Whitely, *Philadelphia Directory*.

26. The Federalists were William Tilghman, president; and William Rawle, vice president. The Republicans were Thomas Leiper, vice president; Samuel Richards, treasurer; and John Harrison, secretary.

27. Here my interpretation differs from that of Albrecht Koschnik, who states that Pennsylvania's protectionist associations were dominated by Republicans. Koschnik, *"Let a Common Interest,"* 233–34.

28. John Forbert to William Young, 6 September 1819, folder 3, box 2, Young Correspondence, HSP.

29. "American Manufactures," *Aurora General Advertiser*, 7 September 1819.

30. "Public Meeting," ibid., 23 August 1819.

31. Mathew Carey correspondence, boxes 22–25, 27, Gardiner Collection, HSP.

32. One example is the *Aurora General Advertiser*, whose editor, William Duane, sat on the board of the Pennsylvania Society.

33. In addition to the Pennsylvania Society, state societies were established in Connecticut, Delaware, Maryland, Massachusetts, New Jersey, New York, Ohio, and Rhode Island. *Circular and Address of the National Institution*, 4.

34. "A Friend to Commerce," *Richmond Enquirer*, 14 March 1820 (reprinted from *Boston Daily Advertiser*).

35. Whitman, 36 Annals of Cong. 2002 (1820).

36. "Roanoke Agricultural Society," *Richmond Enquirer*, 5 May 1820.

37. J. Taylor, *Arator*, 40.

38. For more on Taylor see Shalhope, *John Taylor of Caroline*.

39. Some historians have mistakenly assumed that the United Agricultural Societies was a reorganized version of the Virginia Society. This theory is disproved by James Garnett to Merit Moore Robinson, 11 December 1819, box 30, Cocke Family Papers, ASSSCL. Other useful primary sources on Virginia agricultural societies include the Blow Family Papers, EGSL; *Memoirs of the "Society of Virginia"*; True, "Minute book"; *American Farmer* (Baltimore); and *Richmond Enquirer*.

40. "Constitution of the Roanoke Agricultural Society," *American Farmer*, 4 November 1820.

41. "An Address to the United Agricultural Societies of Virginia, from their delegates, in general meeting assembled," ibid., 19 January 1821. Not all agricultural-society members were so enthusiastic about taking on the protectionists. John Hartwell Cocke declined the presidency of the Virginia Society when it was offered to him in 1819, observing to a friend that "there is a measure on foot . . . to get up a memorial from the Agricultural Society to Congress upon the subject of commercial regulations—which if carried & followed up by similar proceedings will convert the Agricultural Society into a hot bed for hatching politicks." Cocke to J. Cabell, 17 January 1820, folder 4, box 4, Cabell Family Papers, ASSSCL.

42. James M. Garnett, the president of the Fredericksburg Agricultural Society, made this point explicitly. See "An Address to the Virginia Agricultural Society of Fredericksburg," *American Farmer*, 11 and 18 February 1820. On the connection between landowning and republican citizenship in early nineteenth-century Virginia see Curtis, "Reconsidering Suffrage Reform."

43. *Memoirs of the "Society of Virginia*," xi–xiii; "Constitution of the United Agricultural Societies of Virginia," *American Farmer*, 19 January 1821.

44. Blow, speech before the Sussex Agricultural Society, n.d., folder 1, box 14, Blow Family Papers, EGSL.

45. Blow to the editor of the *Farmers' Register* [Edmund Ruffin], n.d., folder 7, box 30, ibid. See also Blow to Ruffin, n.d., folder 5, box 20, ibid.

46. Taylor resigned from the presidency of the Virginia Agricultural Society in 1819 due to infirmity and declined membership in the United Agricultural Societies for the same reason. But old age did not prevent him from publishing three substantial monographs in the years 1820–23 that ranged over a number of subjects, including his opposition to protection: *Construction Construed*; *Tyranny Unmasked*; and *New Views*.

47. The first of Ruffin's three autobiographical volumes, which covers this period of his life, has not survived. He did, however, assist a friend in preparing a sketch of his life for publication in 1851, which includes a brief account of his antitariff activities. See William

Boulware, "Edwin [*sic*] Ruffin, of Virginia, Agriculturalist, Embracing a View of Agricultural Progress in Virginia for the Last Thirty Years. With a Portrait," *De Bow's Review* 11 (1851): 431–36, reprinted in Ruffin, *Incidents of My Life,* app. 1; and Mitchell, *Edmund Ruffin.*

48. Garnett wrote so frequently on the tariff that his old friend John Randolph, representative from Virginia, complained that "time was when I could occasionally get a sight of your Hieroglyphicks, but I believe you now reserve them entirely for the use of Mathew Carey." Randolph to Garnett, 6 July 1823, reel 4, Garnett-Randolph correspondence, Bruce Collection, LV.

49. J. Taylor, *Tyranny Unmasked,* 291.

50. Garnett to Randolph, 27 January 1824, reel 4, Garnett-Randolph correspondence, Bruce Collection, LV.

51. "American Independence," *Richmond Enquirer,* 16 July 1819.

52. "The Memorial Of the 'Virginia Society for promoting Agriculture' to the Congress of the U. States, in opposition to the several Memorials and Petitions praying for additional duties upon Foreign Imports," *Richmond Enquirer,* 19 February 1820; numerous petitions in ASP, 16th Cong., 1st sess.

53. "Congress," *Richmond Enquirer,* 19 May 1820. For more on the practical advantages that the associational model offered as an alternative to parties see Voss-Hubbard, *Beyond Party.*

54. "American Manufactures," *Aurora General Advertiser,* 12 November 1819.

55. *Proceedings of a Convention of the Friends of National Industry,* quotation from 6.

56. *Circular and Address of the National Institution;* Young to Carey, 19 and 25 January 1820, folder 3, box 24, and Jacob T. Walden to Carey, 3 and 22 February 1820, folder 2, box 24, all in Gardiner Collection, HSP.

57. "Proceedings Of a Convention of the *Friends of National Industry,* at a meeting in this city on the 7th instant, and of the *National Institution for the Promotion of Industry,* after it was organized by the Convention," *Patron of Industry* (New York), 28 June 1820.

58. "The Chamber of Commerce of the City of Philadelphia," no. 31, vol. 24, Rush Family Papers, LCP, on deposit at HSP.

59. Circular letter of the Tariff Committee of the Philadelphia Chamber of Commerce, reprinted in "Tariff," *Richmond Enquirer,* 11 August 1820.

60. Philadelphia Chamber of Commerce Tariff Committee scrapbook, 1820, HSP.

61. James Neal et al. (Committee of Correspondence) to John Vaughan, August 1820; unknown writer to Robert Ralston, 22 August 1820; Isaac [?] to Vaughan, 22 July 1820; William Nott to Ralston, 21 August 1820, all in ibid.

62. "Meeting of the citizens of Norfolk and Portsmouth," and Thomas Rutherfoord to Vaughan, 26 October 1820, both in ibid.

63. "At a numerous meeting of the merchants and agriculturalists of Fredericksburg," ibid.

64. For details of the proceedings see "The Tariff," 7 November 1820; untitled report, 10 November 1820; "Philadelphia, Nov. 7," 14 November 1820; untitled editorial, 9 December 1820; and "Address to the Agricultural Society of Virginia," 18 January 1821, all in *Richmond Enquirer.*

65. Untitled editorial, *Patron of Industry,* 19 May 1821 (reprinted from the *Pittsburgh Gazette*).

66. Peter H. Schenck to Carey, 9 December 1819, folder 1, box 24, Gardiner Collection, HSP. For examples of the National Institution's work see "Address, &c.," *Patron of Industry,* 16 December 1820; and "To the Honourable the Senate and House of Representatives of the United States, in Congress Assembled," ibid., 13 January 1821.

67. "Proceedings Of a Convention of the *Friends of National Industry* . . . ," *Patron of Industry,* 28 June 1820.

68. Nord, "Evangelical Origins."

69. The Anti-Masons are credited with holding the first national party convention, in 1830. It was attended by delegates from ten states and one territory, although 70 percent of those present came from New York, Massachusetts, and Pennsylvania. Chase, *Emergence,* 148–49.

70. On the importance of "voluntary federations" throughout the history of the United States see Skocpol, Ganz, and Munson, "Nation of Organizers."

71. "Proceedings Of a Convention of the *Friends of National Industry* . . . ," *Patron of Industry,* 28 June 1820.

72. "Prospectus," ibid.

73. More information on the *Patron* can be found in the letters of Eleazar Lord (the editor) to Mathew Carey, boxes 23 and 24, Gardiner Collection, HSP. Three years later, with the tariff issue once again before Congress, Carey would engage in his own editorial project, a sixteen-page weekly magazine entitled *The Political Economist.* This venture proved even less successful than its predecessor, closing after only four months. Carey, *Auto Biographical Sketches,* 108–11. In Boston, Joseph Buckingham also began publication of a new paper around this time, the *Boston Courier,* whose main function would be to advocate protection. Buckingham, *Personal Memoirs,* 2:3–5.

74. Garnett to Randolph, 3 October 1817, reel 4, Garnett-Randolph correspondence, Bruce Collection, LV.

75. Editorial comments on "A Maryland Farmer," *American Farmer,* 14 July 1820.

76. "Once For All!," ibid., 14 May 1819.

77. Untitled editorial, ibid., 22 March 1822.

78. "A Citizen—but no merchant," writing in the *Richmond Compiler,* quoted in "The Tariff," *Patron of Industry,* 16 August 1820.

79. The meetings are reported in the *Richmond Enquirer,* August–September 1820, and the petitions are reprinted in ASP.

80. Untitled editorial, *Richmond Enquirer,* 22 August 1820.

81. Bailey, *Popular Influence,* 56; Higginson, "Short History," 144–45. Other useful studies of petitioning in the early United States include Bogin, "Petitioning"; Cunningham, *Process of Government,* 294–321; diGiacomantonio, "Petitioners and Their Grievances"; John and Young, "Rites of Passage"; Mark, "The Vestigial Constitution"; and Morgan, *Inventing the People,* 223–30.

82. Pincus, *Pressure Groups,* 53.

83. Memorial of the citizens of New Bedford, no. 680; Memorial of the inhabitants of Nantucket, no. 681; and Memorial of the tallow chandlers and soap boilers of Boston, no. 685, all in ASP, 18th Cong., 1st sess.

84. Carey, *View of the Ruinous Consequences,* x.

85. Baldwin, 37 Annals of Cong. 466–68 (1820). The offending passage from which Baldwin quoted may be founded in *Memorial of the Merchants and Other Citizens of Richmond,* 10.

86. Untitled editorial, *Richmond Enquirer,* 9 December 1820.

87. "A Repentant Citizen," ibid., 12 December 1820.

88. Tyler, 37 Annals of Cong. 673–76 (1820).

89. Ruth Bogin also charts this change in the character of petitions following independence. Bogin, "Petitioning." For the reaction to Tyler's speech see untitled editorial, *Richmond Enquirer,* 21 December 1820. For Baldwin's change in tone see "Report Of the Committee on Manufactures, on the various Memorials praying for, and remonstrating against, an increase of the duties on imports," *Weekly Aurora* (Philadelphia), 5 February 1821, and successive issues. This confrontation apparently marked the beginning of a beautiful friendship between Baldwin and Tyler. See Tyler to John Rutherfoord, 24 November 1858, LV.

90. "A Dream," *Patron of Industry,* 7 March 1821.

91. Smith, 41 Annals of Cong. 738–43 (1824).

92. Jonathan Roberts to Mathew Roberts, 5 May 1820, folder 12, box 3, Roberts Papers, HSP.

93. Smith, quoted in "Extract from a Member of Congress, to the Editor of the Baltimore Patriot, dated Washington, May 7, 1820," *Weekly Aurora,* 22 May 1820.

94. Lord to Carey, 4 April 1820, folder 4, box 23, Gardiner Collection, HSP. See also Henry Baldwin to Carey, 22 February 1820, folder 2, box 23, ibid.; and on the free-trade side, "Address of James M. Garnett, Esq., President of the Fredericksburg Agricultural Society, delivered at their last Semi-annual meeting, at the Farmers' Hotel, in Fredericksburg, on Tuesday the 23d of May, 1820," *American Farmer,* 16 June 1820.

95. See Memorial of the Pennsylvania Society, ASP, 16th Cong., 1st sess., no. 590; and Memorial of the Board of Managers of the Pennsylvania Society, ASP, 18th Cong., 1st sess., no. 703.

96. Memorial of the inhabitants of the city of Philadelphia, no. 572; Memorial of the citizens of Pennsylvania, no. 569; and Memorial of a convention of the friends of national industry, no. 560, all in ASP, 16th Cong., 1st sess.

97. Davis, "Lobbying," 268.

98. Gulian C. Verplanck, *The State Triumvirate, A Political Tale* (New York, 1819), 44, 67–68, quoted in Pasley, "Private Access," 77n. Lobbying in the early republic is still a relatively neglected topic. In addition to the two articles cited above, the best account is Bowers, "From Logrolling to Corruption."

99. Schenck to Carey, 15 December 1819, folder 1, box 24, Gardiner Collection, HSP. For a similar plan see John Harrison to Carey, 13 September 1819, folder 3, box 23, ibid.

100. Some scholars have claimed that both Raguet's mission and the subsequent one of John Harrison were sponsored by the Philadelphia Society, but neither was a member of that organization and no indication of any such payment may be found in its financial records. Receipt Book for the Philadelphia Society, Young Family Papers, HSP.

101. Raguet to Carey and Samuel Jackson, 30 December 1819, folder 8, box 22, Gardiner Collection, HSP.

102. For more on the importance of informal politicking and the opportunity it offered for even disenfranchised groups to participate in public decision making, see Allgor, *Parlor Politics*.

103. John Harrison to Lydia Harrison, 12 January 1820, Leib-Harrison Family Papers, Society Small Collection, HSP.

104. Schenck to Carey, 3 January 1820, folder 1, box 25, Gardiner Collection, HSP; John Harrison to Carey, 24 January 1820, folder 23, box 23, ibid.

105. Lord to Carey, 11 January 1820, folder 4, box 23, ibid.

106. Lord to Carey, 27 February 1820, ibid.

107. See Lord letters to Carey, folders 4–5, ibid.

108. "To C. C. Cambreleng, Esq." (concluded and signed "Marcus" in the next issue), *Aurora General Advertiser*, 23 April 1824. Though this letter relates specifically to the 1824 tariff bill, similar claims reportedly were made about its predecessor in 1820. Stanwood, *American Tariff Controversies*, 1:181–82.

109. Daniel Webster, quoted in Prince and Taylor, "Daniel Webster," 287.

110. "Boston Notions," *Patron of Industry*, 18 October 1820. Webster was not in Congress in 1820, but he did address a public antitariff meeting in Boston that year. See "General Meeting," *Columbian Centinel*, 4 October 1820.

111. Prince and Taylor, "Daniel Webster," 291.

112. Webster to Nathan Appleton, 12 January 1824, and Webster to Edward Everett, 13 February 1824, in Webster, *Papers*, 1:347–48 and 352, quotation from the latter.

113. Perkins to Webster, 26 January 1824, in ibid., 1:348. Even after the bill had passed its third reading in the House, Perkins wrote again to request that Webster delay the new tariff's taking effect in order that his ships might reach port while the duties remained low. Perkins to Webster, 12 May 1824, ibid., 1:360.

114. Nathan Appleton to Samuel Appleton, 1 May 1824, folder 13, box 3, Appleton Family Papers, MHS.

115. Remarkably, the only member of Congress to argue that protection for manufactures was unconstitutional in 1820 was not a southerner but Webster's Massachusetts colleague Ezekiel Whitman. See Whitman, representative from Massachusetts, 36 Annals of Cong. 1998–2008 (1820), and the reply of Henry Clay, representative from Kentucky, 36 Annals of Cong. 2049 (1820).

116. Bowers characterizes lobbying as "both an expression of democracy and a threat to it." "From Logrolling to Corruption," 441.

117. Henry Lee to Carey, 11 February 1820, folder 4, box 23, Gardiner Collection, HSP. The twelve in question were Henry Brush (Rep., OH), Mahlon Dickerson (Sen., NJ), Edward Dowse (Rep., MA), John Holmes (Rep., MA), William Hunter (Sen., RI), Richard M. Johnson (Sen., KY), Thomas Newton (Rep., VA), John Russ (Rep., CT), Nathan Sanford (Sen., NY), Nathaniel Silsbee (Rep., MA), Henry R. Storrs (Rep., NY), and James Wilson (Sen., NJ). Holmes and Silsbee were the only two to vote against the Baldwin bill. William Woodbridge was also on the list, but as a delegate to Congress from the territory of Michigan he was not eligible to vote.

118. Fennimore and Wagner, *Silversmiths to the Nation*, 155–56.

119. "Virginius," *Richmond Enquirer*, 12 May 1820.

120. "Fourth of July," ibid., 14 July 1820.

121. "The Tariff," ibid., 19 September 1820.

122. "Virginius," ibid., 12 May 1820.

123. Virginia 1821 U.S. House of Representatives, District 21, NNV.

124. Untitled editorial, *Patron of Industry*, 22 November 1820.

125. Walden to Carey, 3 February 1820, folder 2, box 24, Gardiner Collection, HSP.

126. Schenck to Carey, 7 March 1821, folder 1, box 25, ibid.

127. Forbert to Young, 22 September 1819, folder 3, box 2, Young Correspondence, HSP.

128. [Carey], *Prefatory Address*.

129. Carey, *Auto Biographical Sketches*, 74. For the opinions of his friends see Schenck to Carey, 15 March 1820, folder 1, box 24, and Hezekiah Niles to Carey, 21 April 1820, folder 6, box 23, Gardiner Collection, HSP.

130. Forbert to Young, 6 September 1819, folder 3, box 2, Young Correspondence, HSP. Forbert does not identify the representative he is referring to.

131. "An Injured Manufacturer," *Weekly Aurora,* 15 May 1820.

132. Untitled editorial in reply to "An Injured Manufacturer," ibid.

133. "Public Meeting," *Aurora General Advertiser,* 28 September 1822.

134. "Public Meeting," ibid., 2 October 1822.

135. "The Election," ibid., 3 October 1822.

136. "Take Your Choice," ibid., 7 October 1822. For two different but equally amusing accounts that suggest the truth of Duane's claims see the entry for 10 August 1819 in Diary of Samuel Breck, vol. 3, Breck Family Papers, LCP, on deposit at HSP; and "Peter Atall," *Hermit in Philadelphia,* 98–111.

137. "The Election," *Aurora General Advertiser,* 9 October 1822.

138. 1822 U.S. House of Representatives, Pennsylvania District 2, NNV. The protectionist vote given here is the combined figure for Adam Seybert and William J. Duane, as two different versions of the ticket were circulated at the polls.

139. "Remarks," *Aurora General Advertiser,* 17 October 1822.

140. See "Election," 8 October 1822; "The Election," 9 October 1822; "The Election," 10 October 1822; and "Remarks," 17 October 1822, all in ibid.

141. Untitled editorial, *Patron of Industry,* 28 April 1821. For more on the New York effort see "Public Meeting," 21 April 1821, and untitled editorial, 25 April 1821, both in ibid.

142. "The Middling Interest," *Aurora General Advertiser,* 16 October 1822. Of course one important difference between Philadelphia and Boston was that popular sentiment in the latter was strongly in favor of free trade. As mentioned in chapter 1, one of the catalysts for the Middling Interest protest was the vote of Boston's congressman *for* the Baldwin bill in 1820.

143. Timothy Fuller to Lemuel Shaw, 7 March 1822, reel 5, Shaw Papers, MHS.

144. "Petition, &c. To the Senate and House of Representatives of the United States, in Congress assembled, the petition of the Agricultural Societies of Prince George, Sussex, Surry, Petersburg, Dinwiddie, Isle of Wight, and Nottoway respectfully sheweth," *American Farmer,* 4 January 1822.

145. "An Inhabitant of the South," *Letter to the Honorable James Brown,* 23–24. For more on the tariff as an issue in the presidential election of 1824 see chapter 4.

146. "Address of J. M. Garnett, Esq. President of the Fredericksburgh Agricultural Society—delivered at their Exhibition at Fredericksburgh, on the 12th and 13th of November last," *American Farmer,* 2 January 1824.

147. "Ruris Consultus," "Letter III—and Last," *American Farmer,* 20 February 1824. Garnett appears to claim authorship of the "Ruris Consultus" series in Garnett to Randolph, 26 December 1823, reel 4, Garnett-Randolph correspondence, Bruce Collection, LV.

148. *Memorial of the Citizens of Richmond and Manchester; Memorial of Sundry Inhabitants of Petersburg.*

149. "An Ex-Member," *Farmers' Register* (Shellbanks), September 1833. On a similar theme see Blow to Ruffin, n.d., folder 7, box 30, Blow Family Papers, EGSL.

150. Carey, *Auto Biographical Sketches*, 71. For more on the breakup of the Philadelphia Society see Carey's correspondence and diary from this period in the Gardiner Collection, HSP.

151. Tilghman's correspondence is at the HSP.

152. See, for example, Memorial of the Board of Managers of the Pennsylvania Society, ASP, 18th Cong., 1st sess., no. 703.

153. Churchill C. Cambreleng, representative from New York, 41 Annals of Cong. 1481 (1824).

154. Hamilton, 42 Annals of Cong. 2206 (1824). See also Cambreleng, 41 Annals of Cong. 1578 (1824).

155. T. Benton, *Thirty Years' View*, 1:34; 41 Annals of Cong. 751 (1824).

156. 42 Annals of Cong. 2429–30 (1824).

157. Webster to Joseph Story, 10 April 1824, in Webster, *Papers*, 1:357.

158. Hays, "Political Parties," 169.

159. [Carey], *Prefatory Address*.

160. "Roanoke Agricultural Society," *Richmond Enquirer*, 5 May 1820.

161. Carey, *View of the Ruinous Consequences*, viii.

4. "YOU MUST ORGANIZE AGAINST ORGANIZATION"

1. Calhoun to George Jackson, 29 December 1823, in Calhoun, *Papers*, 8:430.

2. Silbey, *American Political Nation*, 27–28. See also Aldrich, *Why Parties?*, 4–5; and Schudson, *Good Citizen*, 110.

3. William H. Crawford to Albert Gallatin, 12 March 1817, in Gallatin, *Writings*, 2:27.

4. Untitled editorial, *Kaskaskia Republican*, 6 April 1824.

5. "Address by Senator Benjamin Ruggles," 404.

6. King to Gore, 9 February 1823, in King, *Life and Correspondence*, 6:499.

7. Calhoun to Virgil Maxcy, 2 August 1822, in Calhoun, *Papers*, 7:231.

8. On the model republican candidate see Heale, *Presidential Quest*.

9. *Sketch of the Life of John Quincy Adams*, 16.

10. Entry for 2 May 1820, in Adams, *Memoirs*, 5:90.

11. Calhoun, quoted in "Carolina," *Address to the Citizens of North-Carolina*, 13.

12. "A Citizen of New-York," *Address to the Republicans*, 10.

13. *Nashville Gazette*, quoted in "General Jackson," *Richmond Enquirer*, 30 July 1822.

14. John A. Dix to [George C. Shattuck], 22 February 1824, folder "January–June," box 2, Shattuck Papers, MHS.

15. *Address of the Committee Appointed by a Republican Meeting*, 8.

16. "Wyoming," *Letters of Wyoming*, 67. For more on Crawford's role in the passage of the Tenure of Office Act see Ammon, *James Monroe*, 494–95.

17. According to Richard John, "By *creating* a mechanism for the periodic replacement of a substantial fraction of the civil government, rotation established the material basis for the mass party as a self-perpetuating organization." John, "Affairs of Office." John was of course writing about changes that occurred under Jackson, but his conclusion seems equally applicable to this earlier period. On the importance of patronage to party builders see also Allgor, *Parlor Politics;* and Altschuler and Blumin, *Rude Republic*, 38–46.

18. Entry for 6 January 1822, in Adams, *Memoirs*, 5:482–84.

19. Edwards to Henry Eddy, 22 November 1822, folder 1, box 1, Eddy Papers, IHLC. Article I, Section 6, of the United States Constitution states that "no Senator or Representative shall, during the Time for which he was elected, be appointed to any civil Office under the Authority of the United States which shall have been created, or the Emoluments whereof shall have been increased during such time; and no Person holding any Office under the United States, shall be a Member of either House during his Continuance in Office."

20. Entry for 26 August 1822, in Adams, *Memoirs*, 6:56. See also entries for 28 July and 9 September 1822 in the same volume; and C. Smith, *Press, Politics, and Patronage*, 56–77.

21. Lowndes, quoted in Langdon Cheves to Henry Clay, 9 November 1822, in Clay, *Papers*, 3:314.

22. Fitzpatrick, "Autobiography of Martin Van Buren," 123–24.

23. For a more detailed discussion of Van Buren's political philosophy see Leonard, *Invention of Party Politics*, 35–47; and Wallace, "Changing Concepts."

24. Fitzpatrick, "Autobiography of Martin Van Buren," 131.

25. Mooney, *William H. Crawford*, 240–42.

26. "Address by Senator Benjamin Ruggles," 401–4.

27. "A Republican," *American Mercury* (Hartford), 21 January 1823.

28. "A Republican," "No. IV," *Carolina Gazette* (Charleston), 3 April 1824.

29. Gallatin to Walter Lowrie, 22 May 1824, in Gallatin, *Writings*, 2:290–91.

30. Kane to Jesse B. Thomas, 8 January 1824, folder 4, Thomas Papers, ALPL.

31. Ibid.

32. Jonathan Roberts to Mathew Roberts, 20 December 1823, folder 16, box 3, Roberts Papers, HSP.

33. Hay, "Pillorying of Albert Gallatin."

34. Kane to Thomas, 8 January 1824, folder 4, Thomas Papers, ALPL.

35. Lowell to Otis, 26 February 1823, reel 8, Otis Papers, MHS.

36. This point is important because previous accounts of the emergence of a proparty

philosophy have tended to focus on Van Buren to the exclusion of other sources. See, for example, Leonard, *Invention of Party Politics*.

37. On the disputed etymology of the Radical label see Rigali, "Restoring the Republic," 56–61.

38. Calhoun to Joseph G. Swift, 26 October 1823, in Calhoun, *Papers*, 8:329.

39. Calhoun to Swift, 14 October 1823, in ibid., 8:313.

40. Calhoun to George Jackson, 29 December 1823, in ibid., 8:430.

41. Calhoun to Samuel D. Ingham, 25 June 1823, in ibid., 8:131.

42. Calhoun to Cass, 14 October 1823, in ibid., 8:312.

43. "Questions and Answers on the Presidency," *Aurora General Advertiser*, 27 September 1824 (reprinted from the *Cincinnati Gazette*).

44. *Sketch of the Life of John Quincy Adams*, 16, 25.

45. "Gen. Jackson," *Aurora General Advertiser*, 13 April 1824.

46. Remini, *Andrew Jackson*, 77–78. See also Hay, "Case for Andrew Jackson."

47. "Wyoming," *Letters of Wyoming*, 89, 23. In fact, Jackson would soon be in Washington too, for he was elected to the United States Senate by the Tennessee legislature a few months after the "Letters" were first serialized in the press.

48. Ibid., 62, 71, 46.

49. Clay, quoted in Remini, *Henry Clay*, 252.

50. "Wyoming," *Letters of Wyoming*, 22.

51. Jackson to Andrew Jackson Donelson, 6 August 1822, in Jackson, *Papers*, 5:213.

52. Eaton to John Coffee, 20 November 1823, John Coffee Papers, Tennessee Historical Society, Nashville, quoted in Coens, "Formation of the Jackson Party," 182.

53. Entry for 25 April 1824, in Adams, *Memoirs*, 6:307. See also Lowe, "John H. Eaton."

54. Clay, *Papers*, vol. 3.

55. See correspondence between Johnston and Clay in ibid.; and Johnston Papers, HSP.

56. Johnston to Clay, 22 September 1824, in Clay, *Papers*, 3:844–45.

57. See, for example, Wilentz, *Rise of American Democracy*, chap. 9, "The Aristocracy and Democracy of America."

58. Joseph Hopkinson to Louisa Catherine Adams, [1822], in Adams, *Memoirs*, 6:130–32.

59. Adams to Hopkinson, 23 January 1823, in ibid., 6:132–37.

60. Adams, *Memoirs*, vols. 5 and 6. On his wife's contribution to the campaign see Allgor, *Parlor Politics*, 147–89.

61. Entry for 26 August 1822, in Adams, *Memoirs*, 6:56.

62. Ames and Olson, "Washington's Political Press," 346–49.

63. Adams to Hopkinson, 23 January 1823, in Adams, *Memoirs*, 6:135.

64. Calhoun to Maxcy, 14 April and 25 November 1823, both in Calhoun, *Papers*, 8:20, 379.

65. Calhoun to Samuel L. Gouverneur, 25 May 1823, in ibid., 8:74.

66. Calhoun to Swift, 16 November 1823, in ibid., 8:367.

67. "Roanoke Agricultural Society," *Richmond Enquirer*, 5 May 1820; Coles to Birkbeck, 29 January 1824, reprinted in Washburne, "Sketch of Edward Coles," 149.

68. For more on the notion of "partisan antipartisanship" see A. Smith, *No Party Now*, 15–20; and Waldstreicher, *In the Midst*, 201–16.

69. Chase, *Emergence*, 1–66.

70. "Virginius," *Richmond Enquirer*, 6 August 1824.

71. "Declaration of New York Republican Caucus," 398.

72. Entry for 19 November 1823, in Adams, *Memoirs*, 6:191.

73. Entry for 24 January 1824, in ibid., 6:235.

74. See, for example, Calhoun to Ingham, 1 June 1823, in Calhoun, *Papers*, 8:81.

75. For a typical example of Jackson's opinions on this subject see Andrew Jackson to John Donelson, 9 February 1824, in Jackson, *Papers*, 5:354–55. For evidence that Jackson's friends were less consistent in their opposition to caucuses see Isaac L. Baker to Jackson, 14 February 1823, in Jackson, *Correspondence*, 3:187.

76. Daniel Webster to Ezekiel Webster, 4 December 1823, in Webster, *Papers*, 1:337. See also "A Caucus," *Trenton Federalist*, 24 November 1823.

77. "A South-Carolinean," *Some Objections to Mr. Crawford*, 19.

78. *Proceedings of the Convention, assembled at Harrisburg*, 8.

79. "The Caucus," *Richmond Enquirer*, 19 February 1824.

80. Untitled article, *Richmond Enquirer*, 10 February 1824 (reprinted from the *National Intelligencer*).

81. *Niles' Weekly Register* (Baltimore), 13 March 1824, cited in Remini, *Henry Clay*, 236–37.

82. "The Caucus," *New-England Galaxy*, 27 February 1824. The nominations received by Crawford's opponents are detailed in Chase, *Emergence*, 51.

83. "Belthazar," *Baltimore Patriot & Mercantile Advertiser*, 29 October 1823.

84. "Caucus and Convention," *Washington Republican*, 16 February 1824, cited in Coens, "Formation of the Jackson Party," 175.

85. *National Gazette* (Philadelphia), 26 February 1824, cited in ibid., 193.

86. "Atticus," *A few considerations*, 7.

87. Chase, *Emergence*, 52–58.

88. This point is emphasized in R. P. McCormick, *Second American Party System*, 94–95, 346–49; and Pessen, "We Are All Jeffersonians," 21–22. It is important because subscribers to the celebratory narrative tend to take the populist rhetoric of the anticaucus, proconvention contingent at face value.

89. Timothy Fuller, representative from Massachusetts, quoted in entry for 2 May 1820, in Adams, *Memoirs*, 5:89.

90. "Nominations," *Columbian Centinel,* 2 October 1824; "Presidential Election Prospects," ibid., 16 October 1824.

91. "Adams Meeting in Boston," ibid., 27 October 1824; "Adams Vote Distributors," ibid., 30 October 1824.

92. Henry Shaw to Clay, 4 October 1824, in Clay, *Papers,* 3:858.

93. "Presidential Election Prospects," *Columbian Centinel,* 16 October 1824.

94. "To the Federal Republicans of Massachusetts," October 1824, ABE.

95. Untitled editorial, *Boston Patriot & Daily Mercantile Advertiser,* 21 October 1824.

96. For this and all other voting figures for the 1824 presidential election given in this chapter see Dubin, *United States Presidential Elections.*

97. Entry for 3 January 1822, in Adams, *Memoirs,* 5:478.

98. Henry Shaw to Clay, 11 February 1823, in Clay, *Papers,* 3:373.

99. "Boston Federalists," *Columbian Centinel,* 27 October 1824.

100. "Political," *New-England Galaxy,* 29 October 1824.

101. Johnston to Clay, 19 August 1824, in Clay, *Papers,* 3:816.

102. Hamilton, *Reminiscences,* 62. Hamilton rejected Calhoun's advances in favor of Crawford.

103. Klein, *Pennsylvania Politics,* 166–69.

104. Wire, "John M. Clayton," 259–60.

105. Daniel Webster to Jeremiah Mason, 9 May 1824, in Webster, *Papers,* 1:358.

106. Edward Patchell to James Hall, 4 September 1823, folder 2, box 1, Eddy Papers, IHLC. The role played by Federalists in the 1824 election is discussed in Livermore, *Twilight of Federalism,* 132–96.

107. The power of the Richmond Junto is debated by Ammon, "Richmond Junto"; and F. Miller, "Richmond Junto."

108. Calhoun to John George Jackson, 29 December 1823, in Calhoun, *Papers,* 8:430. Albany Regency was another name given to Van Buren's Bucktails by their critics.

109. "Legislative Caucus," *Richmond Enquirer,* 24, 26, 28 February 1824.

110. "To the People of Virginia" and "Circular," 18 June 1824; "Crawford Ticket," 1 October 1824; "Address to the Citizens of Virginia" and "To the County Committees," 16 October 1824; and "To the People of Virginia," 19 October 1824, all in ibid.

111. "To the County Committees," ibid., 16 October 1824.

112. Newsome, *Presidential Election.*

113. Daniel Call to Clay, 30 June 1824, and Francis T. Brooke to Clay, 12 July 1824, in Clay, *Papers,* 3:789–90 and 793–94.

114. "Henry Clay," *Richmond Enquirer,* 12 March 1824. On attendance at the Clay caucus see Thomas Rutherfoord to Andrew Stevenson, 4 April 1824, vol. 1, Stevenson Papers, LC.

115. Brooke to Clay, 15 October 1824, in Clay, *Papers*, 3:867.

116. Calhoun had by this point been removed from contention by events elsewhere, as we will see shortly.

117. "Fredericksburg, June 18," *Richmond Enquirer*, 18 June 1824.

118. "Jackson Convention" and untitled editorial, both in ibid., 3 August 1824.

119. "To the friends of John Quincy Adams in Virginia," ibid., 8 August 1824.

120. Clifft, "Politics of Transition," app. 2. See also *Richmond Enquirer*, March–October 1824.

121. Untitled editorial, *Richmond Enquirer*, 6 August 1824.

122. "A Looker-On," ibid., 23 March 1824.

123. "Roanoke," in *Presidential Election* (n.p., n.d), 11. See also Rufus King to J. A. King, January 1823, in King, *Life and Correspondence*, 6:496–97.

124. This is evident from both the private correspondence of the candidates and the public statements issued by their supporters on their behalf in pamphlets and newspapers.

125. Garnett to Randolph, 27 January 1824, reel 4, Garnett-Randolph correspondence, Bruce Collection, LV. Edmund Ruffin made a similar complaint against Crawford in the columns of the *Enquirer*. See "A Farmer," *Richmond Enquirer*, 13 June 1823.

126. *Pennsylvania Intelligencer*, 1 April 1823, quoted in Phillips, "Pennsylvania Origins," 503.

127. It is not clear how many clubs were founded during the campaign, but certainly they were active in Philadelphia and in Baltimore. See Scharf and Westcott, *History of Philadelphia*, 1:610; and "Jackson Meeting," *Baltimore Patriot & Mercantile Advertiser*, 7 January 1824, quotation from the latter.

128. Robert Patterson to Ingham, 31 December 1823, in Calhoun, *Papers*, 8:438.

129. "A Democrat of '98," *Franklin Gazette* (Philadelphia), 6 February 1824, quoted in Phillips, "Pennsylvania Origins," 503.

130. *Proceedings of the Convention, assembled at Harrisburg.*

131. Jonathan Roberts to Mathew Roberts, 5 March 1824, folder 18, box 3, Roberts Papers, HSP.

132. Untitled report, *Aurora General Advertiser*, 13 August 1824; "Crawford Convention," ibid., 18 August 1824 (reprinted from the *Harrisburg Chronicle*).

133. See *Aurora General Advertiser*, September–November 1824; and correspondence between Clay and Johnston, August–October 1824, in Clay, *Papers*, vol. 3.

134. Fitzpatrick, "Autobiography of Martin Van Buren," 240.

135. "General Jackson," *Mercury* (Pittsburgh), 12 August 1823.

136. Jackson to Littleton H. Coleman, 26 April 1824, in Jackson, *Papers*, 5:398.

137. Clay, quoted in Fitzpatrick, "Autobiography of Martin Van Buren," 240.

138. Van Buren, c. 1824, quoted in T. Benton, *Thirty Years' View*, 1:34. It is striking that Van Buren, often identified as the chief architect of the modern political party, should urge the separation of policymaking from the vagaries of partisan competition.

139. Entries for 21 March 1823 and 29 March 1823, Diary of Mathew Carey, UoP.

140. William Ingalls to Johnston, 18 September 1824, folder 6, box 2, Johnston Papers, HSP; Johnston to Clay, 19 August, 4 September, and 11 September 1824, in Clay, *Papers*, 3:814–16, 829, 836–37. Johnston's efforts to recruit Carey presumably were not helped by the fact that four months previously he had been rebuked by the Philadelphian for voting against the 1824 tariff bill. See Carey to Johnston, 8 May 1824, folder 2, box 2, Johnston Papers, HSP.

141. Kehl, *Ill Feeling*, 213–22; Joseph Nancrede to James Ronaldson, 29 July 1829, Stern Papers, UoD.

142. Thomas I. Wharton to Clay, 13 August 1823, in Clay, *Papers*, 3:467.

143. [?] Sheppard to Andrew Stevenson, 20 April 1824, vol. 1, Stevenson Papers, LC.

144. Clay to Johnston, 3 September 1824, in Clay, *Papers*, 3:827.

145. James Jackson to Andrew Jackson, 24 July 1822, in Jackson, *Papers*, 5:204.

146. "General Jackson," 17 April 1824; "General Jackson in Illinois," 24 April 1824; "Jackson in Illinois," 18 September 1824; and "Many Jacksonians of the 3d Electoral District," 2 October 1824, all in *Illinois Gazette*.

147. "Presidential Election," ibid., 25 September 1824.

148. "To the friends of Gen. *Jackson*, in the Wabash District" and "National Nomination," both in ibid., 9 October 1824. In fact, even Field wrote privately that he believed "J. Q. Adams would make the ablest President," that his support for Jackson was predicated on the assumption that "Adams would stand no chance of getting the vote in this part of the State," and that he "would willingly relinquish any favorite candidate and unite on one that would stand the best chance of beating the radical faction." A. P. Field to D. P. Cook, 31 August 1824, folder 6, box 2, Edwards Papers, CHM.

149. Untitled reports, *Edwardsville Spectator*, 7 and 14 September 1824.

150. Untitled reports, ibid., 21 September and 12 October 1824 (quotation); untitled editorial, ibid., 26 October 1824.

151. Untitled editorial, ibid., 6 April 1824.

152. Coles's allegiance to Crawford is particularly interesting in light of Adams's suspicions that the treasury secretary actively supported the plot to legalize slavery in Illinois. See entry for 3 March 1820, in Adams, *Memoirs*, 5:3–12. There is no evidence to corroborate this allegation, although Crawford was certainly close to proslavery Illinois politicians such as Thomas and Kane.

153. Untitled reports, *Edwardsville Spectator*, 14 September 1824.

154. Untitled editorial, ibid., 2 November 1824.

155. Memorandum in Rufus King's handwriting, in King, *Life and Correspondence,* 6:507.

156. Garrison, *Letters,* 1:4.

157. Peter B. Porter to Clay, 17 November 1823, in Clay, *Papers,* 3:523.

158. Unidentified publication, quoted in Chase, *Emergence,* 64. See also *Short Appeal from the Decrees of King Caucus.*

159. Calhoun to Swift, 26 October 1823, in Calhoun, *Papers,* 8:329.

160. Jackson to George Washington Martin, 2 January 1824, in Jackson, *Papers,* 5:334.

161. Fitzpatrick, "Autobiography of Martin Van Buren," 142.

162. Ibid., 144.

163. Weed, *Autobiography,* 1:104–38.

164. Fitzpatrick, "Autobiography of Martin Van Buren," 149.

165. On Calhoun in North Carolina see Newsome, *Presidential Election.*

166. For events in Louisiana see Clay to Porter, 26 December 1824, in Clay, *Papers,* 3:904–5.

167. "So you see the *Judas* of the West has closed the contract and will receive the thirty pieces of silver—his end will be the same. Was there ever witnessed such a bare faced corruption in any country before?" Jackson to William Berkeley Lewis, 14 February 1825, in Jackson, *Papers,* 6:29–30.

168. The figure 29 percent includes only the eighteen states that chose their electors by popular vote.

169. Taylor to Bernard, 8 April 1824, Taylor Papers, LV.

170. Entry for 22 May 1820, in Adams, *Memoirs,* 5:128.

171. Actually, as Donald Ratcliffe points out, if a popular vote had been held in the six states where electors were chosen by the legislature, the likely level of support for Adams, particularly in New York, might well have placed him above Jackson in the final count. Ratcliffe, "Andrew Jackson."

172. Leonard, *Invention of Party Politics,* 38.

173. Van Buren later admitted that he had switched his support to Jackson in 1828 with the object of "adding the General's personal popularity to the strength of the old Republican party." Fitzpatrick, "Autobiography of Martin Van Buren," 198.

174. "Most often rival candidates appear in campaign biographies to be as alike as Tweedledum and Tweedledee." W. B. Brown, *People's Choice,* 140.

175. On this point see Howe, *What Hath God Wrought,* 283; and Rigali, "Restoring the Republic," 257.

176. "The commonly held impression of universal disdain for the Adams administration is a myth that was deliberately created by his Jacksonian successors." Forbes, *Missouri Compromise,* 188. See also John, *Spreading the News,* 207; and Larson, *Internal Improvement,* 161.

177. See, for example, Ratcliffe, *Politics of Long Division,* 146–59.

178. Adams, *First Annual Message.*

179. Adams, *Inaugural Address;* Formisano, *For the People,* 66–67.

180. Mooney, *William H. Crawford,* 289; Fitzpatrick, "Autobiography of Martin Van Buren," 198, 233. For an account that stresses the antiparty tone of Jackson's 1824 campaign in the context of party building see Coens, "Formation of the Jackson Party."

CONCLUSION

1. Adams, *Inaugural Address.*

2. It might be argued that it was the conduct of the local Federalist Party in particular that provoked the Middling Interest in Boston, but it must be remembered that the protestors considered both parties to be "the same in purpose, the same in effect" and chose to make their opposition through a third party rather than support the existing Republican organization. It might also be argued that this situation was unique to Massachusetts, as the unusual persistence of Federalism there delayed the democratizing reforms embraced by Republicans elsewhere in the nation. Yet we have already witnessed the disregard that Martin Van Buren's Bucktails showed for popular sentiment in New York during the 1824 presidential campaign. As for Thomas Jefferson's own Virginia, it was the only state to retain property qualifications for voting, which barred roughly half of adult white males from participating in elections, into the 1850s, as the legislature consistently blocked popular efforts to obtain a more equitable reapportionment of political power. Evidently the fulminations against "mere force of numbers" by critics of the wooden-buildings scheme would have been just as sympathetically received by the Republican planter aristocracy of Virginia as they were by the Federalist merchant princes of Massachusetts. Quotations from "Our Representative to Congress," *New-England Galaxy,* 3 November 1820; and "One of the Remonstrants against any wooden houses," *Boston Daily Advertiser,* 6 March 1822.

3. These characteristics of a two-party system are discussed in Robertson, "Look on This Picture . . . ."

4. R. P. McCormick, *Second American Party System.* For the turnout figures see appendix 1.

5. "Public Meeting," *Aurora General Advertiser,* 2 October 1822.

6. "Middling Interest," *Boston Patriot & Daily Mercantile Advertiser,* 16 May 1822.

7. Entry for 22 May 1820, in Adams, *Memoirs,* 5:128. This widespread disillusionment with the existing parties is discussed in Ratcliffe, *Politics of Long Division,* xii–xiii; and Rigali, "Restoring the Republic," 20–32.

8. In this regard, parallels might be drawn with the 1850s, when popular dissatisfaction caused the collapse of the Democrat-Whig party system, with northerners turning to various partisan and nonpartisan alternatives, while many southerners lost faith in

the political process entirely. See Holt, *Political Crisis;* Ethington, *Public City,* 43–169; and Voss-Hubbard, *Beyond Party.*

9. The potential for multiple meanings and manifestations of antipartisanship is discussed in Baker, "Midlife Crisis."

10. "Federal Caucus," *New-England Galaxy,* 12 April 1822.

11. [Carey], *Prefatory Address.*

12. Calhoun to Swift, 14 October 1823, in Calhoun, *Papers,* 8:313.

13. *Middling Interest* ([Boston, April 1822]).

14. Here I disagree with both Joel Silbey's claim that "nonconformist political movements played little role electorally or in policy making in a culture textured by the partisan imperative" and Walter Dean Burnham's argument that "the antipartisan tradition . . . has not infrequently prevailed [in American history], but always at a major cost to effective governmental performance." Silbey, *American Political Nation,* 196; Burnham, "Elections as Democratic Institutions," 57.

15. This point has been made by Sorauf, "Political Parties," 44.

16. Altschuler and Blumin, *Rude Republic,* 270. Similar conclusions are reached by Bensel, *American Ballot Box;* and Schudson, "Good Citizens and Bad History." The importance of elections in maintaining the "fiction" of popular sovereignty is discussed in Morgan, *Inventing the People.*

17. Monroe, *Second Inaugural Address.*

18. Ford, *History of Illinois,* 53. The *Washington City Gazette* reported on 19 April 1825 that "[Henry] Clay has been burned in effigy 153 times in the different states of the union, and buried formally 7 times." Quoted in Coens, "Formation of the Jackson Party," 205.

19. [Sullivan], *Defence of the Exposition,* 15.

20. Two excellent narratives that do look beyond parties and elections are Brooke, *Columbia Rising;* and Formisano, *For the People.*

21. See, for example, Keyssar, *Right to Vote;* and, for a specific case in which political parties actively promoted this disenfranchisement, Klinghoffer and Elkis, "Petticoat Electors."

22. Some of the more recent additions to the ever-expanding literature on this topic include Dunbar, *Fragile Freedom;* Newman, "Protest in Black and White"; Portnoy, "Female Petitioners"; Rael, *Black Identity;* Zaeske, *Signatures of Citizenship;* Zagarri, *Revolutionary Backlash;* and Zagarri, "Women and Party Conflict." While the focus of their studies differs from my own, I have certainly been influenced by the arguments of these scholars that political participation does not begin and end at the ballot box.

23. Unknown writer to George W. Lyman, 19 April 1822, reel 1, Lyman Family Papers, MHS. Eliza Quincy's journals corroborate the suggestion that her mother exercised an important influence over her father's political career, although she is silent on the subject

of the 1822 election in this respect. See Eliza Susan Quincy, "Extracts from Old Journals," entry for 1820, reel 5, Quincy, Wendell, Holmes, and Upham Family Papers, MHS. A similar rumor of improper female influence circulated regarding the vote of Stephen Van Rensselaer that swung the New York delegation, and thus the entire House of Representatives, in favor of the election of John Quincy Adams for president in February 1825. See Hunt, *Forty Years*, 184–85, 193. These examples support the thesis of Allgor, *Parlor Politics*.

24. "Morgan County," *Edwardsville Spectator*, 20 September 1823, emphasis added.

25. "Good Example," *Patron of Industry*, 23 June 1821; *Columbian Observer* (Philadelphia), 21 August 1824, quoted in Coens, "Formation of the Jackson Party," 196.

26. "M," "Convention Letter Factories," *Edwardsville Spectator*, 18 May 1824.

27. "Fildelia Flimsey," ibid., 30 March 1824.

28. Leonard, *Invention of Party Politics*, 231–32. For a critique of the comparable tendency among political scientists to treat the two-party system as timeless and unchanging rather than the product of specific choices and circumstances see Disch, *Tyranny of the Two-Party System*.

29. In addition to Leonard, *Invention of Party Politics*, see also Kruman, "Second American Party System"; and A. Smith, *No Party Now*, 9–24.

30. According to Richard John, "Even rotation in office—the most avowedly democratic of the Jacksonians' innovations—did little to increase the access of previously underrepresented groups to public office." John, "Affairs of Office," 73.

31. Brooke, *Columbia Rising*, 295.

32. Aldrich, *Why Parties?*, 3.

33. Skocpol, *Diminished Democracy*, subtitle and 11. On the same point see Neem, *Nation of Joiners*, 172–80.

BIBLIOGRAPHY

MANUSCRIPT COLLECTIONS
Abraham Lincoln Presidential Library, Springfield, Illinois
    Berry Family Papers, 1819–1847
    Buckmaster-Curran Family Papers, 1801–1940
    Coles, Edward, Letters, 1815–1842
    Dunlop, James and John, Papers, 1818–1853
    Harlan-Sargent Family Papers, 1820–1940
    Larwill, Joseph, Papers, 1818, 1828, 1838
    Newhall, Horatio, Letters and Journal
    Reynolds, John, Papers, 1823–1858
    Riggin Family Papers, 1822–1903
    Shaw Family Papers, 1822–1916
    Thomas, Jesse Burgess, Papers, 1785–1866

Albert and Shirley Small Special Collections Library, University of Virginia, Charlottesville
    Cabell, Joseph Carrington, Family Papers, 1790–1890. Accession# 38-111-c.
    Cocke Family Papers, 1689–1968. Accession# 9513.

Chicago History Museum
    Coles, Edward, Papers, 1809–1858, 1881–1883. Microfilm; originals at CHM.
    Edwards, Ninian, Papers, 1798–1833
    Flower, George, Family Papers, 1812–1974
    Kane, Elias Kent, Papers, 1808–1835
    Mather, Thomas, Papers

Earl Gregg Swem Library, College of William & Mary, Williamsburg, Virginia
    Blow Family Papers, 1770–1875

Edwardsville Public Library, Illinois
    Genealogy Collection

Historical Society of Pennsylvania, Philadelphia
    Coles Family Papers, 1760–1921
    Gardiner, Edward Carey, Collection, 1673–1949
    Johnston, Josiah Stoddard, Papers, 1821–1839

Bibliography

Leib-Harrison Family Papers, Society Small Collection, 1769–1975
Philadelphia Chamber of Commerce Tariff Committee scrapbook, 1820
Roberts, Jonathan, Papers, 1780–1930
Sergeant, John, Papers, 1783–1897
Tilghman, William, Correspondence, 1772–1827
Vaux Family Papers, 1684–1923
Young, William, Correspondence, 1792–1827
Young, William, Family Papers, 1745–1850

Illinois History and Lincoln Collections, University of Illinois at Urbana-Champaign
Eddy, Henry, Papers, 1822–1848
Lippincott, Thomas, Papers, 1860, 1864–1865
Williams-Woodbury Papers, 1820–1900

Library Company of Philadelphia
Breck Family Papers, 1679–1888. On deposit at HSP.
Rush Family Papers, 1748–1876. On deposit at HSP.

Library of Congress, Washington, DC
Crawford, William Harris, Papers, 1810–1914
Stevenson, Andrew, and Stevenson, J. W., Papers, 1756–1882

Library of Virginia, Richmond
Bruce, William Cabell, Collection, 1713–1924. Microfilm; originals at LV.
Cabell, Nathaniel Francis, Papers, 1722–1879
Garnett-Mercer-Hunter Families Papers, 1713–1853
Ruffin Family Papers, 1811–1892. Microfilm; originals at Huntington Library, San Marino, California.
Taylor, John, Papers, 1798–1824
Tazewell Family Papers, 1623–1930
Tyler, John, letter to John Rutherfoord, 24 November 1858. Accession# 24726.

Massachusetts Historical Society, Boston
Appleton Family Papers
Lyman Family Papers. Microfilm, originals at MHS.
Otis, Harrison Gray, Papers. Microfilm; originals at MHS.
Quincy, Wendell, Holmes, and Upham Family Papers. Microfilm; originals at MHS.
Shattuck, George Cheyne, Papers
Shaw, Lemuel, Papers. Microfilm; originals at MHS.
Washington Benevolent Society Records
Williams, Moses, Papers

Rare Book and Manuscript Library, University of Pennsylvania, Philadelphia
  Carey, Matthew, Diary of, 1822–1826

University of Delaware Library, Newark
  Stern, Madeline B., Papers related to Joseph de Nancrede, 1972–1977

Virginia Historical Society, Richmond
  Blow Family Papers, 1653–1905 (Mss1 6235a)

NEWSPAPERS
Connecticut
  American Mercury (Hartford), 1822–23 [AHN]

Illinois
  Alton Telegraph, 1864–65 [ALPL]
  Edwardsville Spectator, 1821–25 [AHN]
  Illinois Gazette (Shawneetown), 1822–25 [19CUSN/ALPL]
  Illinois Intelligencer (Vandalia), 1823–24 [LC]
  Illinois Republican (Edwardsville), 1824 [ALPL/LC]
  Kaskaskia Republican, 9 March 1824–28 December 1824. See also *Republican Advocate*
    [ALPL/LC]
  Republican Advocate (Kaskaskia), 1823–2 March 1824 [ALPL/LC]

Maryland
  American Farmer (Baltimore), 1819–25 [BL]
  Baltimore Patriot & Mercantile Advertiser, 1823–24 [AHN]

Massachusetts
  Boston Commercial Gazette, 1820, 1822, 1824 [AHN]
  Boston Daily Advertiser, 1822–23 [AHN]
  Bostonian & Mechanics' Journal, 1822–23 [BPL]
  Boston Patriot & Daily Mercantile Advertiser, 1820–24 [BPL]
  Columbian Centinel (Boston), 1817, 1820–24 [AHN]
  New-England Galaxy (Boston), 1820–25 [BPL]

New Jersey
  Trenton Federalist, 1823–24 [AHN]

New York
  Patron of Industry (New York), 1820–21 [AHN]

Bibliography

Pennsylvania

    Aurora General Advertiser (Philadelphia), 1815, 1819, 1822, 1824–25 [LCP]

    Mercury (Pittsburgh), 1816, 1818–24 [Van Pelt Library, University of Pennsylvania]

    Political Economist (Philadelphia), 1824 [New York Public Library]

    Weekly Aurora (Philadelphia), 1820–21 [AHN]

South Carolina

    Carolina Gazette (Charleston), 1823–24 [AHN]

Virginia

    The Farmers' Register (Shellbanks), 1833–40 [BL]

    Richmond Enquirer, 1819–24 [AHN]

OTHER ARCHIVAL SOURCES

Adams, John Quincy. *The Duplicate Letters, the Fisheries and the Mississippi.*
    Washington, DC, 1822. [SA]

———. *Letter of the Hon. John Quincy Adams, in reply to a letter of the Hon. Alexander
    Smyth, to his constituents.* N.p., 1823. [LC]

*Address of the Committee Appointed by a Republican Meeting in the County of Hunterdon,
    Recommending Gen. Andrew Jackson, of Tennessee, to the People of New-Jersey, as
    President of the United States.* Trenton, NJ, 1824. [LC]

An Address to the People of Maryland, on the Subject of the Presidential Election. N.p., n.d.
    [LC]

*An Address to the People of Ohio, on the Important Subject of the Next Presidency; by the
    Committee appointed for that purpose, at a Convention of Delegates from the Different
    Sections of the State, assembled at Columbus, on Wednesday, the 14th day of July, 1824.*
    Cincinnati, [1824]. [LC]

*An Address to the People of the United States, drawn up by order of the National Institution
    for the Promotion of Industry, established in June, 1820, by delegates from New-York,
    New-Jersey, Pennsylvania, Connecticut, Massachusetts, Rhode-Island, Ohio, and
    Delaware.* New York, 1820. [LC]

An American System for the Protection of American Industry. Cincinnati, OH, [1824].
    [LC]

"Americanus." See Cooper, Thomas.

"Atticus." *A few considerations, in relation to the choice of President, written with a view
    to the approaching Election, and respectfully offered to the Citizens of the United States.*
    N.p., 1822. [LC]

Benton, Jesse. *An Address to the People of the United States on the Presidential Election.*
    Nashville, 1824. [LC]

Birkbeck, Morris. *An Appeal to the People of Illinois, on the Question of a Convention.* Shawneetown, IL, 1823. [ALPL]

Carey, Mathew. *Address delivered before the Philadelphia Society for Promoting Agriculture, at its Meeting, on the Twentieth of July, 1824.* Philadelphia, 1824. [LCP]

———. "Address to the Farmers of the United States, on the Ruinous Consequences to their Vital Interests, of the Existing Policy of this Country." In Carey, *Essays on Political Economy.* [SA]

———. *An Appeal to Common Sense and Common Justice or, Irrefragable Facts opposed to Plausible Theories: Intended to prove the extreme injustice, as well as the utter impolicy, of the existing tariff.* 3rd ed. Philadelphia, 1822. [NYHS]

———. Circular letter, 2 March 1824. [ABE]

———. "Circular letter from the committee appointed at a meeting of the citizens of Philadelphia, held October 2, 1819." In Carey, *Essays on Political Economy.* [SA]

———. *Collectanea: Displaying the Rise and Progress of the Tariff System of the United States.* 2nd ed. Philadelphia, 1833. [LCP]

———. *Essays on Political Economy.* Philadelphia, 1822. [SA]

———. "The New Olive Branch." In Carey, *Essays on Political Economy.* [SA]

———. "Report on American Manufactures to a meeting of the citizens of the city and county of Philadelphia, 2 October 1819." In Carey, *Essays on Political Economy.* [SA]

———. *Sketches Towards A History of the Present Session of Congress, from December 6, 1819, to April 15, 1820.* Philadelphia, 1820. [LCP]

———. *Three Letters on the Present Calamitous State of Affairs. Addressed to J. M. Garnett, Esq. President of the Fredericsburg Agricultural Society.* Philadelphia, 1820. [VHS]

———. *A View of the Ruinous Consequences of a Dependence on Foreign Markets for the Sale of the Great Staples of this Nation, Flour, Cotton, and Tobacco: Address to the Congress of the United States, read before, and ordered to be printed by, the Board of Manufactures of the Pennsylvania Society for the Promotion of American Manufactures.* Philadelphia, 1820. [LC]

——— ["Guatimozin," pseud.]. "The Farmer's & Planter's Friend." In Carey, *Essays on Political Economy.* [SA]

——— ["Hamilton," pseud.]. Letters, Series I–IX. 1822–25. [LCP/NYHS]

——— ["Necker," pseud.]. "Strictures on Mr. Cambreleng's Work, entitled, 'An examination of the New Tariff.'" In Carey, *Essays on Political Economy.* [SA]

——— ["Pennsylvanian," pseud.]. *Address to the Senate and House of Representatives of the United States, on the Subject of the Tariff.* Philadelphia, 1822. [LC]

——— ["Pennsylvanian," pseud.]. *Considerations on the Impropriety and Inexpediency of Renewing the Missouri Question.* Philadelphia, 1820. [SA]

——— ["Pennsylvanian," pseud.]. *The Crisis: A Solemn Appeal to the President, the Senate*

and House of Representatives, and the Citizens of the United States, on the Destructive
Tendency of the Present Policy of this Country, on its Agriculture, Manufactures,
Commerce, and Finances. Philadelphia, 1823. [SA]

—— ["Pennsylvanian," pseud.]. *Desultory Facts, and Observations, Illustrative of the
Past and Present Situation and Future Prospects of the United States: embracing A View
of the causes of the late Bankruptcies in Boston.* Philadelphia, 1822. [NYHS]

—— ["Pennsylvanian," pseud.]. *Examination of a Tract on the Alteration of the Tariff,
Written by Thomas Cooper, M. D.* Philadelphia, 1824. [NYHS]

—— ["Pennsylvanian," pseud.]. *Twenty-One Golden Rules to Depress Agriculture,
Impede the Progress of Manufactures, Paralize Commerce, Impair National Resources,
Produces a Constant Fluctuation in the Value of Every Species of Property, and Blight
and Blast the Bounties of Nature, How Bounteously Soever Lavished on a Country.*
Philadelphia, 1824. [LCP]

[Carey, Mathew]. *Constitution Of the Society for the dissemination of correct principles
relative to the Foreign Intercourse of the United States.* N.p., [1823]. [LCP]

——. *A Defence of Direct Taxes, and of Protective Duties for the Encouragement of
Manufactures.* Philadelphia, 1822. [LC]

——. *Prefatory Address. To the Artists, Mechanics, and Manufactures of the United
States.* N.p., [1820]. [LCP]

——. *A Warning Voice to the Cotton and Tobacco Planters, Farmers, and Merchants
of the United States, on the pernicious consequences to their respective interests of the
existing policy of the country.* Philadelphia, 1824. [LCP]

Carey, Mathew; and Samuel Jackson. "Addresses of the Philadelphia Society for the
Promotion of National Industry." In Carey, *Essays on Political Economy.* [SA]

"Carolina." *An Address to the Citizens of North-Carolina, on the Subject of the Presidential
Election.* N.p., 1823. [LC]

"Cassius" [Mahlon Dickerson]. *An Examination of Mr. Calhoun's Economy and an Apology
for those Members of Congress who have been denounced as Radicals.* N.p., 1823. [LC]

*Circular and Address of the National Institution for Promoting Industry in the United
States, to their Fellow-Citizens.* New York, 1820. [SA]

"Citizen." *The Election of President of the United States, Considered.* Boston, 1823. [LC]

——. *Political Thoughts. No. I—Idea of a Patriot President.* Washington, DC, 1823. [SA]

"Citizen" [Isaac Winslow]. *Old and New Tariffs Compared.* Boston, 1820. [BPL]

"Citizen of New-York." *An Address to the Republicans and People of New-York,
Pennsylvania, and Virginia, upon the State of Presidential Parties.* New York, 1824.
[SA]

——. *Measures, Not Men. Illustrated by Some Remarks upon the Public Conduct and
Character of John C. Calhoun.* New York, 1823. [SA]

"Citizen of Rhode-Island." *Principles and Men: Considered with reference to the approaching Election of President.* Providence, 1823. [SA]

"Citizen of the South." *A Concise View of the Rise and Progress of the United States, and of their Present Condition.* Washington, DC, 1824. [LC]

Clark, John. *Considerations on the Purity of the Principles of William H. Crawford, Esq.* New York, 1823. [LC]

The Constitution of the Middling Interest Association. Boston, 1822. [MHS]

Cooper, Thomas. *A Tract on the Proposed Alteration in the Tariff. Submitted to the Consideration of the Members from South Carolina in Congress.* New York, 1824. [NYHS]

——— ["Americanus," pseud.]. *Strictures Addressed to James Madison on the Celebrated Report of William H. Crawford, recommending the Intermarriage of Americans with the Indian Tribes.* Philadelphia, 1824. First published 1816. [SA]

Election of President in the House of Representatives. N.p., [late 1824 or early 1825]. [LC]

An Exposition of the Principles and Views of the Middling Interest. Boston, May 1822. [LC]

A Full and Authentic Report of the Debates in Faneuil Hall, Dec. 31, Jan. 1, & 2, 1821–2; On changing the form of Government of the Town of Boston. Boston, 1822. [BA]

Garnett, James M. *An Address Delivered before the Virginia Agricultural Society, of Fredericksburg, at the Organization Thereof, October 28, 1818: by James M. Garnett, Esq. President of the Society.* N.p., n.d. [VHS]

"Guatimozin." See Carey, Matthew.

"Hamilton." See Carey, Matthew.

An Historical View of the Public Celebrations of the Washington Society, and those of the Young Republicans. Boston, 1823. [SA]

"Inhabitant of the South." *A Letter to the Honorable James Brown, Senator in Congress from the state of Louisiana, on the Tariff.* Washington, DC, 1823. [LC]

The Injurious Effects of Slave Labour: An Impartial Appeal to the Reason, Justice, and Patriotism of the People of Illinois on the Injurious Effects of Slave Labour. London, 1824. [ALPL]

Jenkins, Joseph. *An Address delivered before the Massachusetts Charitable Mechanick Association, December 17, 1818, being the Anniversary of the Choice of Officers, and Fourth Triennial Celebration of their Public Festival.* Boston, 1819. [BL]

[Lippincott, Thomas, John Peck, Edward Coles ("Aristides"), and Daniel P. Cook ("Laocoon")]. *To the People of Illinois.* [Edwardsville, IL, 1824]. [ALPL]

"Massachusetts." *The Treaty of Ghent, and the Fisheries; or the Diplomatic Talents of John Quincy Adams, candidly examined.* Boston, 1824. [LC]

Melish, John. *Letter to James Monroe, Esq. President of the United States, on the State of the Country: with a Plan for Improving the Condition of Society.* Philadelphia, 1820. [LCP]

——. *Views on Political Economy, from the Description of the United States.* N.p., 1822. [HSP]

Memoirs of the "Society of Virginia for Promoting Agriculture:" containing Communications on Various Subjects in Husbandry and Rural Affairs. Richmond, 1818. [VHS]

Memorial of Sundry Citizens of Hampshire County, State of Virginia. Washington, DC, 1821. [VHS]

Memorial of Sundry Inhabitants of Petersburg, in Virginia, upon the Subject of the Proposed Tariff. Washington, DC, 1824. [VHS]

The Memorial of the Board of Manufactures of the Pennsylvania Society for the Encouragement of American Manufactures. Philadelphia, 1822. [NYHS]

Memorial of the Citizens of Richmond and Manchester, in Virginia, upon the subject of the Proposed Tariff, now before Congress. Washington, DC, 1824. [LV]

Memorial of the Merchants and Agriculturalists, of Fredericksburg and its Vicinity, Virginia. Washington, DC, 1820. [LV]

Memorial of the Merchants and Other Citizens of Richmond and its Vicinity, against An increase of the Tariff of Import Duties, a discontinuation of credits on Revenue Bonds, the abolition of Drawbacks, and other restrictions on Commerce. Washington, DC, 1820. [VHS]

The Middling Interest. Boston, [March] 1822. [ABE]

Middling Interest. [Boston, April 1822]. [AAS]

Middling Interest. Boston, May 1822. [ABE]

"Millions." *Some Reasons why the Votes of the State of New-York ought to be given to Henry Clay, for President of the United States.* [New York, 1824]. [NYHS]

"Necker." See Carey, Matthew.

"One of the People" [Churchill C. Cambreleng]. *An Examination of the New Tariff proposed by the Hon. Henry Baldwin, a Representative of Congress.* New York, 1821. [LCP]

"Pennsylvanian." See Carey, Matthew.

"Peter Atall" [Robert Waln]. *The Hermit in Philadelphia.* 2nd ser. Philadelphia, 1821. [BL]

"Philo-Jackson." *The Presidential Election, written for the benefit of the People of the United States, but particularly for those of the State of Kentucky.* 2nd ser. Louisville, KY, 1823. [LC]

——. *The Presidential Election, written for the benefit of the People of the U. States, but particularly for those of the State of Kentucky; relating to the Seminole War, and the Vindication of General Jackson.* 3rd ser. Frankfort, KY, 1824. [LC]

——. *The Presidential Election, written for the benefit of the People of the United States, but particularly for those of the State of Kentucky.* 4th ser. Frankfort, KY, 1824. [LC]

———. *The Presidential Election, written for the benefit of the People of the United States, but particularly for those of the State of Kentucky; relating, also, to South America, a war with the Holy Allies; and to an Alliance with Great Britain.* 5th ser. Frankfort, KY, 1824. [LC]

———. *The Presidential Election, written for the benefit of the People of the United States, but particularly for those of the State of Kentucky; relating, also, to the Constitution of the United States, and to Internal Improvements.* 6th ser. Frankfort, KY, 1824. [SA]

"Plain Sense" [John Woodward]. *Plain Sense, on National Industry.* New York, 1820. [SA]

Presidential Election. N.p., n.d. [LC]

The Proceedings of a Convention of the Friends of National Industry, assembled in the City of New-York, November 29, 1819, consisting of delegates from the States of Massachusetts, Rhode Island, Connecticut, New-York, New-Jersey, Pennsylvania, Delaware, Maryland, and Ohio. New York, 1819. [NYHS]

Proceedings of the Convention, assembled at Harrisburg, March 4, 1824, for the purpose of forming an Electoral Ticket, to be supported by the Democratic Republicans of Pennsylvania, at the ensuing Election for President and Vice President of the United States. N.p., 1824. [LC]

Remarks Addressed to the Citizens of Illinois, on the Proposed Introduction of Slavery. N.p., n.d. [ALPL]

Report of the Committee of Merchants and Others, of Boston; on the Tariff. Boston, 1820. [BL]

"Rusticus." *Hints for the People, with some thoughts on the Presidential Election.* N.p., 1823. [LC]

Short Appeal from the Decrees of King Caucus and the Albany Regency, to the People. [New York, 1824]. [LC]

A Sketch of Several Distinguished Members of the Woodbee Family. New York, 1823. [SA]

Sketch of the Life of John Quincy Adams; taken from the Port Folio of April, 1819, to which are added, the Letters of Tell: Originally Addressed to the Editor of the Baltimore American. N.p., 1824. [LC]

"South-Carolinean." *Some Objections to Mr. Crawford as a Candidate for the Presidential Chair, with a Few Remarks on the Charges Preferred against South Carolina as being "in error, and uncertain in her Politics."* N.p., n.d. [LC]

[Sullivan, George]. *Defence of the Exposition of the Middling Interest, on the Right of Constituents to give Instructions to their Representatives, and the Obligation of these to obey them.* Boston, July 1822. [SA]

Taylor, John. *Construction Construed, and Constitutions Vindicated.* Richmond, 1820. [SA]

———. *New Views of the Constitution of the United States.* Washington, DC, 1823. [SA]

————. *Tyranny Unmasked.* Washington, DC, 1822. [SA]

To the Federal Republicans of Massachusetts. N.p., 1824. [ABE]

To Your Tents O Israel! [Boston], 1820. [ABE]

[Webster, Redford]. *Selections from the Chronicle of Boston and from the Book of Retrospections & Anticipations.* N.p., 1822. [MHS]

Woods, John. *Two Years' Residence in the Settlement on the English Prairie, in the Illinois Country, United States.* London, 1822. [BL]

"Wyoming" [John H. Eaton]. *The Letters of Wyoming, to the People of the United States, on the Presidential Election, and in favour of Andrew Jackson.* Philadelphia, 1824. [SA]

PUBLISHED SOURCES

Adams, John Quincy. *First Annual Message.* 6 December 1825. http://www.presidency. ucsb.edu/ws/index.php?pid=29467. Accessed 14 November 2010.

————. *Inaugural Address.* 4 March 1825. http://www.bartleby.com/124/pres22.html. Accessed 14 November 2010.

————. *Memoirs of John Quincy Adams, Comprising Portions of His Diary from 1795 to 1848.* Edited by Charles Francis Adams. 12 vols. Philadelphia, 1874–77.

"Address by Senator Benjamin Ruggles to the Republicans of the United States, Washington, February 21, 1824." In Schlesinger, *History of American Presidential Elections, 1789–1968.*

Aldrich, John H. *Why Parties? The Origin and Transformation of Political Parties in America.* Chicago: University of Chicago Press, 1995.

Allgor, Catherine. *Parlor Politics: In Which the Ladies of Washington Help Build a City and a Government.* Charlottesville: University of Virginia Press, 2000.

Altschuler, Glenn C., and Stuart M. Blumin. *Rude Republic: Americans and Their Politics in the Nineteenth Century.* Princeton, NJ: Princeton University Press, 2000.

Alvord, Clarence Walworth, ed. *Governor Edward Coles.* Springfield: Illinois State Historical Library, 1920.

Ames, William E., and S. Dean Olson. "Washington's Political Press and the Election of 1824." *Journalism Quarterly* 40 (Summer 1963): 343–50.

Ammon, Harry. *James Monroe: The Quest for National Identity.* New York: McGraw-Hill, 1971.

————. "The Richmond Junto, 1800–1824." *Virginia Magazine of History and Biography* 61 (October 1953): 395–418.

Annals of the Congress of the United States. 42 vols. Washington, DC: Gales & Seaton, 1834–55.

Babcock, Rufus, ed. *Forty Years of Pioneer Life: Memoir of John Mason Peck D.D. Edited from His Journals and Correspondence.* Carbondale: Southern Illinois University Press, 1965.

Bailey, Raymond C. *Popular Influence upon Public Policy: Petitioning in Eighteenth-Century Virginia.* Westport, CT: Greenwood, 1979.

Baker, Paula, "The Midlife Crisis of the New Political History." *Journal of American History* 86 (June 1999): 158–66.

Bartlett, Irving H. *John C. Calhoun: A Biography.* New York: Norton, 1993.

Beck, Lewis C. *A Gazetteer of the States of Illinois and Missouri.* Albany, NY, 1823.

Bemis, Samuel Flagg. *John Quincy Adams and the Union.* New York: Knopf, 1956.

Bensel, Richard Franklin. *The American Ballot Box in the Mid-Nineteenth Century.* Cambridge: Cambridge University Press, 2004.

Benton, Thomas Hart. *Thirty Years' View; or, A History of the Working of the American Government for Thirty Years, from 1820 to 1850.* Vol. 1. 1954. Reprint, New York: Greenwood, 1968.

Bogin, Ruth. "Petitioning and the New Moral Economy of Post-Revolutionary America." *William and Mary Quarterly* 45 (July 1988): 392–425.

Bogue, Allan G. "The Quest for Numeracy: Data and Methods in American Political History." *Journal of Interdisciplinary History* 21 (Summer 1990): 89–116.

The Boston Directory. Boston, 1820.

Bourke, Paul F., and Donald A. DeBats. *Washington County: Politics and Community in Antebellum America.* Baltimore: John Hopkins University Press, 1995.

Bowers, Douglas E. "From Logrolling to Corruption: The Development of Lobbying in Pennsylvania, 1815–1861." *Journal of the Early Republic* 3 (Winter 1983): 439–74.

Bowling, Kenneth R., and Donald R. Kennon, eds. *The House and Senate in the 1790s: Petitioning, Lobbying, and Institutional Development.* Athens: Ohio University Press, 2002.

Bridges, Roger D., ed. "John Mason Peck on Illinois Slavery." *Illinois Historical Journal* 75 (Autumn 1982): 179–217.

Brooke, John L. "Ancient Lodges and Self-Created Societies: Voluntary Association and the Public Sphere in the Early Republic." In *Launching the "Extended Republic": The Federalist Era,* edited by Ronald Hoffman and Peter J. Albert. Charlottesville: University of Virginia Press, 1996.

———. *Columbia Rising: Civil Life on the Upper Hudson from the Revolution to the Age of Jackson.* Chapel Hill: University of North Carolina Press, 2010.

———. "To be 'Read by the Whole People': Press, Party, and Public Sphere in the United States, 1789–1840." *Proceedings of the American Antiquarian Society* 110 (2000): 41–118.

Brown, Richard D. "The Emergence of Urban Society in Rural Massachusetts, 1760–1820." *Journal of American History* 61 (June 1974): 29–51.

———. *The Strength of a People: The Idea of an Informed Citizenry in America, 1650–1870.* Chapel Hill: University of North Carolina Press, 1996.

Brown, William Burlie. *The People's Choice: The Presidential Image in the Campaign Biography.* Baton Rouge: Louisiana State University Press, 1960.

Brown, William H. "An Historical Sketch of the Early Movement in Illinois for the Legalization of Slavery." *Fergus Historical Series* 4 (1876): 1–31.

Buckingham, Joseph T. *Annals of the Massachusetts Charitable Mechanic Association.* Boston, 1853.

———. *Personal Memoirs and Recollections of Editorial Life.* 2 vols. Boston, 1852.

———. *Specimens of Newspaper Literature: with Personal Memoirs, Anecdotes, and Reminiscences.* 2 vols. Boston, 1850.

Burnham, J. H., and J. F. Snyder. "Forgotten Statesmen of Illinois." *Transactions of the Illinois State Historical Society* 8–11 (1903–6).

Burnham, Walter Dean. "The Changing Shape of the American Political Universe." *American Political Science Review* 59 (March 1965): 7–28.

———. "Elections as Democratic Institutions." In *Elections in America,* edited by Kay Lehman Schlozman. Boston: Allen & Unwin, 1987.

———. "Table I: Summary: Presidential Elections, USA, 1788–2004." *Journal of the Historical Society* 7 (December 2007): 521–80.

———. "Those High Nineteenth-Century American Voting Turnouts: Fact or Fiction?" *Journal of Interdisciplinary History* 16 (Spring 1986): 613–44.

Burstein, Andrew. *America's Jubilee.* New York: Vintage Books, 2001.

Calhoun, John C. *The Papers of John C. Calhoun.* Edited by Robert L. Meriwether, W. Edwin Hemphill, Shirley A. Cook, Clyde N. Wilson, et al. 28 vols. Columbia: University of South Carolina Press, 1959–2003.

Carey, Mathew. *Auto Biographical Sketches. In a Series of Letters Addressed to a Friend.* Philadelphia, 1829.

———. *The Olive Branch; or Faults on Both Sides, Federal and Democratic.* 9th ed. Winchester, VA, 1817.

Carter, Edward C. "The Birth of a Political Economist: Mathew Carey and the Recharter Fight of 1810–1811." *Pennsylvania History* 33 (July 1966): 274–88.

———. "Mathew Carey and 'The Olive Branch,' 1814–1818." *Pennsylvania Magazine of History and Biography* 89 (October 1965): 399–415.

Carwardine, Richard J. *Evangelicals and Politics in Antebellum America.* Knoxville: University of Tennessee Press, 1997.

A Catalogue of the City Councils of Boston 1822–1908, Roxbury 1846–1867, Charlestown 1847–1873, and of the Selectmen of Boston, 1634–1822, also of various other town and municipal officers. Boston: City of Boston Printing Department, 1909.

Cayton, Andrew R. L. "The Fragmentation of 'A Great Family': The Panic of 1819 and the Rise of the Middling Interest in Boston, 1818–1822." *Journal of the Early Republic* 2 (Summer 1982): 143–67.

Census for 1820. Washington, DC, 1821.

Chambers, William Nisbet, and Walter Dean Burnham, eds. *The American Party Systems: Stages of Political Development*. Oxford: Oxford University Press, 1967.

Chambers, William Nisbet, and Philip C. Davis. "Party, Competition, and Mass Participation: The Case of the Democratizing Party System, 1824–1852." In *The History of American Electoral Behavior*, edited by Joel H. Silbey, Allan G. Bogue, and William H. Flanigan. Princeton, NJ: Princeton University Press, 1978.

Chase, James S. *Emergence of the Presidential Nominating Convention, 1789–1832*. Urbana: University of Illinois Press, 1973.

Clay, Henry. *The Papers of Henry Clay*. Edited by James F. Hopkins, Robert Seager II, Melba Porter Hay, et al. 11 vols. Lexington: University Press of Kentucky, 1959–92.

Clifft, Joseph Clinton. "The Politics of Transition: Virginia and North Carolina and the 1824 Presidential Election." PhD diss., University of Tennessee, 1999.

Coens, Thomas M. "The Formation of the Jackson Party, 1822–1825." PhD diss., Harvard University, 2004.

Cohen, Joanna. "'The Right to Purchase Is as Free as the Right to Sell': Defining Consumers as Citizens in the Auction-house Conflicts of the Early Republic." *Journal of the Early Republic* 30 (Spring 2010): 25–62.

Coles, Edward. *History of the Ordinance of 1787*. Philadelphia, 1856.

Crocker, Matthew H. *The Magic of the Many: Josiah Quincy and the Rise of Mass Politics in Boston, 1800–1830*. Amherst: University of Massachusetts Press, 1999.

Cunningham, Noble E., Jr. *The Process of Government under Jefferson*. Princeton, NJ: Princeton University Press, 1978.

Curtis, Christopher M. "Reconsidering Suffrage Reform in the 1829–1830 Virginia Constitutional Convention." *Journal of Southern History* 74 (February 2008): 89–124.

Dangerfield, George. *The Awakening of American Nationalism, 1815–1828*. New York: Harper Torchbooks, 1965.

———. *The Era of Good Feelings*. London: Methuen, 1953.

Davis, Rodney O. "Lobbying and The Third House in the Early Illinois General Assembly." *Old Northwest* 14 (1988): 267–84.

"Declaration of New York Republican Caucus, April 22, 1823." In Schlesinger, *History of American Presidential Elections, 1789–1968*.

Demaree, Albert Lowther. *The American Agricultural Press, 1819–1860*. New York: Columbia University Press, 1941.

Desilver, Robert. *The Philadelphia Directory for 1824*. Philadelphia, 1824.

diGiacomantonio, William C. "Petitioners and Their Grievances: A View from the First Federal Congress." In Bowling and Kennon, *House and Senate in the 1790s.*

Disch, Lisa Jane. *The Tyranny of the Two-Party System.* New York: Columbia University Press, 2002.

Doyle, Don Harrison. *The Social Order of a Frontier Community: Jacksonville, Illinois, 1825–70.* Urbana: University of Illinois Press, 1978.

Dubin, Michael J. *United States Congressional Elections, 1788–1997: The Official Results of the Elections of the 1st through 105th Congresses.* Jefferson, NC: McFarland, 1998.

———. *United States Gubernatorial Elections, 1776–1860: The Official Results by State and County.* Jefferson, NC: McFarland, 2003.

———. *United States Presidential Elections, 1788–1860: The Official Results by County and State.* Jefferson, NC: McFarland, 2002.

Dunbar, Erica Armstrong. *A Fragile Freedom: African American Women and Emancipation in the Antebellum City.* New Haven, CT: Yale University Press, 2008.

Eames, Charles M. *Historic Morgan and Classic Jacksonville.* Jacksonville, IL, 1885.

Eaton, Clement. "Southern Senators and the Right of Instruction, 1789–1860." *Journal of Southern History* 18 (August 1952): 303–19.

"Edward Coles, Second Governor of Illinois—Correspondence with Rev. Thomas Lippincott." *Journal of the Illinois State Historical Society* 3 (1911): 59–63.

Einhorn, Robin L. *American Taxation, American Slavery.* Chicago: University of Chicago Press, 2006.

Eiselen, Malcolm Rogers. *The Rise of Pennsylvania Protectionism.* Philadelphia: Porcupine, 1974.

Ellis, Richard E. "The Market Revolution and the Transformation of American Politics, 1801–1837." In Stokes and Conway, *Market Revolution in America.*

Emerson, Ralph Waldo. *The Letters of Ralph Waldo Emerson.* Edited by Ralph L. Rusk. Vol. 1. New York: Columbia University Press, 1939.

Ethington, Philip J. *The Public City: The Political Construction of Urban Life in San Francisco, 1850–1900.* Berkeley: University of California Press, 2001.

Fennimore, Donald L., and Ann K. Wagner. *Silversmiths to the Nation: Thomas Fletcher and Sidney Gardiner, 1800–1842.* [Winterthur, DE?]: Henry Francis du Pont Winterthur Museum, 2007.

Fifth census; or enumeration of the inhabitants of the United States, corrected at the Department of State. 1830. Washington, DC, 1832.

Finkelman, Paul. "Evading the Ordinance: The Persistence of Bondage in Indiana and Illinois." *Journal of the Early Republic* 9 (Spring 1989): 21–51.

Fischer, David Hackett. *The Revolution of American Conservatism: The Federalist Party in the Era of Jeffersonian Democracy.* New York: Harper & Row, 1965.

Fitzpatrick, John C., ed. *The Autobiography of Martin Van Buren.* Vol. 2 of *Annual Report of the American Historical Association for the Year 1918.* Washington, DC: GPO, 1920.

Flower, George. *History of the English Settlement in Edwards County Illinois, founded in 1817 and 1818, by Morris Birkbeck and George Flower.* Chicago, 1882.

Forbes, Robert Pierce. *The Missouri Compromise and Its Aftermath: Slavery and the Meaning of America.* Chapel Hill: University of North Carolina Press, 2007.

Ford, Thomas. *A History of Illinois, from its Commencement as a State in 1818 to 1847.* Chicago, 1854.

Formisano, Ronald P. "Boston, 1800–1840: From Deferential-Participant to Party Politics." In *Boston 1700–1980: The Evolution of Urban Politics,* edited by Ronald P. Formisano and Constance K. Burns. Westport, CT: Greenwood, 1984.

———. "The Concept of Political Culture." *Journal of Interdisciplinary History* 31 (Winter 2001): 393–426.

———. "Deferential-Participant Politics: The Early Republic's Political Culture, 1789–1840." *American Political Science Review* 68 (June 1974): 473–87.

———. *For the People: American Populist Movements from the Revolution to the 1850s.* Chapel Hill: University of North Carolina Press, 2008.

———. "The 'Party Period' Revisited." *Journal of American History* 86 (June 1999): 93–120.

———. "Political Character, Antipartyism and the Second Party System." *American Quarterly* 21 (Winter 1969): 683–709.

———. *The Transformation of Political Culture: Massachusetts Parties, 1790s–1840s.* Oxford: Oxford University Press, 1983.

Fritz, Christian G. *American Sovereigns: The People and America's Constitutional Tradition before the Civil War.* Cambridge: Cambridge University Press, 2008.

"From the Diary of William Plumer." In *American Presidential Campaigns and Elections,* edited by William G. Shade and Ballard C. Campbell, vol. 1. Armonk, NY: Sharp Reference, 2003.

Gallatin, Albert. *The Writings of Albert Gallatin.* Edited by Henry Adams. Vol. 2. Philadelphia, 1879.

Garrison, William Lloyd. *The Letters of William Lloyd Garrison.* Vol. 1. Edited by Walter M. Merrill. Cambridge, MA: Harvard University Press, 1971.

Gienapp, William E. "'Politics Seem to Enter into Everything': Political Culture in the North, 1840–1860." In *Essays on American Antebellum Politics, 1840–1860,* edited by Stephen E. Maizlish and John J. Kushma. College Station: Texas A&M University Press, 1982.

Ginsburg, Gerald. "Computing Antebellum Turnout: Methods and Models." *Journal of Interdisciplinary History* 16 (Spring 1986): 579–611.

Grob, Gerald N. "The Political System and Social Policy in the Nineteenth Century: Legacy of the Revolution." *Mid-America* 58 (January 1976): 5–19.

Guasco, Suzanne Cooper. "'The Deadly Influence of Negro Capitalists': Southern Yeomen and Resistance to the Expansion of Slavery in Illinois." *Civil War History* 48 (March 2001): 7–29.

———. "'To Put into Complete Practice Those Hallowed Principles': Edward Coles and the Crafting of Antislavery Nationalism in Early Nineteenth-Century America." *American Nineteenth Century History* 11 (March 2010): 17–45.

Gustafson, Sandra M. *Imagining Deliberative Democracy in the Early American Republic.* Chicago: University of Chicago Press, 2011.

Hair, James T. *Gazetteer of Madison County.* Alton, IL, 1866.

Hamilton, Alexander, James Madison, and John Jay. *The Federalist Papers.* Edited by Lawrence Goldman. Oxford: Oxford University Press, 2008.

Hamilton, James. *Reminiscences of James A. Hamilton; or, Men and Events, at Home and Abroad, during Three Quarters of a Century.* New York, 1869.

Hay, Robert P. "The Case for Andrew Jackson in 1824: Eaton's *Wyoming Letters.*" *Tennessee Historical Quarterly* 29 (Summer 1970): 139–51.

———. "The Pillorying of Albert Gallatin: The Public Response to his 1824 Vice-Presidential Nomination." *Western Pennsylvania Historical Magazine* 65 (July 1982): 181–202.

Hays, Samuel P. "Political Parties and the Community-Society Continuum." In Chambers and Burnham, *American Party Systems.*

———. "Politics and Society: Beyond the Political Party." In *The Evolution of American Electoral Systems,* by Paul Kleppner, Walter Dean Burnham, Ronald P. Formisano, Samuel P. Hays, Richard Jensen, and William G. Shade. Westport, CT: Greenwood, 1981.

Heale, Michael J. *The Presidential Quest: Candidates and Images in American Political Culture, 1787–1852.* London: Longman, 1982.

Hemberger, Suzette. "A Government Based on Representations." *Studies in American Political Development* 10 (Fall 1996): 289–332.

Higginson, Stephen A. "A Short History of the Right to Petition Government for the Redress of Grievances." *Yale Law Journal* 96 (November 1986): 142–66.

History of Madison County, Illinois. Edwardsville, IL, 1882.

Hofstadter, Richard. *The Idea of a Party System: The Rise of Legitimate Opposition in the United States, 1780–1840.* Berkeley: University of California Press, 1970.

Holt, Michael F. *The Political Crisis of the 1850s.* New York: Norton, 1983.

———. "The Primacy of Party Reasserted." *Journal of American History* 86 (June 1999): 151–57.

Hooper, Leonard John, Jr. "Decade of Debate: The Polemical, Political Press in Illinois, 1814–1824." PhD diss., Southern Illinois University, 1964.

Hopkins, James F. "Election of 1824." In Schlesinger, *History of American Presidential Elections, 1789–1968.*

Howe, Daniel Walker. *What Hath God Wrought: The Transformation of America, 1815–1848.* Oxford: Oxford University Press, 2007.

Hubbard, James Mascarene. "Boston's Last Town Meetings and First City Election." *Bostonian Society Publications* 6 (1910): 91–118.

Hunt, Gaillard, ed. *Forty Years of Washington Society: Portrayed by the Family Letters of Mrs. Samuel Harrison Smith (Margaret Bayard).* London, 1906.

Huston, James L. "Virtue Besieged: Virtue, Equality, and the General Welfare in the Tariff Debates of the 1820s." *Journal of the Early Republic* 14 (Winter 1994): 523–47.

Huston, Reeve. "Popular Movements and Party Rule: The New York Anti-Rent Wars and the Jacksonian Political Order." In Pasley, Robertson, and Waldstreicher, *Beyond the Founders.*

Jackson, Andrew. *Correspondence of Andrew Jackson.* Edited by John Spencer Bassett. Vol. 3. Washington, DC: Carnegie Institute of Washington, 1928.

———. *The Papers of Andrew Jackson.* Edited by Harold D. Moser, Daniel Feller, et al. 8 vols. to date. Knoxville: University of Tennessee Press, 1980–.

John, Richard R. "Affairs of Office: The Executive Departments, The Election of 1828, and the Making of the Democratic Party." In *The Democratic Experiment: New Directions in American Political History,* edited by Meg Jacobs, William J. Novak, and Julian E. Zelizer. Princeton, NJ: Princeton University Press, 2003.

———. "Governmental Institutions as Agents of Change: Rethinking American Political Development in the Early Republic, 1787–1835." *Studies in American Political Development* 11 (Fall 1997): 347–80.

———. *Spreading the News: The American Postal System from Franklin to Morse.* Cambridge, MA: Harvard University Press, 1998.

John, Richard R., and Christopher J. Young. "Rites of Passage: Postal Petitioning as a Tool of Governance in the Age of Federalism." In Bowling and Kennon, *House and Senate in the 1790s.*

Journal of the House of Representatives of the State of Illinois. Third General Assembly, 1st sess. Springfield, IL, 1823.

Kehl, James A. *Ill Feeling in the Era of Good Feeling: Western Pennsylvania Political Battles, 1815–1825.* Pittsburgh: University of Pittsburgh Press, 1956.

Keller, Morton. *America's Three Regimes: A New Political History.* Oxford: Oxford University Press, 2007.

Keyssar, Alexander. *The Right to Vote: The Contested History of Democracy in the United States.* New York: Basic Books, 2000.

Kielbowicz, Richard B. *News in the Mail: The Press, Post Office, and Public Information, 1700–1860s.* Westport, CT: Greenwood, 1989.

King, Charles R., ed. *Life and Correspondence of Rufus King.* Vol. 6. New York: G. P. Putnam's Sons, 1900.

Klein, Philip Shriver. *Pennsylvania Politics, 1817–1832: A Game Without Rules.* Philadelphia: Historical Society of Pennsylvania, 1940.

Klinghoffer, Judith Apter, and Lois Elkis. "'The Petticoat Electors': Women's Suffrage in New Jersey, 1776–1807." *Journal of the Early Republic* 12 (Summer 1992): 159–93.

Kornblith, Gary J. "Becoming Joseph T. Buckingham: The Struggle for Artisanal Independence in Early-Nineteenth-Century Boston." In *American Artisans: Crafting Social Identity, 1750–1850,* edited by Howard B. Rock, Paul A. Gilje, and Robert Asher. Baltimore: John Hopkins University Press, 1995.

Koschnik, Albrecht. "The Democratic Societies of Philadelphia and the Limits of the American Public Sphere, circa 1793–1795." *William and Mary Quarterly* 58 (July 2001): 615–36.

———. *"Let a Common Interest Bind Us Together": Associations, Partisanship, and Culture in Philadelphia, 1775–1840.* Charlottesville: University of Virginia Press, 2007.

Kruman, Marc W. "The Second American Party System and the Transformation of Revolutionary Republicanism." *Journal of the Early Republic* 12 (Winter 1992): 509–37.

Larson, John Lauritz. *Internal Improvement: National Public Works and the Promise of Popular Government in the Early United States.* Chapel Hill: University of North Carolina Press, 2001.

Leichtle, Kurt E. "The Rise of Jacksonian Politics in Illinois." *Illinois Historical Journal* 82 (Summer 1989): 93–107.

Leonard, Gerald. *The Invention of Party Politics: Federalism, Popular Sovereignty, and Constitutional Development in Jacksonian Illinois.* Chapel Hill: University of North Carolina Press, 2002.

Lewis, James E., Jr. *The American Union and the Problem of Neighborhood: The United States and the Collapse of the Spanish Empire, 1783–1829.* Chapel Hill: University of North Carolina Press, 1998.

Livermore, Shaw, Jr. *The Twilight of Federalism: The Disintegration of the Federalist Party, 1815–1830.* Princeton, NJ: Princeton University Press, 1962.

Lowe, Gabriel L., Jr. "John H. Eaton, Jackson's Campaign Manager." *Tennessee Historical Quarterly* 11 (June 1952): 99–147.

Madison, James. *Letters and Other Writings of James Madison.* Vol. 3. Philadelphia, 1865.

Mark, Gregory A. "The Vestigial Constitution: The History and Significance of the Right to Petition." *Fordham Law Review* 66 (1997–98): 2153–2231.

Massachusetts Constitution. 1780. http://www.mass.gov/legis/const.htm. Accessed 16 November 2009.

McCaughey, Robert A. "From Town to City: Boston in the 1820s." *Political Science Quarterly* 88 (June 1973): 191–213.

———. *Josiah Quincy, 1772–1864: The Last Federalist.* Cambridge, MA: Harvard University Press, 1974.

McCormick, Richard L. "The Party Period and Public Policy: An Exploratory Hypothesis." *Journal of American History* 66 (September 1979): 279–98.

McCormick, Richard P. "New Perspectives on Jacksonian Politics." *American Historical Review* 65 (January 1960): 288–301.

———. *The Second American Party System: Party Formation in the Jacksonian Era.* Chapel Hill: University of North Carolina Press, 1966.

Miller, F. Thornton. "The Richmond Junto: The Secret All-Powerful Club—or Myth." *Virginia Magazine of History and Biography* 99 (January 1991): 63–80.

Mitchell, Betty L. *Edmund Ruffin: A Biography.* Bloomington: Indiana University Press, 1981.

Monroe, James. *Second Inaugural Address.* 5 March 1821. http://www.bartleby.com/124 /pres21.html. Accessed 13 August 2012.

Mooney, Chase C. *William H. Crawford, 1772–1834.* Lexington: University Press of Kentucky, 1974.

Morgan, Edmund S. *Inventing the People: The Rise of Popular Sovereignty in England and America.* New York: Norton, 1988.

Morison, Samuel Eliot. *The Life and Letters of Harrison Gray Otis, Federalist, 1765–1848.* 2 vols. Boston: Houghton Mifflin, 1913.

Neem, Johann N. *Creating a Nation of Joiners: Democracy and Civil Society in Early National Massachusetts.* Cambridge, MA: Harvard University Press, 2008.

Newman, Richard. "Protest in Black and White: The Formation and Transformation of an African American Political Community during the Early Republic." In Pasley, Robertson, and Waldstreicher, *Beyond the Founders.*

Newsome, Albert Ray. *The Presidential Election of 1824 in North Carolina.* Chapel Hill: University of North Carolina Press, 1939.

Nord, David Paul. "The Evangelical Origins Of Mass Media in America, 1815–1835." *Journalism Monographs* 88 (May 1984): 1–30.

Norton, W. T., ed. *Centennial History of Madison County, Illinois, and Its People, 1812 to 1912.* Vol. 1. Chicago: Lewis, 1912.

Oberholtzer, Ellis Paxson. *Philadelphia: A History of the City and its People.* 4 vols. Philadelphia: S. J. Clarke, 1912.

Onuf, Peter S. *Statehood and Union: A History of the Northwest Ordinance.* Bloomington: Indiana University Press, 1987.

Parsons, Lynn Hudson. *The Birth of Modern Politics: Andrew Jackson, John Quincy Adams, and the Election of 1828.* Oxford: Oxford University Press, 2009.

Pasley, Jeffrey L. "The Cheese and the Words: Popular Political Culture and Participatory Democracy in the Early American Republic." In Pasley, Robertson, and Waldstreicher, *Beyond the Founders.*

———. "Party Politics, Citizenship, and Collective Action in Nineteenth-Century America: A Response to Stuart Blumin and Michael Schudson." *Communication Review* 4 (2000): 39–54.

———. "Private Access and Public Power: Gentility and Lobbying in the Early Congress." In Bowling and Kennon, *House and Senate in the 1790s.*

———. *"The Tyranny of Printers": Newspaper Politics in the Early American Republic.* Charlottesville: University of Virginia Press, 2001.

Pasley, Jeffrey L., Andrew W. Robertson, and David Waldstreicher, eds. *Beyond the Founders: New Approaches to the Political History of the Early American Republic.* Chapel Hill: University of North Carolina Press, 2004.

Pease, Theodore Calvin. *Centennial History of Illinois.* Vol. 2, *The Frontier State, 1818–1848.* Chicago: A. C. McClurg, 1922.

———, ed. *Illinois Election Returns, 1818–1848.* Springfield: Illinois State Historical Library, 1923.

Peskin, Lawrence A. "How the Republicans Learned to Love Manufacturing: The First Parties and the 'New Economy.'" *Journal of the Early Republic* 22 (Summer 2002): 235–62.

———. *Manufacturing Revolution: The Intellectual Origins of Early American Industry.* Baltimore: John Hopkins University Press, 2003.

Pessen, Edward. "We Are All Jeffersonians, We Are All Jacksonians: or A Pox on Stultifying Periodizations." *Journal of the Early Republic* 1 (Spring 1981): 1–26.

Phillips, Kim Tousley. "The Pennsylvania Origins of the Jackson Movement." *Political Science Quarterly* 91 (Autumn 1976): 489–508.

Pincus, Jonathan J. *Pressure Groups and Politics in Antebellum Tariffs.* New York: Columbia University Press, 1977.

Pole, J. R. *Political Representation in England and the Origins of the American Republic.* Berkeley: University of California Press, 1971.

Portnoy, Alisse Theodore. "'Female Petitioners Can Lawfully Be Heard': Negotiating Female Decorum, United States Politics, and Political Agency, 1829–1831." *Journal of the Early Republic* 23 (Winter 2003): 573–610.

Preyer, Norris Watson. "Southern Support of the Tariff of 1816—A Reappraisal." *Journal of Southern History* 25 (August 1959): 306–22.

Prince, Carl E., and Seth Taylor. "Daniel Webster, the Boston Associates, and the U.S. Government's Role in the Industrializing Process, 1815–1830." *Journal of the Early Republic* 2 (Autumn 1982): 283–99.

Quincy, Edmund. *Life of Josiah Quincy of Massachusetts*. Boston, 1867.

Quincy, Josiah. *A Municipal History of the Town and City of Boston, during Two Centuries*. Boston, 1852.

Quincy, Josiah, Jr. *Figures of the Past: From the Leaves of Old Journals*. Boston, 1883.

Rael, Patrick. *Black Identity and Black Protest in the Antebellum North*. Chapel Hill: University of North Carolina Press, 2002.

Ratcliffe, Donald J. "The Crisis of Commercialization: National Political Alignments and the Market Revolution, 1819–1844." In Stokes and Conway, *Market Revolution in America*.

———. *Party Spirit in a Frontier Republic: Democratic Politics in Ohio, 1793–1821*. Columbus: Ohio State University Press, 1998.

———. *The Politics of Long Division: The Birth of the Second Party System in Ohio, 1818–1828*. Columbus: Ohio State University Press, 2000.

———. "Voter Turnout in Early Ohio." *Journal of the Early Republic* 7 (Autumn 1987): 223–51.

———. "Was Andrew Jackson really the people's choice in 1824?" *Myths of the Lost Atlantis*, 10 October 2008. http://www.common-place.org/pasley/?p=590#more-590. Accessed 9 May 2010.

Remini, Robert V. *Andrew Jackson and the Course of American Freedom, 1822–1832*. New York: Harper & Row, 1981.

———. *Henry Clay: Statesman for the Union*. New York: Norton, 1991.

Ress, David. *Governor Edward Coles and the Vote to Forbid Slavery in Illinois, 1823–1824*. Jefferson, NC: McFarland, 2006.

Reynolds, John. *My Own Times: Embracing Also the History of My Life*. Chicago, 1879.

Rigali, James Henry. "Restoring the Republic of Virtue: The Presidential Election of 1824." PhD diss., University of Washington, 2004.

Robertson, Andrew W. "1828 as the Dawn of the 'Age of the Common Man.'" *Myths of the Lost Atlantis*, 7 October 2008. http://www.common-place.org/pasley/?p=704#more-704. Accessed 9 May 2010.

———. "'Look on This Picture . . . And on This!': Nationalism, Localism, and Partisan Images of Otherness in the United States, 1787–1820." *American Historical Review* 106 (October 2001): 1263–80.

———. "Voting Rites and Voting Acts: Electioneering Ritual, 1790–1820." In Pasley, Robertson, and Waldstreicher, *Beyond the Founders*.

Rohrbach, Lewis Bunker, ed. *Boston Taxpayers in 1821*. Camden, ME: Picton, 1988.

Rothbard, Murray N. *The Panic of 1819: Reactions and Policies.* New York: Columbia University Press, 1962.

Rowe, Kenneth Wyer. *Mathew Carey: A Study in American Economic Development.* Baltimore: John Hopkins University Press, 1933.

Ruffin, Edmund. *Incidents of My Life: Edmund Ruffin's Autobiographical Essays.* Edited by David F. Allmendinger Jr. Charlottesville: University of Virginia Press, 1990.

Saltonstall, Leverett. *The Papers of Leverett Saltonstall, 1816–1845.* Vol. 1. Edited by Robert E. Moody. Boston: Massachusetts Historical Society, 1978.

Scharf, J. Thomas, and Thompson Westcott. *History of Philadelphia, 1609–1884.* 3 vols. Philadelphia, 1884.

Schlesinger, Arthur M., ed. *History of American Presidential Elections, 1789–1968.* Vol. 1. New York: Chelsea House, 1971.

Schoen, Brian. *The Fragile Fabric of Union: Cotton, Federal Politics, and the Global Origins of the Civil War.* Baltimore: John Hopkins University Press, 2009.

Schudson, Michael. *The Good Citizen: A History of American Civic Life.* New York: Free Press, 1998.

———. "Good Citizens and Bad History: Today's Political Ideals in Historical Perspective." *Communication Review* 4 (2000): 1–19.

Selinger, Jeffrey S. "Rethinking the Development of Legitimate Party Opposition in the United States, 1793–1828." *Political Science Quarterly* 127 (2012): 263–87.

Shade, William G. "Commentary: Déjà Vu All Over Again: Is There a New New Political History?" In Pasley, Robertson, and Waldstreicher, *Beyond the Founders.*

Shalhope, Robert E. *John Taylor of Caroline: Pastoral Republican.* Columbia: University of South Carolina Press, 1980.

Shankman, Andrew. *Crucible of American Democracy: The Struggle to Fuse Egalitarianism and Capitalism in Jeffersonian Pennsylvania.* Lawrence: University Press of Kansas, 2004.

Silbey, Joel H. *The American Political Nation, 1838–1893.* Stanford, CA: Stanford University Press, 1991.

———. "The Incomplete World of American Politics, 1815–1829: Presidents, Parties and Politics in the Era of Good Feelings." *Congress & the Presidency* 11 (Spring 1984): 1–17.

Simeone, James. *Democracy and Slavery in Frontier Illinois: The Bottomland Republic.* DeKalb: Northern Illinois University Press, 2000.

Skeen, C. Edward. "An Uncertain 'Right': State Legislatures and the Doctrine of Instruction." *Mid-America* 73 (January 1991): 29–47.

Skocpol, Theda. *Diminished Democracy: From Membership to Management in American Civic Life.* Norman: University of Oklahoma Press, 2003.

———. "The Tocqueville Problem: Civic Engagement in American Democracy." *Social Science History* 21 (Winter 1997): 455–79.

Skocpol, Theda, Marshall Ganz, and Ziad Munson. "A Nation of Organizers: The Institutional Origins of Civic Voluntarism in the United States." *American Political Science Review* 94 (September 2000): 527–46.

Smith, Adam I. P. *No Party Now: Politics in the Civil War North.* Oxford: Oxford University Press, 2006.

Smith, Culver H. *The Press, Politics, and Patronage: The American Government's Use of Newspapers, 1789–1875.* Athens: University of Georgia Press, 1977.

Smith, Kimberly K. *The Dominion of Voice: Riot, Reason, and Romance in Antebellum Politics.* Lawrence: University Press of Kansas, 1999.

Sorauf, Frank J. "Political Parties and Political Analysis." In Chambers and Burnham, *American Party Systems.*

Stanwood, Edward. *American Tariff Controversies in the Nineteenth Century.* Vol. I. London: Archibald Constable, 1904.

Stokes, Melvyn, and Stephen Conway, eds. *The Market Revolution in America: Social, Political, and Religious Expressions, 1800–1880.* Charlottesville: University of Virginia Press, 1996.

Story, Ronald. *The Forging of an Aristocracy: Harvard and the Boston Upper Class, 1800–1870.* Middletown, CT: Wesleyan University Press, 1980.

Sutton, Robert M. "Edward Coles and the Constitutional Crisis in Illinois, 1822–1824." *Illinois Historical Journal* 82 (Spring 1989): 33–46.

Sydnor, Charles S. "The One-Party Period of American History." *American Historical Review* 51 (April 1946): 439–51.

Taussig, F. W. *The Tariff History of the United States.* 8th ed. New York: G. P. Putnam's Sons, 1931.

Taylor, Alan. "'The Art of Hook & Snivey': Political Culture in Upstate New York during the 1790s." *Journal of American History* 79 (March 1993): 1371–96.

Taylor, John. *Arator; being a series of Agricultural Essays, Practical & Political.* 3rd ed. Baltimore, 1817.

Tocqueville, Alexis de. *Democracy in America.* Ware, UK: Wordsworth Editions, 1998.

True, Rodney C., ed. "Minute book of the Albemarle (Va.) Agricultural Society." In *Annual Report of the American Historical Association for the Year 1918,* 1:261–349. Washington, DC: GPO, 1920.

Van Buren, Martin. *Inquiry into the Origin and Course of Political Parties in the United States.* New York, 1867.

Vernon, James. *Politics and the People: A Study in English Political Culture, c. 1815–1867.* Cambridge: Cambridge University Press, 1993.

Voss-Hubbard, Mark. *Beyond Party: Cultures of Antipartisanship in Northern Politics before the Civil War.* Baltimore: John Hopkins University Press, 2002.

——. "The 'Third Party Tradition' Reconsidered: Third Parties and American Public Life, 1830–1900." *Journal of American History* 86 (June 1999): 121–50.

Waldstreicher, David. *In the Midst of Perpetual Fetes: The Making of American Nationalism, 1776–1820.* Chapel Hill: University of North Carolina Press, 1997.

Wallace, Michael. "Changing Concepts of Party in the United States: New York, 1815–1828." *American Historical Review* 74 (December 1968): 453–91.

Washburne, E. B., ed. *The Edwards Papers: Being a portion of the collection of the letters, papers, and manuscripts of Ninian Edwards.* Chicago, 1884.

——. "Sketch of Edward Coles, Second Governor of Illinois, and of the Slavery Struggle of 1823–4." In Alvord, *Governor Edward Coles.*

Webster, Daniel. *The Papers of Daniel Webster: Correspondence.* Vol. 1, *1798–1824.* Edited by Charles Wiltse. Hanover, NH: University Press of New England, 1974.

Weed, Thurlow. *Autobiography of Thurlow Weed.* Edited by Harriet A. Weed. 2 vols. Boston, 1883.

Whitely, Edward. *The Philadelphia Directory and Register, for 1820.* Philadelphia, [1820].

Wilentz, Sean. *The Rise of American Democracy: Jefferson to Lincoln.* New York: Norton, 2005.

Williams, Gary M. "Colonel George Blow: Planter and Political Prophet of Antebellum Sussex." *Virginia Magazine of History and Biography* 90 (October 1982): 432–55.

Williams, William Henry, ed. "Ten Letters from William Harris Crawford to Martin Van Buren." *Georgia Historical Quarterly* 49 (March 1965): 65–81.

Winkle, Kenneth J. "The U.S. Census as a Source in Political History." *Social Science History* 15 (Winter 1991): 565–77.

Wire, Richard Arden. "John M. Clayton and the Rise of the Anti-Jackson Party in Delaware, 1824–1828." *Delaware History* 15 (1972–73): 256–68.

Wood, Gordon S. *Empire of Liberty: A History of the Early Republic, 1789–1815.* Oxford: Oxford University Press, 2011.

Zaeske, Susan. *Signatures of Citizenship: Petitioning, Antislavery, and Women's Political Identity.* Chapel Hill: University of North Carolina Press, 2003.

Zagarri, Rosemarie. *Revolutionary Backlash: Women and Politics in the Early American Republic.* Philadelphia: University of Pennsylvania Press, 2007.

——, "Women and Party Conflict in the Early Republic." In Pasley, Robertson, and Waldstreicher, *Beyond the Founders.*

DATABASES

American Broadsides and Ephemera. Readex e-database.

American State Papers, 1789–1838. Readex e-database.

America's Historical Newspapers. Readex e-database.

Biographical Directory of the United States Congress, 1774–Present. http://bioguide
.congress.gov/biosearch/biosearch.asp.

A New Nation Votes: American Election Returns, 1787–1825. http://elections.lib.tufts
.edu/aas_portal/index.xq.

19th Century U.S. Newspapers. Gale e-database.

Sabin Americana. Gale e-database.

United States Elections Project, http://elections.gmu.edu/index.html.

INDEX

abolitionism, 10, 88, 133, 143

Adams, Benjamin, 98

Adams, John, 38

Adams, John Quincy, 111, 114, 141; antipartisanship of, 116, 119, 121, 138, 139, 146; and congressional caucus, 121; and "convention question," 133, 197n152; 1824 presidential campaign of, 109–10, 116, 119–20, 121, 135; —, in Illinois, 132–33, 197n148; —, in Massachusetts, 124–26; —, in New York, 135; —, in Pennsylvania, 130; —, in Virginia, 128–29; 1824 presidential election outcome and, 13, 136–38, 143, 146, 198n171, 200–201n23; on "Era of Good Feelings," 139–40; and Federalist Party, 109–10, 113, 116, 126; and slavery, 133–34

Adams, Louisa Catherine Johnson, 119, 193n60

Albany Regency (New York), 110, 112, 127, 134–35, 195n108, 199n2

American Bible Society, 54, 58

American Farmer (Baltimore), 89, 104, 106. *See also* Skinner, John

American Society for the Encouragement of Domestic Manufactures, 95

American Statesman (Boston), 18, 126

American System, 110, 137–38

American Tract Society, 54, 58

anticonventionists. *See* "convention question" (Illinois)

antipartisanship, 9, 16, 46, 108, 137, 138, 139, 141–42, 146–47; in "convention question," 9–11, 47, 48–49, 59–62, 62–63, 64–68, 68–69, 70–71, 120, 142,

145; 1824 presidential election and, 13, 108, 109–10, 110–11, 111, 114, 115–17, 119, 120, 121–24, 126–27, 127, 130–31, 134–35, 137–38, 142, 146; Middling Interest and, 8–9, 15–16, 18, 19, 21, 23, 26, 27, 28, 29, 30, 31–32, 33–34, 36–41, 42, 45–46, 61, 102, 140, 142, 199n2; and tariff policy, 11–13, 73, 78, 79–80, 83–84, 88, 89, 97, 99, 100–103, 106, 131, 142

Appleton, Nathan, 96

Articles of Confederation, 77

association: in "convention question," 10, 47, 52–62, 62–63, 64, 68, 70–71, 71–72, 142, 144–45; interstate, 85–88, 106, 142; legitimacy of disputed, 40–41, 59–62, 62–63, 64, 68, 70–71, 99–100; Middling Interest and, 39–41, 59; origins of, 10, 47, 54, 58, 59; partisan functions of, 10–11, 19, 80; political importance of, 10–11, 12–13, 40–41, 47, 54, 58–59, 62, 68, 71–72, 73–74, 81, 84–85, 88, 99, 102–3, 105, 106–7, 109, 142–43, 147, 179n73; and tariff policy, 12, 73–74, 78–89, 90, 98–100, 104–5, 106–7, 142–43, 145, 183n27

Aurora General Advertiser (Philadelphia), 100, 101, 117. *See also* Duane, William; Duane, William J.

Baldwin, Henry, 75, 187n89; as chairman of House Committee on Manufactures, 84, 97, 103, 104; 1824 presidential election and, 131; and lobbying, 94, 95; and petitioning, 91–92. *See also* tariff bill, 1820

Barbour, Philip B., 103

Birkbeck, Morris, 53, 54, 57, 61, 62

Recent Books in the JEFFERSONIAN AMERICA SERIES